WITNESSES
TO MYSTERY

ignatius press

GRZEGORZ GÓRNY
JANUSZ ROSIKOŃ

WITNESSES TO MYSTERY

Investigations into Christ's relics

PROLOGUE

Every person on this planet leaves behind him a material imprint of his existence, and so did the man who arguably exerted the greatest influence on the history of mankind: Jesus Christ. Indeed, even our calendar is shaped according to the date of Christ's birth.

Despite the attempts once made by Communist propaganda to convince us otherwise, there is much reliable historical evidence, both Christian and pagan, that confirms the existence of a Jewish teacher called Jesus of Nazareth who lived 2,000 years ago. This begs the question, however, of whether genuine artifacts associated with His life have remained with us to this day.

One would assume that if the Apostles truly recognized Jesus as their Messiah, their Savior, and the Son of God, the material vestiges of His life would have been treated with the utmost reverence. The earliest Christian communities made concerted efforts to preserve the memory of Jesus' life, through both the spoken and the written word. Why should their efforts, however, have been limited to preserving their Savior's teaching when it was also possibile to preserve His earthly legacy?

We are born with an inherent desire to collect, to preserve. We seek to uphold the memory of our closest relations, often by retaining possession of their personal effects. Without doubt, the Apostles' closest relationship was with Christ, for whom (with the exception of St. John) each of the Twelve gave his life, becoming a martyr in death.

It's worth noting that Jesus' material legacy became an influential element in spreading the fledgling Christian faith. German scientific researcher Michael Hesemann elaborates: "The first Christians were by no means ignorant. Certainly, they might have expected that the Kingdom of God would come about even in their own lifetimes. Until that time, however, they had a difficult task to fulfill: to spread the gospel. This was founded on the words and deeds of a Nazarene, whose example they had witnessed. He was not a myth, like the sons of pagan deities; He lived, preached, and really existed. The early Christians encountered opponents; their message was met with skepticism, and their testimony was often discredited. Regardless of how strong their faith was in the Holy Spirit, they knew that every person expected proof, with which they could then find Christ on their own terms. Jesus' physical legacy backed up His words; it contained within itself a sign of the Lord's saving grace and might, and it served as a material inheritance. These objects became silent witnesses to the events that Christians believe had such a redemptive influence on the course of human history. Because of them, the stories of these events became revitalized, since religion is not just an intellectual exercise in understanding, but rather an all-encompassing and bodily experience."

In describing these attitudes held by the early Christians, Hesemann remarks upon an aspect of their faith that is reflected in the Church's own teachings about relics. A belief in the physical power of holy objects was born out of events in Jesus' own life. In his Gospel St. Mark recounts the following episode: "A great multitude followed Him and thronged Him. Now a certain woman had a flow of blood for 12 years, had suffered many things from many physicians, and had spent all that she had and was no better, but rather grew worse. When she heard about Jesus, she came behind Him in the crowd and touched His garment. For she said, 'If only I may touch His clothes, I shall be made well.' Immediately the flow of her blood stopped, and she felt in her body that she was healed of the affliction. And Jesus, immediately knowing in Himself that power had gone out of Him, turned around in the crowd and said, 'Who touched My clothes?' But His disciples said to Him, 'You see the multitude thronging You, and You say, "Who touched Me?"' And He looked around to see her who had done this thing. But the woman, fearing and trembling, knowing what had happened to her, came and fell down before Him and told Him the whole truth. And He said to her, 'Daughter, your faith has made you well. Go in peace, and be healed of your affliction'" (Mk 5 :24b–34).

Jesus did not chastise the woman; rather, He praised her actions. On the basis of this story, Christians became convinced of the power found in holy objects. This wasn't a case of fetishism or belief in magic, however. In this account, there are three elements worth noting: first, God's power, which acts as the healing force; second, the woman's faith in seeking help; and third, the mediation of a concrete object. It is on this evidence that Christians developed a belief in the power of relics as objects that, through physical contact, mediate between this mortal world and the Kingdom of Heaven.

During the Middle Ages, relics were misused and forged. Europe became littered with a multitude of fake relics, which had been sold by corrupt pardoners along with indulgences. There are numerous accounts written by pilgrims describing how in the course of one pilgrimage the same relic was found in as many as three places. Such examples include the shoulder of St. Thomas in Rhodes, Rome, and Maastricht, and the body of St. Matthias in Padua, Rome, and Trier. This sort of fraud resulted in gradually increasing skepticism toward Christian relics. The incredulity was compounded further by the Reformation, the Enlightenment, and positivist thought: with the advent of a scientifically minded civilization, relics were confined to the world of superstition.

Does not the presence of numerous forgeries, however, suggest the existence of an original? Are mass reproductions evidence of attempts at imitating a genuine relic? The term *simulacrum* in postmodernist use indicates a copy without an original. Could Christ's relics be regarded as simulacra, as reproductions of things that don't exist? Or are they in fact real objects, with which Jesus of Nazareth once had contact?

Janusz Rosikoń and I tried to answer this question, spending two years traveling around the world in search of Christ's relics. Almost everywhere we went, we were confronted with the same remarkable phenomenon: these relics seemed to attract the attention of academics more than that of religious devotees. They have been analyzed by world-renowned specialists in such fields as history, archaeology, philology, Bible studies, patristics, law, anthropology, Oriental studies, numismatics, paleography, chemistry, physics, biology, forensic medicine, anatomy, genetics, spectrography, and optical science. Special investigative teams—boasting experts in criminology, hematology, palynology, mathematics, computer science, and polarized imaging—were called in for just one reason: to find out whether a given relic was indeed genuine.

We tracked down these efforts more as investigative journalists than as pilgrims. We spent more time learning from scientists equipped with highly modernized machinery than we did listening to the stories of religious believers past or present. Yet it turned out that these two perspectives often found common ground. The results of numerous time-consuming and comprehensive analyses, conducted using the most technologically advanced equipment available, seemed to coincide with assertions prevalent in Christian tradition. Science and religion, it would seem, need not contradict each other.

In addition some of the objects that were tested exhibit characteristics that completely challenge contemporary scholarship and research on the subject of relics. From a scientific point of view, it's practically impossible to account for the way in which they came into being. Likewise startling is the fact that, despite the technology we have available to us today, these relics cannot be copied. Quite unexpectedly, we saw how contemporary science, in the words of its own luminaries, must admit to ignorance and open itself up to the mysteries of faith. Similarly, after two years of research, we feel that we were given the opportunity to examine nothing less than the silent witnesses to Christ's Mysteries.

We invite you on our journey,

Grzegorz Górny and Janusz Rosikoń

7

✠

CONTENTS

8

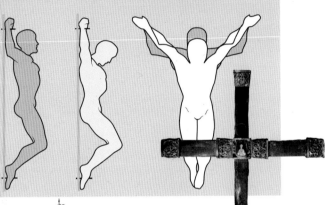

Aachen
Essen
Kornelimünster
Prüm
Argenteuil
Paris
Santo Toribio de Liébana
Cahors
Turin
Oviedo

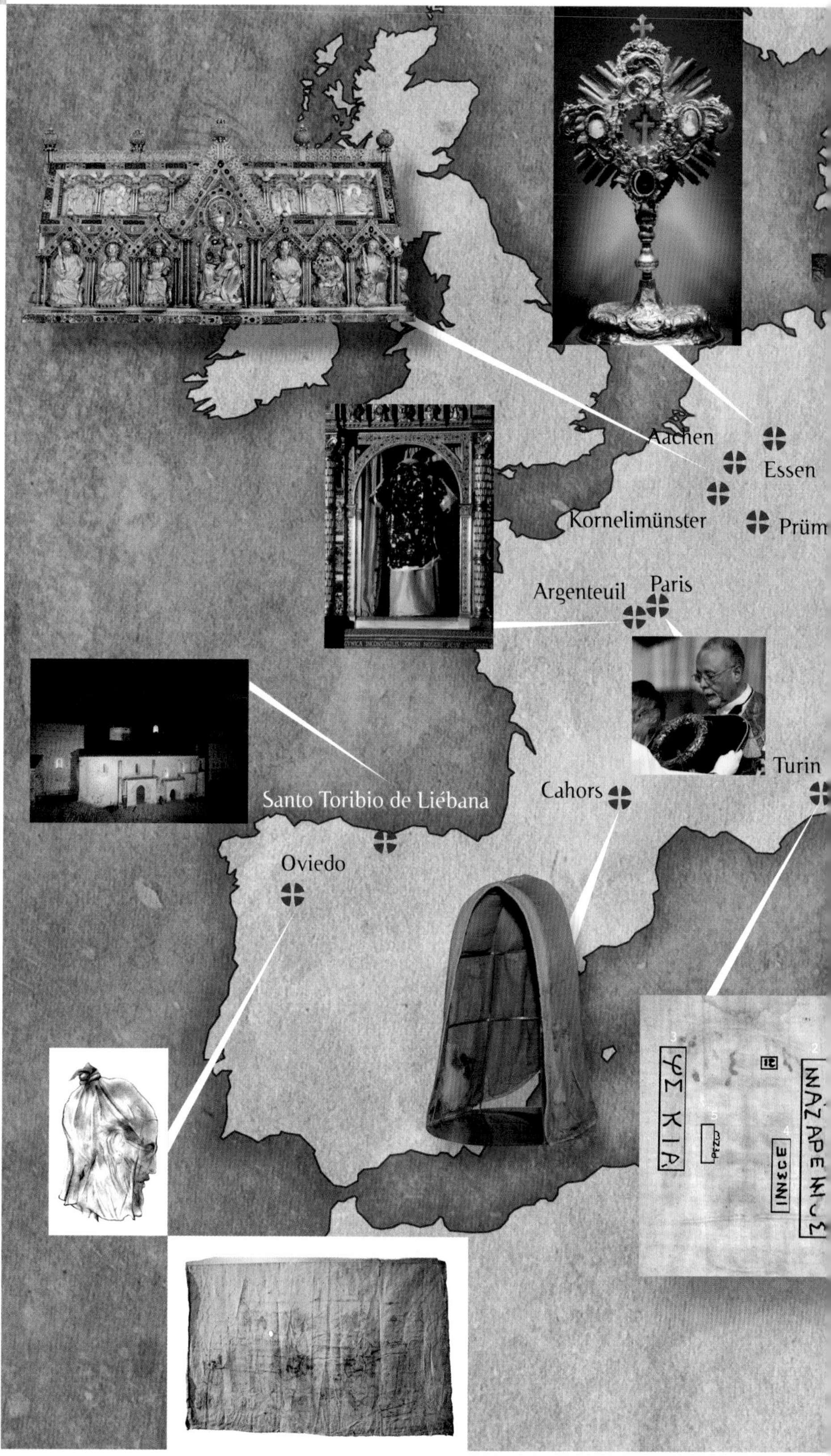

RELICS MAP

Vilnus

Strzelno

Góra Kalwaria

Boćki

Częstochowa

Święty Krzyż

Karlštejn

Cracow

Trier

Venice

Milan

Florence

Colle Val d'Elsa

Pisa

Manoppello

Siena

Rome

Monte Gargano

Castel Sant' Elia

Jerusalem

THE STATIONS OF THE CROSS

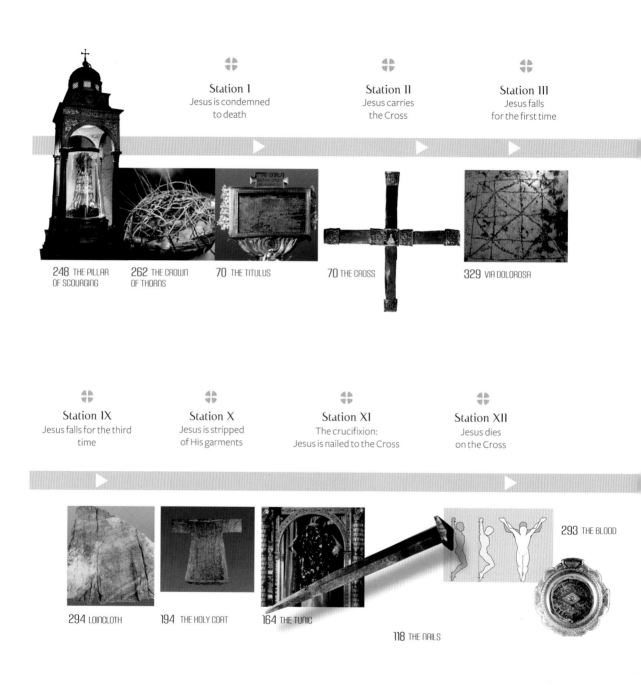

Station I
Jesus is condemned
to death

Station II
Jesus carries
the Cross

Station III
Jesus falls
for the first time

248 THE PILLAR
OF SCOURGING

262 THE CROWN
OF THORNS

70 THE TITULUS

70 THE CROSS

329 VIA DOLOROSA

Station IX
Jesus falls for the third
time

Station X
Jesus is stripped
of His garments

Station XI
The crucifixion:
Jesus is nailed to the Cross

Station XII
Jesus dies
on the Cross

294 LOINCLOTH

194 THE HOLY COAT

164 THE TUNIC

118 THE NAILS

293 THE BLOOD

Station IV
Jesus meets
His Mother

Station V
Simon of Cyrene helps
Jesus to carry the Cross

Station VI
Veronica wipes the
face of Jesus

Station VII
Jesus falls for the
second time

Station VIII
Jesus meets the holy
women of Jerusalem

308 MARY

290 THE SANDALS

216 THE VEIL

329 VIA DOLOROSA

Station XIII
Jesus is taken down
from the Cross

Station XIV
Jesus is laid
in the tomb

Station XV
The Resurrection
of Jesus

216 VERA EIKON

142 THE SUDARIUM

14 THE SHROUD

304 THE CAP

294 THE CLOTH   308 THE TOMB

13

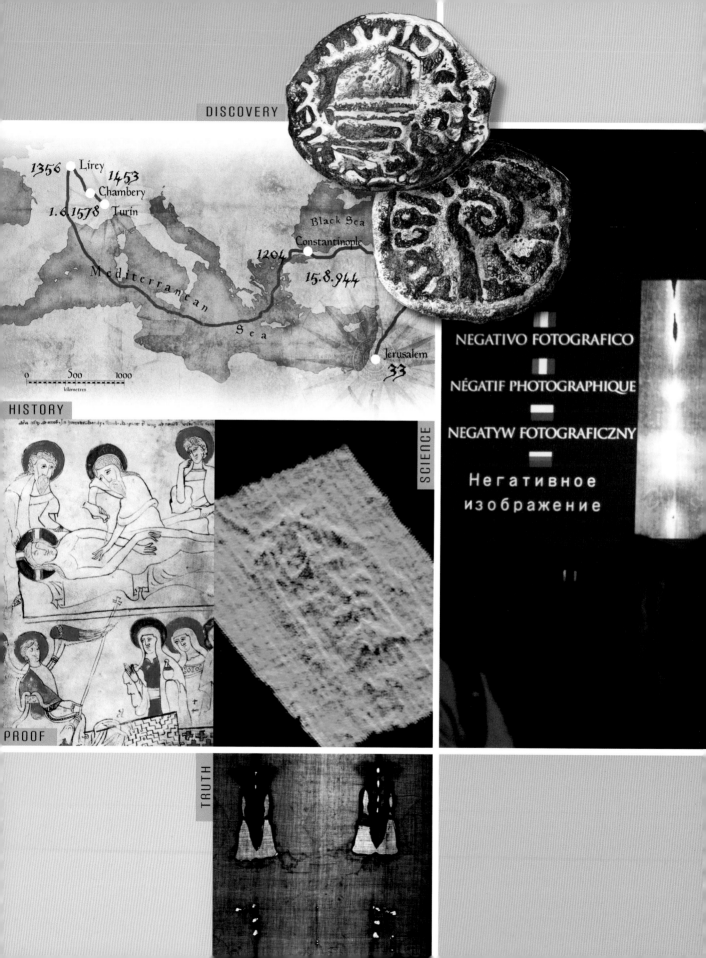

DISCOVERY

1356 Lirey
1453 Chambery
1.6.1578 Turin

Black Sea
Constantinople
1204
15.8.944

Mediterranean

Sea

Jerusalem
33

0   500   1000
kilometres

HISTORY

PROOF

SCIENCE

NEGATIVO FOTOGRAFICO

NÉGATIF PHOTOGRAPHIQUE

NEGATYW FOTOGRAFICZNY

Негативное
изображение

TRUTH

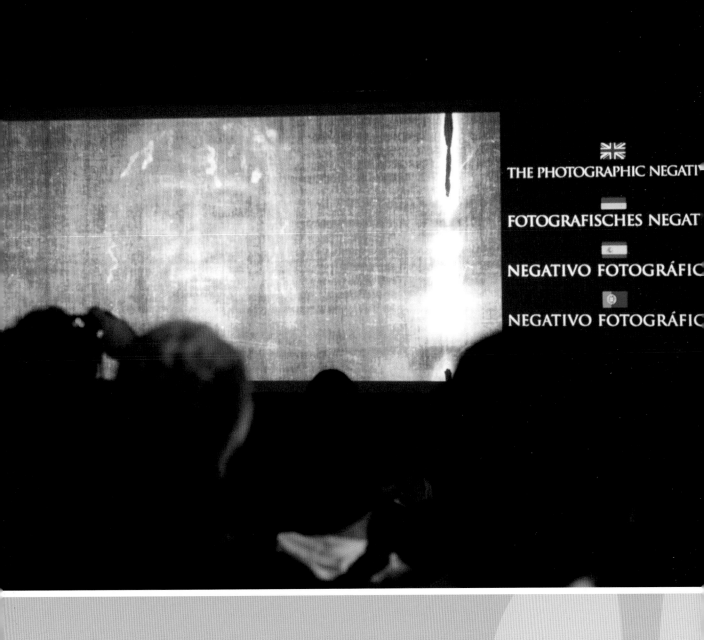

CHAPTER I

THE TURIN SHROUD

A shiver went down Secondo Pia's spine as he examined his photographic plates one evening in his workshop in Turin. The Italian photographer surely never expected that this day—May 28, 1898—would change his life. Earlier that afternoon, as he peered through the lens of his camera, he had barely noticed the image imprinted upon the shroud he was attempting to photograph. Lacking any definitive shape, the image was

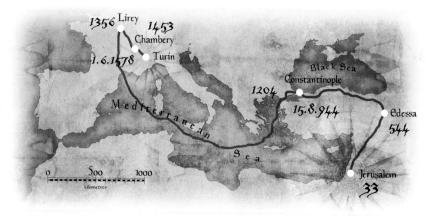

16

JOURNEY TAKEN BY THE TURIN SHROUD from the Holy Sepulchre in Jerusalem to St. John's Cathedral in Turin.

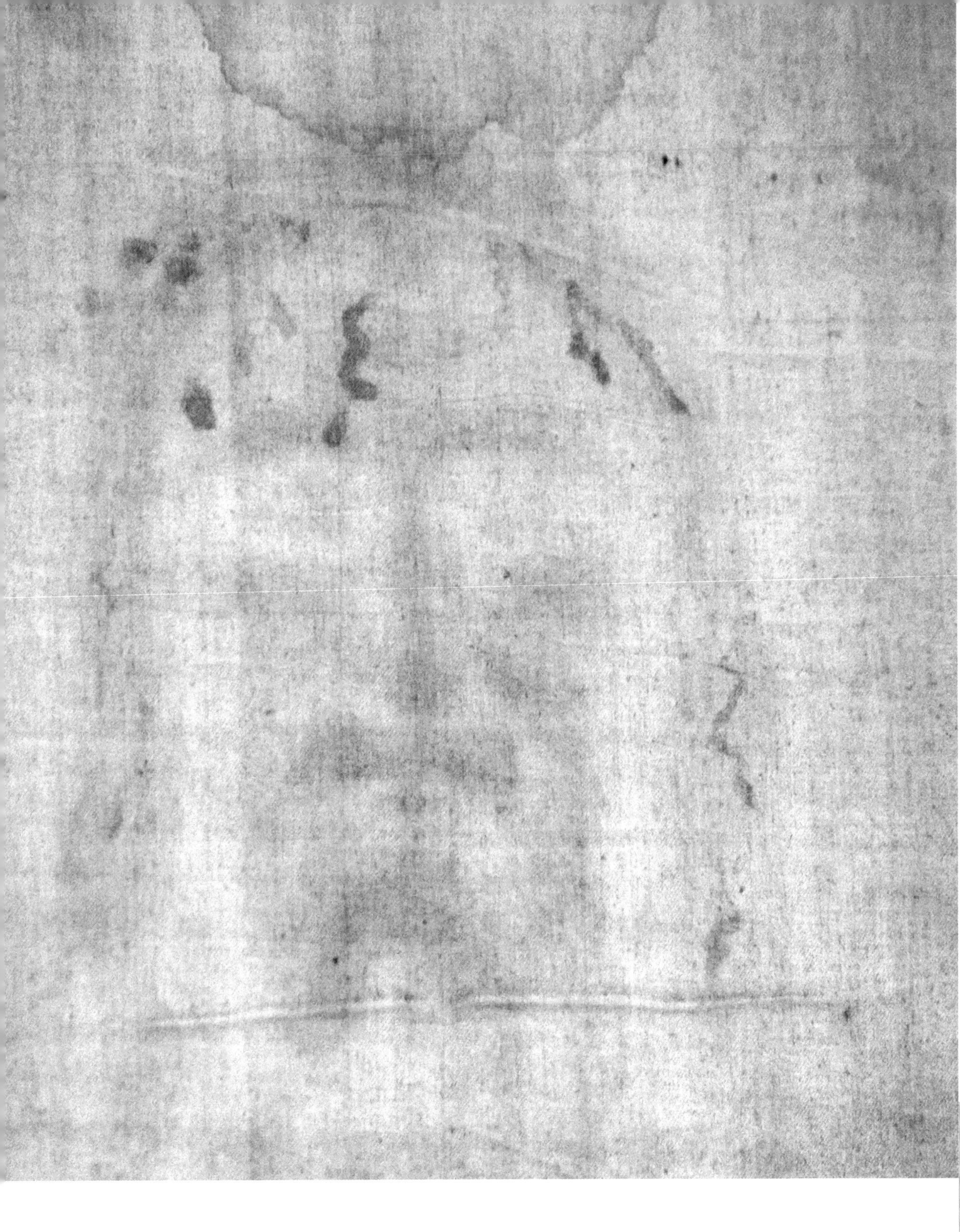

THE VISAGE ON THE SHROUD is an example of an effect that art historians call *sfumato*, in which the mind's eye is not able to grasp pictures because of their softened outlines and blurred form. As a result, the eye is unable to see the image's details when observed close up. They are more visible from afar.

SECONDO PIA
(1855–1941) was
a respected Turin
lawyer as well
as an amateur
photographer. He
produced his famous
photo of the Turin
Shroud in 1898.

SECONDO PIA'S PHOTOGRAPH prompted shock and disbelief as it revealed an imprint of Christ in the form of a photographic negative.

obscure against the background of the yellowing fabric, creating only a faded contrast. The closer the photographer had approached his subject, the less detail he was able to make out with his own eyes.

Now, poring over the plates in his home laboratory, he watched in wonder as his developing photograph revealed the outline of a figure gradually emerging on the linen cloth. "As I developed my photographs, I was overcome with emotion", wrote Secondo Pia in his memoirs. "I saw a holy visage appear, which was so clear that I was taken aback." His amazement was compounded by the fact that the picture that appeared on the negative looked more like a positive image. This was a phenomenon that contradicted everything within the field of scientific knowledge. The Italian photographer surely never expected that his discovery would make such a great impact on the world's scientific community.

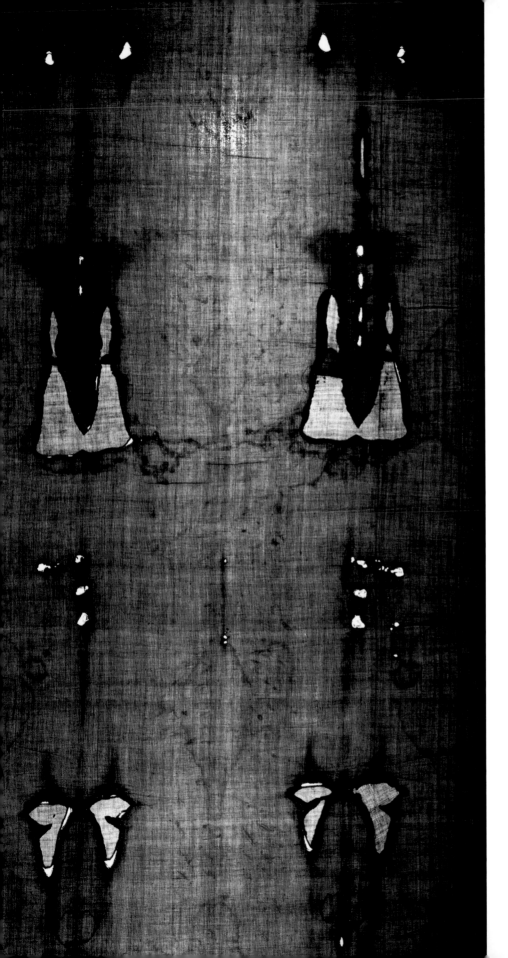

ILLUMINATED FROM BEHIND, the shroud exhibits amazing characteristics. The image of the man disappears and only the traces of blood remain visible. Experts believe this is proof that the image was not painted, since paint – like blood – is not translucent. The cloth also has burn marks made as a result of the fire in 1532, as well as staining caused by the water used to extinguish the fire.

COMPARE
pages ▶ 46–47

THE SHROUD AND CONFORMITY WITH THE GOSPELS

THE IMAGE VISIBLE on the Turin Shroud exhibits a number of details that correspond with the circumstances of Christ's death, as described in the Gospels. The image on the shroud is of a man who was evidently flogged in accordance with the Roman practice of scourging (by the use of a flagellum) and crowned with a headpiece of thorns. His body bears the signs of multiple injuries and beatings. The sentenced man was crucified in accordance with the technique used in Roman executions. Contrary to the widespread medieval belief regarding crucifixion, the condemned was not nailed to the cross through the palms, but through the wrists. Neither were his shins broken, as was commonly practiced in Roman times. On the right side of the imprinted figure's body, between the fifth and sixth ribs, one can discern a large wound that would have been caused by a spearhead. It pierced the pleura, the pericardium, and the heart's right atrium. The blow to the heart from the right, and not from the left, was in keeping with Roman infantrymen's training, as Julius Caesar describes in his *Commentaries on the Gallic War*: because their opponents would have covered their hearts by holding their shield in their left hands, Roman legionnaires were trained to thrust their spear from the right.

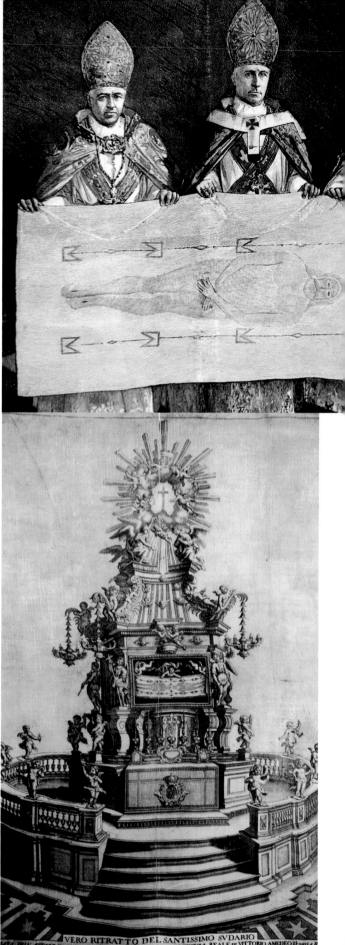

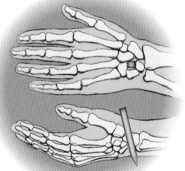

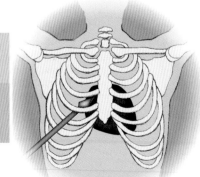

ANATOMICAL RECON-STRUCTIONS prove that the person imprinted on the shroud had nails driven through his wrists and a spear pierce his side between the fifth and sixth ribs.

20

VERO RITRATTO DEL SANTISSIMO SVDARIO

THE SHROUD DISPLAYED in 1898. It is held by five bishops: Manacorda of Fossano, Pampirio of Vercelli, Richelmy of Turin, Reggio of Genoa, and Duc of Aosta.

Since that time, no other item has been the subject of such systematic and thorough examination as the Turin Shroud. It has even brought about the creation of a new scientific discipline—sindonology (from the Greek *sindon*, meaning "shroud")—concerned exclusively with investigating the phenomenon hidden in this seemingly unremarkable linen cloth. Its study encompasses numerous fields of research, including history, archaeology, philology, Bible studies, patristics, law, anthropology, Oriental studies, numismatics, paleography, chemistry, physics, biology, forensic medicine, anatomy, genetics, spectrography, and optical science. Some of the world's most renowned scientific authorities have spent many years attempting to discover the truth behind this mysterious cloth.

Of particular interest is the fact that numerous world-renowned academics have engaged with a Christian relic and therefore an object of religious devotion. From the time of the Enlightenment, the paths of science and religion have become increasingly divergent from one another as materialism, technocratism, and scientism began to predominate at universities. One of the leading proponents of this emerging nineteenth-century trend was Ernest Renan, who wrote: "Indeed, the only discipline that has any real worth is one that is able to replace religion. I ascribe to scientific learning just one achievement: that is to solve problems, to provide the final word in any debate, to enlighten people and provide them, in the name of the only

THEOLOGICAL TREATISE on the Turin Shroud written by Agaffino Solaro (bishop of the Fossano and Saluzzo dioceses), published in 1627, two years after the author's death.

ALTAR OF THE HOLY SHROUD in the Guarini Chapel, Turin Cathedral. The Illustration was produced in Lyon in 1737.

MYSTERIOUS MANUSCRIPT CONTRADICTS THEORY REGARDING THIRTEENTH/FOURTEENTH-CENTURY FORGERY

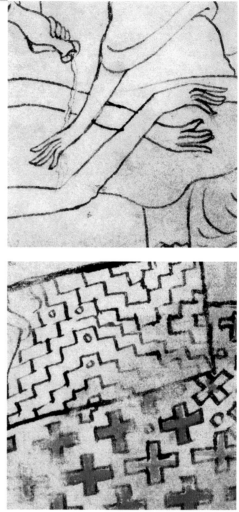

COMPARE
page ▶ 122

A UNIQUE COLLECTION of medieval manuscripts is preserved in the National Széchényi Library in Budapest. It is known as the Pray Codex, after György Pray, who discovered it in 1770. The parchment, which dates back to between 1192 and 1195, is the oldest known example of continuous prose text in Hungarian.

One of the five illustrations in the codex is of Christ's burial. The depiction of Christ exhibits details identical to those on the image on the Turin Shroud. The body is shown lying on its back, naked, which is unprecedented in medieval religious painting. Whether in paintings, frescoes or illuminations, Jesus was always shown wearing a loincloth. Depicting Christ totally naked would have been unthinkable and blasphemous. If an artist decided to take this step, he must have been inspired by some incontrovertible piece of evidence, which could only have been the Turin Shroud.

This is by no means the only similarity between the codex and shroud images. In both cases the figure's wrists are crossed over on the pelvis and the hands have only four fingers each, missing thumbs. This is not merely a mistake made by the illuminator, since the other figures in the illustration all have five fingers. Rather, the illuminator copied a reality of crucifixion recorded by the shroud: that the nailing of the wrists to the cross severed a central nerve and forced each thumb to contract within the palm. With the onset of rigor mortis, the thumbs of the figure remained folded over in a way that made them seemingly invisible.

Another illustration shows three women arriving at the tomb with fragrances to anoint Christ's body. There they encounter an angel who points not toward heaven, as was common practice in this sort of depiction, but toward two burial cloths: a folded scarf and an outspread shroud. The depiction of the larger cloth in particular is very detailed. The artist has replicated the herringbone pattern of the fabric, which corresponds exactly with the weaving pattern of the Turin Shroud.

The Pray Codex, dating from between 1192 and 1195, therefore, contradicts the theory that the Turin Shroud was produced some time between 1260 and 1390 (the alleged fabrication date established through carbon dating tests). The manuscripts date back to the rule of King Béla III, who was raised in Constantinople and related to the Byzantine ruling family. (He was brother-in-law to Emperor Manuel I Komnenos, and his daughter Margaret was married to Isaac II Angelos. Upon Isaac's death, Margaret married the leader of the Fourth Crusade, Boniface of Montferrat.) While living in the Byzantine capital, Béla was able to see the shroud when it was displayed to the public every Friday.

ILLUSTRATIONS from the Pray Codex clearly show Christ with four fingers, while the cloth wrapped around His body has a herringbone weave – the same as on the Turin Shroud.

HERRINGBONE WEAVE on the Turin Shroud. Photograph by Mark Evans, 1978.

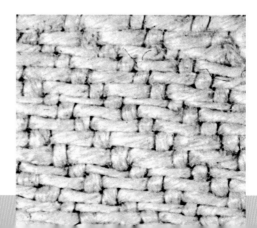

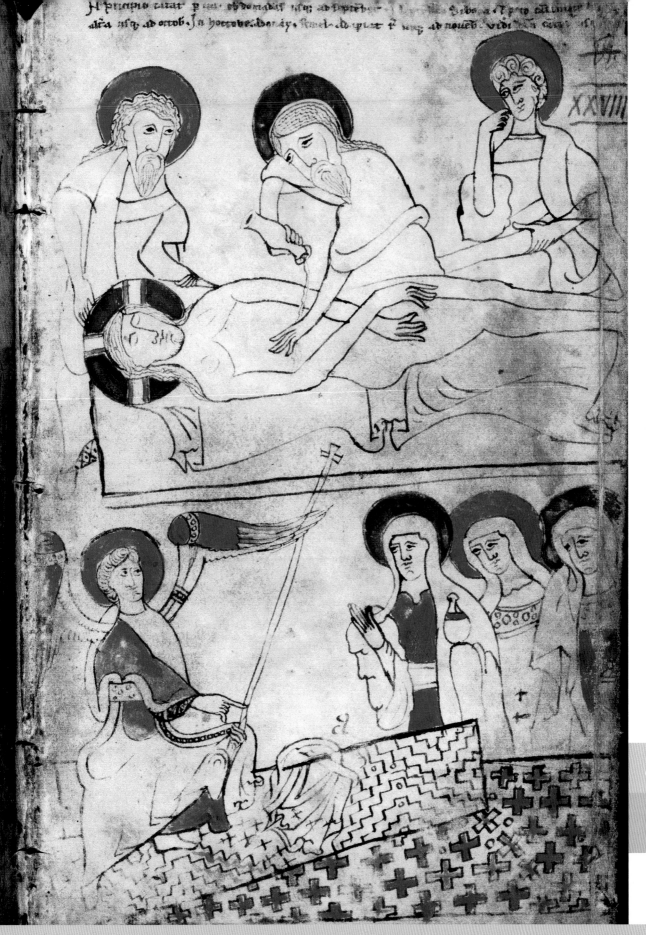

MODERN RECONSTRUCTION of Christ's tomb. It was hollowed out from rock and was made of two rooms, with a large stone sealing its entrance.

truly legal authority, with a complete insight into the nature of man. This was once the prerogative of religion, which we can no longer accept."

In sharing Renan's opinion, many scientists referred to Christianity as mere superstition. The main argument put forth against this religion had to do with its reverence of relics alongside its faith in miracles—in other words, occurrences that have no rational explanation. What Christians believed, they decided, was at total odds with common sense.

On that May 1898 night in Turin, however, the paths of science and religion crossed unexpectedly. An unassuming object, derided by scientists as a relic of a backward and bygone era, suddenly launched a challenge to reason. Since 1578 this relic had been worshipped in Turin Cathedral as the burial clothing of Jesus of Nazareth. But how did it make its way from the Holy Land all the way to Piedmont's capital city?

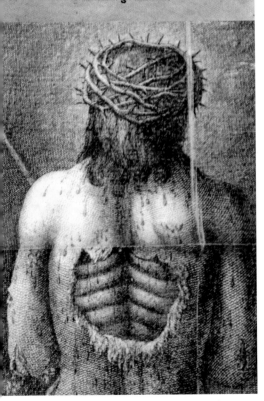

PHILIBERTI PINGONII SABAVDI· CVSIACEN. BARONIS.

SINDON EVANGE-LICA.

Accesserunt Hymni aliquot,
Insignis Bulla
Pontificia.

Elegans Epist. Francisci Adorni
Ies. de Peregrinatione
memorabili.

AVGVSTÆ TAVRINORVM,
Apud hæredes Nicolai Beuilaquæ.1581.
Cum Priuilegio decennali.

MONOGRAPH ON THE TURIN SHROUD by Emmanuel Philibert Pingon, baron of Cusiaco, entitled *The Gospel Shroud*, published in Turin in 1581.

DEPICTION OF CHRIST AFTER SCOURGING, venerated in a Franciscan chapel in Genoa, and based on the image of Christ imprinted on the Turin Shroud.

ITALIAN SCIENTIST INVENTS GLASSES TO VIEW TURIN SHROUD

IN MAY 2010, the last time the Turin Shroud was displayed to the public, pilgrims were able to look at the relic using specially constructed glasses. Even Pope Benedict XVI tried them on. Their inventor is the Italian professor Bruno Fabbiani, of the Polytechnic University of Turin. He described how he came up with the idea in the following passage:

"I saw the shroud in 2000, when it was last displayed. An old woman stood next to me with her grandson. At one point, the young boy asked his grandmother why the lower half of Jesus' legs had been cut off. I understood then that many people couldn't make out the pale outline of Christ's body exactly and often imagined they were looking at parts of His body where nothing was actually imprinted. In particular, many people's eyes are drawn to the marks made as a result of the fire in 1532. Some even think they constitute parts of Christ's body. Since I am a specialist in optics, I decided to design a pair of glasses with which one could see details on the shroud that remain difficult to perceive with the naked eye. The traces of blood are made much more visible through the left eyeglass, while the right makes it easier to trace the body's anatomical features."

Fabbiani—a student of the Hungarian physicist Dennis Gabor, who invented holography and was a recipient of the Nobel Prize in Physics—began his study of the Turin Shroud in 1998. To this day, he does not know how the imprinted image was formed: "The more tests I carry out on the shroud, the more mysteries it seems to yield."

In answer to the question of whether the same could be said of any scientifically tested object, Fabbiani replies: "Oh no! From a scientific point of view, physical objects at this level are entirely explicable. There are those objects, however, that remain a mystery. In the course of my career, I have encountered only two such articles: the Turin Shroud and the image of Our Lady of Guadalupe. These are two depictions about which one can say with certainty that they were not produced by human hand."

PROF. BRUNO FABBIANI, creator of the glasses worn by Pope Benedict XVI to look at the Turin Shroud.

"MY DEATH YOUR LIFE" is the Latin inscription appearing on an anonymous sixteenth-century illustration of Christ's tomb.

DRAWING OF THE TURIN SHROUD from a book on the relic written by Jean Jacob Chifflet, published in Antwerp in 1624.

There is a great dearth of documentary evidence recording Christianity's early years. We are left with a huge gap, therefore, in what we know of the shroud's history, as well as that of other relics associated with the Passion. During this time, Jesus' followers were living in fear of being captured by those hostile to their faith. They had no choice but to keep their faith a complete secret. Objects such as the shroud were in particular danger of being destroyed, both by Romans and by Jews. For the Romans, the cloth's holy depiction was a direct challenge to the empire's political religious system, while for the Jews it amounted to flagrant idolatry. For this reason, the location of the shroud's hiding place remained a closely guarded secret in the early years of the Christian Church.

We know from the Gospels that before it was laid in the tomb, Jesus' body was wrapped in a shroud. This was in accordance with Jewish burial rites, which dictated that the eyes be closed and the jaw shut (so as to stop the tongue from protruding). The body was washed and anointed with fragrances and wrapped in white linen. The head was draped with a veil.

Contemporary researchers, among them Italian scientist Gino Zaninotti, believe that Jesus' body was prepared for burial in the following manner: first, a cap (*pathil*) was placed upon His head, with a strap around His chin. His body was then wrapped lengthwise in a linen shroud (*sindon*) and tied horizontally with two pieces of cloth (*othonia*). Finally, a veil (*sudarion*) was placed over His

PAINTING BY GIOVANNI BATTISTA DELLA ROVERE (1575–1640), depicting how the shroud was wrapped around Christ, exhibited today in the Savoy Gallery, Turin.

IL VERISSIMO RITRATTO DEL SANTISSIMO SVDARIO
DEL NOSTRO SALVATORE GIESV CHRISTO

OREMVS
DEVS QVI NOBIS IN SANCTA SINDONE, QVA CORPVS TVVM SACRATISSIMV

1

COMPARE
pages ▶ 236–237

THE **PROTOTYPE**

MANY IMAGES OF CHRIST

created by artists over the centuries are reminiscent of the visage imprinted on the Turin Shroud. Such examples include:

1) The gold coin, called a solidus, minted in the reign of the Byzantine emperor Michael III (842–867).

2) The painting of Christ by Simone Martini (1284–1344).

3) The Deesis Mosaic located in the Hagia Sophia in Istanbul, Turkey, dating to 1261.

face. Jewish custom prescribed that a person sentenced to death had to be buried on the day he died: "If a man has committed a sin deserving of death, and he is put to death, and you hang him on a tree, his body shall not remain overnight on the tree, but you shall bury him that day for he who is hanged is accursed of God" (Deut 21: 22–23).

Since Jesus died with barely three hours left before sunset, which on that particular day was the beginning of the Sabbath, the burial rites had to be conducted quickly. According to some experts, the lack of time meant that Jesus' body could not be washed before being laid to rest. Others, however, make the observation that religious custom forbade the washing of a body stained with blood. Indeed, Jews believed that blood was the most life-giving part of the body—"For the life of the flesh is in the blood" (Lev 17:11)—which was why it had to be buried with the deceased. Jesus' body was not washed, in that case, but was anointed with myrrh and aloe before being laid in the tomb.

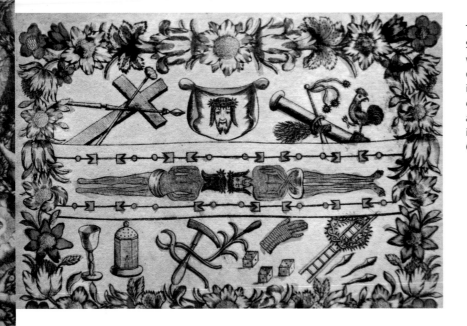

THE TURIN
SHROUD
was often the
central motif in
iconographic
depictions of the
arma Christi, or
instruments of
Christ's torture.

Aloe (*Aloe vera* or *Aloe succotrina*) is a plant whose sap was used as medicine in the ancient world. It tautens the skin and prevents decay; hence its use in anointing bodily remains. Likewise myrrh (*Balsamodendron* or *Commiphora abyssinica*) was known for its tautening and antiseptic qualities and was also used in ancient medicine.

The Torah states that a dead body is unclean. Everything that comes into direct contact with it is also made unclean, which is why it was necessary to destroy any such impure object. For Christians, this particular custom changed following Jesus' Resurrection. Now that He lived once again, all those apparently unclean objects were no longer so. What's more, when the Apostles became convinced that Jesus was indeed the Son of God, they treasured His personal effects as cherished reminders of their Savior.

While no sources exist on this particular topic, according to Christian tradition it was Jesus' disciples who took His burial clothes for safekeeping. Among them, St. John is the most likely candidate to have done so: not only was he at Jesus' grave on the morning of the third day, but he also spent the most time writing about Jesus' burial clothes in his Gospel. The apocryphal *Gospel of the Hebrews*, dating from the second century A.D., maintained that the risen Jesus Himself gave St. Peter His *sindon* for safekeeping.

It's difficult to say where the shroud was hidden. Some historians suppose that it might have been kept either in Jerusalem or in grottoes by the Dead ▶

THE HAGIA SOPHIA in Constantinople (modern-day Istanbul) was the most important Byzantine church, as well as the patriarch's cathedral and the imperial coronation site. When the Turks captured the city in 1453, the church was made into a mosque, with four minarets built around it.

THE DOME IN THE HAGIA SOPHIA was the world's first dome built on a square base, supported by four pillars. It reached 62 meters above floor level and had a diameter of 33 meters.

THE WORLD'S **CAPITAL CITY**

AT THE TIME OF ITS EXPANSION, Constantinople was Europe's largest and richest city. It was a cultural beacon and the economic powerhouse of the entire Mediterranean Basin. It was founded by Constantine the Great, who made it his new capital city in A.D. 324. Its location was of strategic importance, lying on the Bosporus, at the junction of two major trade routes of the ancient world: the Balkan Peninsula to Asia Minor and the Mediterranean Sea to the Black Sea.

With a largely Greek population, the city soon became one of the world's most important Christian centers. After the Roman Empire was divided into East and West, Constantine declared Constantinople the capital of the Byzantine Empire. It was invaded twice by foreign armies: first in 1204 by the Knights of the Fourth Crusade (who founded the Latin Empire of Constantinople, which lasted until 1261) and then— definitively—by the Ottoman Turks in 1453.

For over 11 centuries, Constantinople served as the capital for Christian emperors. In those days, monarchs were considered rulers by divine providence. In other words, their rule was legitimized by God. Indeed, for the Byzantine emperors, the Passion relics served as divine evidence of God's legitimization of their rule. For centuries, Constantinople drew pilgrims from all over the continent, boasting as it did the world's largest collection of relics associated with Jesus Christ, including the True Cross, the Holy Nail, the Crown of Thorns, the Longinus Spear, the Mandylion of Edessa (otherwise known as the Turin Shroud), and the Veil of Camulia (or the Veil of Manoppello).

The city's wealth attracted the attention of other countries, among them the Venetian Republic, which organized and led the Fourth Crusade. Constantinople was invaded and pillaged by the Crusaders, who also plundered many of the city's relics. The Byzantine capital would never regain its former holiness.

INTERIOR OF THE HAGIA SOPHIA, which was turned into a mosque after the Muslim conquest of Constantinople. The building became a museum in 1935 under Kemal Atatürk.

33

TREATISE BY ALFONSO PALEOTTI, archbishop of Bologna, entitled *Wounds of the Crucified Jesus Christ Imprinted on the Holy Shroud,* published in Venice in 1606.

The Turin Shroud

34

PILGRIMS praying before the shroud. The illustration, with its inscription of *"Blessed are the eyes which see what you see.* Luke 10:23", come from a book published in 1769.

Sea or in Pella on the eastern shore of the River Jordan or even in Lebanon, but this all just conjecture. What is known, however, is that the shroud eventually found its way to Edessa, which was once the ancient capital of the Kingdom of Osroene and today is the Turkish city of Urfa.

But when exactly did the shroud arrive in Edessa? In his *Ecclesiastical History*, Eusebius of Caesarea states that it arrived at the court of King Abgar V, "the Black", of Edessa soon after the death of Christ. Eusebius, who lived from 263 to 339, was the first writer to remark upon the existence of a piece of cloth bearing Jesus' imprint. It seems also that the people of Edessa knew about the shroud but could not comment on the circumstances under which the image was made. They deduced that the shroud first appeared in their city during the reign of Abgar V, who ruled the Kingdom of Osroene from A.D. 13 to 50. In time, the legend of "Abgar's Mandylion", which sought to explain how the shroud's imprint came into being, was born. This story, quoted by Eusebius, relates how Abgar, who was suffering from leprosy, sent Jesus a letter asking for help. Since He was not able to come and see the king personally, Jesus sent him His portrait, and Abgar was healed.

There is some truth in this legend. Various historical and archaeological investigations testify to the fact that Abgar was actually baptized and endorsed the spread

Beati oculi, qui vident, quæ vos videtis. LUC. X. 23.

Vendibili presso la Lit.ª Verdoni, via S. Tommaso, Nº 26.

VERO DISEGNO DEL SS. SUDARIO
ESPOSTO NELLA CATTEDRALE DI S. GIOVANNI IN TORINO
1868

PUBLIC SHOWING of the Turin Shroud in 1868, which took place during the rule of Italy's first king, Victor Emmanuel II, of the House of Savoy.

ILLUSTRATION from Archbishop Alfonso Paleotti's book, showing St. Jerome contemplating the Turin Shroud.

of Christianity throughout his kingdom. It's highly likely, therefore, that in an attempt to escape repression, many Christians journeyed from Judea to nearby Osroene. They could in that case have brought the shroud with them, especially since Edessa seemed at that time to be the safest place for keeping the relic, under the eye of a receptive monarch and far from either Roman or Jewish spheres of influence. Over time, however, Abgar's successors abandoned Christianity, and Edessa itself came under Roman rule. According to legend, one of the city's bishops hid the shroud within the city walls, fearing it would otherwise end up being destroyed.

The shroud was next unearthed in 544, during the Persian ruler Khosrau I's siege of Edessa. Evagrius

THE CATHEDRAL OF ST. JOHN in Turin was built in the Renaissance style from 1491 to 1498. The shroud has been kept inside the cathedral since 1578. Guarino Guarini erected a chapel to house the relic toward the end of the seventeenth century.

Scholasticus, a Syrian historian, documented the event and was the first to claim that the shroud's imprint was "divinely wrought" (*Theotokos Eikon*—"God-bearing image"). He described it as an image "made without human hand" (*acheiropoietos*), a phrase that has since been used to refer to any such miraculous images. The shroud has also been called the *tetradiplon*, because it was folded in half three times, resulting in four double layers of cloth. The folding had something to do with the way the shroud was exhibited, allowing devotees to see only that part of the cloth bearing the imprint of Christ's face. The most popular name for the relic in the Christian world, however, became the Mandylion of Edessa, as St. John of Damascus, St. Theodor the Studite, St. Theofanes the Confessor, and John of Antioch all referred to it. The shroud was kept in Edessa's Hagia Sophia (the Church of Holy Wisdom) for almost 400 years, remaining there even when the Muslims conquered the city in 639. Their only condition for keeping it there was that the shroud would not be copied or paraded around during festivals.

The shroud's fame spread throughout the world. In the tenth century the Byzantine emperor Romanos I Lekapenos sent his finest general, John

PILGRIMS IN TURIN CATHEDRAL during the last showing of the shroud, between April 10 and May 23, 2010. A multimedia presentation accompanied the display.

Kourkouas, to seize the relic and bring it to Constantinople. The mission was a success; the Muslims were comprehensively beaten, and the citizens of Edessa were forced to surrender the shroud.

Kourkouas and his men returned triumphantly to the Byzantine capital on August 15, 944. The shroud was paraded around the city, first to St. Mary's Church in the district of Blacherne, then to the Hagia Sophia and the emperor's Boukoleon Palace, and finally to the Church of the Virgin of the Pharos, where it remained. In later years Emperor Constantine VII Porphyrogennetos, who enjoyed fashioning icons, judged the shroud to have been "produced without painting".

The shroud stayed in Constantinople for the next 260 years, during which time its history was comparatively well documented. We know that in 1147 Louis VII of France paid tribute to the relic while visiting the Byzantine ruler. The emperor's *skeuophylax* (or *skeuophylakion*—guard to the treasury), Nicholas Mesarites, wrote about the shroud in 1201 while it was housed in the church of St. Mary in Blacherne: "Christ's burial sheets are made of linen, which is typical of that period; they still retain an odor; they have withstood damage, because they enveloped a wholly mysterious and anointed body." ▷

PREVIOUS PAGES:
THE RELIC IS
SHOWN alongside a
text containing parts
from the Bible relating
Christ's Passion.

Just three years after those words were written, Constantinople fell to the Venetians and the Franks of the Fourth Crusade. Rather than marching on the Holy Land to face the Muslims, the Crusaders hit Constantinople, seizing it on April 13, 1204. The capital's citizens were massacred, the churches desecrated, and the treasury plundered. As had previously been agreed between the crusading factions, anything wrought from gold would go to the Venetians, and all relics—including the Mandylion—would become the property of the Franks.

The shroud's fate during this time is largely unknown. Pope Innocent III condemned the pillaging of Constantinople, excommunicating those responsible. No one was ever found boasting about relics they owned, and cursed was the man who admitted to having stolen any. Unsurprisingly, for a long time afterward, many of the relics that were looted in Constantinople simply disappeared.

TURIN CATHEDRAL is
filled with visitors from
all over the world on
days when the shroud is
displayed to the public.
According to Vatican
Radio, 2.1 million
pilgrims came to see
the shroud in 2010.

As far as the Mandylion's fate is concerned, it was most likely stolen by the Fourth Crusade's leader Boniface I, marquess of Montferrat, who then passed it on to one of his most trusted aides, the Burgundian knight Otto de la Roche. De la Roche then took it with him to Greece, where he became the first ruler of the Duchy of Athens, before transporting it to France. When Boniface I died while fighting the Bulgarians in 1207, de la Roche became the shroud's sole owner.

Some historians believe that during the thirteenth and fourteenth centuries, the shroud was in the hands of the Knights Templar, who nevertheless made every attempt to conceal this fact. One theory states that at the time of his death, Otto de la Roche bequeathed the shroud to the Templars in the form of a deposit. We know from various historical sources that some of the order's highest-ranking members venerated a mysterious relic in the shape of a head, both in Montpellier and in Carcassonne. This in itself was enough of a pretext for the French king Philip IV, "the Fair", to confront the order and abscond with its riches. He accused the Templars of secretly worshipping a pagan deity by the name of Baphomet, and in 1312 the order was formally disbanded, with Philip claiming its assets for his own. Two years later, 54 higher-ranking Templars, including Grand Master Jacques de Molay, were burned at the stake for heresy.

Some historians surmise that the pagan deity the Templars supposedly venerated was in fact the Turin Shroud. The Italian historian Antonio Lombatti writes that "while we know that this deity was exhibited in a great variety of ways, almost all of its manifestations—as a relic, a painting on paper or on a wall, a head, a head with four legs, or a man with a beard—relate in some way to the shroud."

Lombatti goes on to write that "the trade of relics between East and West prompted the Christian authorities present at the Fourth Council of the Lateran in 1215 to order an

THE KNIGHTS TEMPLAR were most probably the shroud's owners during the thirteenth and fourteenth centuries. Their symbol was a red cross, and their crest showed two knights riding on one horse.

official decree banning their transportation. Such practice, they claimed, was both sacrilegious and simoniacal. In such circumstances, the Knights Templar would have been hard pressed to account for how they came to own an authentic Christ-bearing image and why it was then illegally transported to France. Without doubt, anyone who freely admitted to being at fault would have been burned at the stake. In keeping quiet, many Templars were at least able to save their own lives, if not their honor. Like the Templars, who presumably regarded the shroud as being genuine, the relic's first official owners were also forced to keep their prized acquisition a secret."

For the next 150 years or so, the shroud's exact whereabouts are unknown. However, it resurfaced midway through the fourteenth century in the French town of Lirey, not far from Troyes, in the Champagne region. We do not know how its owner, the Crusader Geofrroi de Charny, was able to procure it, but we do know that the shroud was put on public display for the first time in the West in 1357, in the Lirey collegiate church. It remained in the Charny family for almost a hundred years and was housed variously in Montfort, Saint-Hippolyte, Chimay, and Germolles. In 1453, six years before her death, Geoffroi's granddaughter and the family's last remaining heir, Marguerite de Charny, gave the shroud to her friend Louis, the duke of Savoy. The shroud was to remain with the Savoyard dynasty until 1983.

This does not mean, however, that the relic was left entirely untroubled throughout that time. Due to a frequently strained political climate and resulting wars, the shroud was often transferred from one place to another, including Geneva, Vercelli, Ivrea, Moncalieri, Pinerolo, Susa, Avigliana, Rivoli, Savigliano, Pont-d'Ain, Brissac, Milan and Nice. The shroud spent most of its time, however, on public display at Chambéry—the capital of the duchy ruled by the House of Savoy.

The relic was in fact almost destroyed in Chambéry, on the night of December 3, 1532. The chapel in which it was kept caught fire; its interior was completely destroyed, and its facade was razed. Luckily the shroud, which was folded in 48 layers and kept in a solid silver reliquary, escaped largely unscathed: one corner was charred by a few drops of molten silver, and one side of the shroud was slightly discolored. It was rescued by four men, including two Franciscans, who used buckets of water to cool the reliquary before dragging it out of the burning chapel.

According to the Italian scientist Giorgio Tessiore, the temperature inside the chapel during the fire was as high as 500 degrees centigrade, while the temperature inside the reliquary was almost 280 degrees. "Based on my calculations as well as several

COMMEMORATIVE MEDAL FRAGMENT, dated pre-1356. It shows the Turin Shroud and the de Charny family crest. The medal was almost certainly produced to mark when the relic was displayed in Lirey. This only surviving example was found in the Seine.

✤

reconstructions, I am convinced", writes Tessiore, "that a drop of molten silver would have fallen at an angle of 45 degrees in relation to the reliquary's base, and did so precisely at the moment when the casket was dragged out of the chapel." It might have been only a matter of seconds, therefore, before the shroud was completely destroyed.

Between April 16 and May 2, 1532, the shroud underwent restoration by the Poor Clares in Chambéry. The sisters patched up the relic in 16 places and lined it with Holland cloth to strengthen the fabric.

The shroud found its permanent home in 1578, when Duke Emmanuel Philibert decided to transfer it to Piedmont's capital, Turin. From that moment on, the so-called Mandylion of Edessa became increasingly known as the Turin Shroud. In 1694 the shroud was placed in a special chapel built for it beside St. John's Cathedral. Thereafter, it left Turin only twice in the next 300 years: the first time in 1706, when the city was besieged by the French, and then from 1939 to 1946, when it was hidden in the monastery at Montevergine, not far from Avellino. When the Second World War broke out, the original plan was to move the shroud to the abbey at Monte Cassino, but this was decided against at the last minute.

For almost 500 years, the Turin Shroud remained in the possession of the House of Savoy, who ruled Italy between 1861 and 1946. Italy's last monarch, Humbert II, was dethroned in June 1946 as a result of a constitutional referendum. Before

TESTS ON THE TURIN SHROUD were carried out in October 1978 by a team of 40 American scientists, including the photographer Barrie Schwortz. His colleagues Ray Rogers and Robert Dinegar, based in Los Alamos, collected pollen samples and other surface particles using adhesive tape made of pure carbon.

The Turin Shroud

43

✠

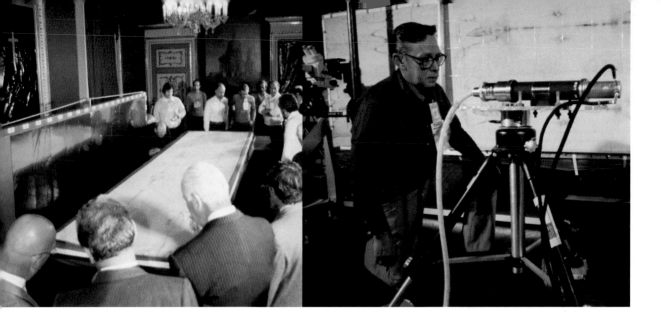

THE TURIN SHROUD was unfolded on an aluminum table covered with magnetic film, which was constructed so that the cloth could be turned over on its vertical axis, and be studied lengthways as well as horizontally. The tests were carried out in the library of the Royal Palace of Turin.

RON LONDON, an American scientist at the Sandia National Laboratories, while carrying out radiographic tests on the Turin Shroud.

he died in Geneva in 1983 he declared that the shroud should become the charge of the Holy See.

Although the relic was regularly placed on public display from 1706, it never attracted much scientific interest. The turning point came in 1898, when Secondo Pia published his photographs. The task of proving that the shroud was a fake fell to the French zoologist Yves Delage, who was also known to be an agnostic and an anticleric. He announced the results of his tests during a meeting of the Scientific Academy in Paris in 1902. To everyone's surprise, he declared that both the figure's anatomical details and the traces of wounds found on the cloth were, from a medical perspective, too exact to be attributed to a painter. According to Delage, the Turin Shroud was imprinted with a genuine image of Christ. The likelihood of its being anyone else, he claimed, was 1 in 10 billion.

Furthermore, Delage stated that "in order for the likeness to be imprinted, and then not fade, the body must have been wrapped in the linen for at least 24 hours—in other words, the length of time needed for an imprint to be made—but not longer than a few days, after which it would have started to decompose, thereby destroying both the image and the cloth itself . This is exactly what, according to tradition (which is more or less apocryphal, in my opinion), happened to Christ, who died on a Friday, and disappeared on the Sunday."

The French medical doctor Paul Vignon was the next to conduct tests on the Turin Shroud. He determined that there were as many as 15 shared characteristics between the image found on the relic and those images of Christ found in religious icons. This strongly suggested the existence of some "master icon"; in other words, a model depiction ▷

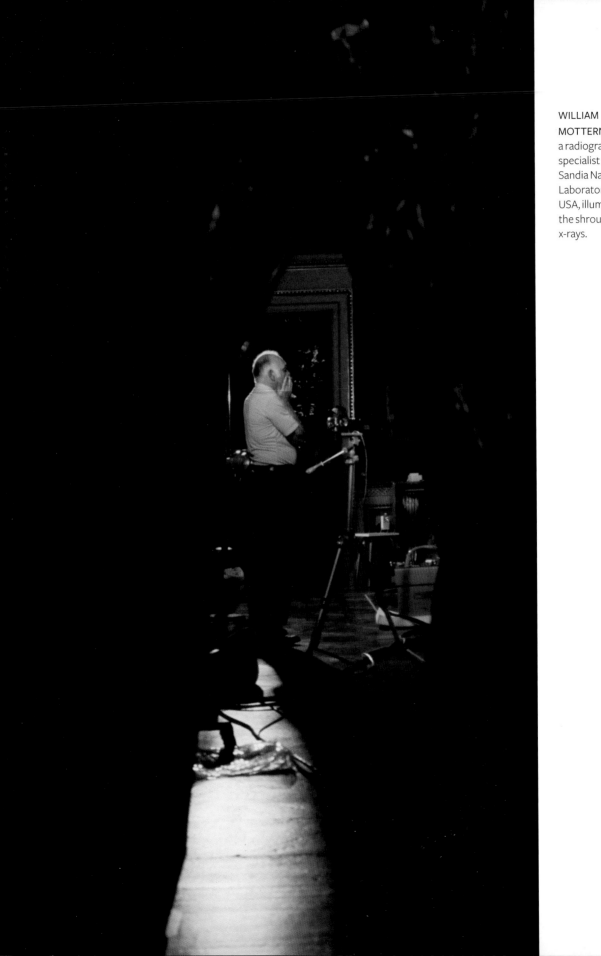

WILLIAM MOTTERN, a radiography specialist at the Sandia National Laboratories in the USA, illuminates the shroud using x-rays.

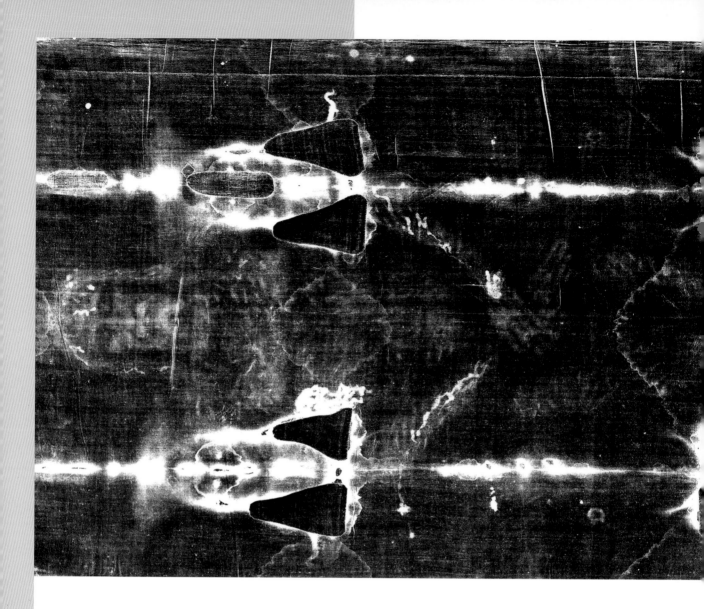

SHROUD IMPRINT
FRONT

FRONT OF THE TURIN SHROUD IMAGE
The following details can be observed:

1. Burn marks resulting from the 1532 fire

2. Staining caused by water used
   to extinguish the fire

3. Image of a male figure

4. Injuries sustained as a result of scourging

5. Bloodstains caused by lacerations

6. Bloodstain caused by nailing of the left wrist

7. Blood flowing from the wrists down
   the length of the forearms

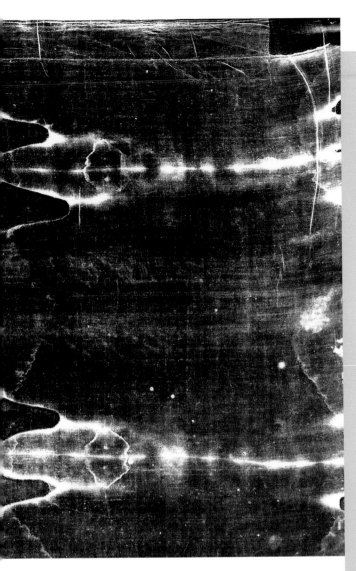

8. Bloodstain caused by piercing of the body's right side

9. Bloodstain caused by nailing of the right foot

COMPARE
page ▶ 19

47

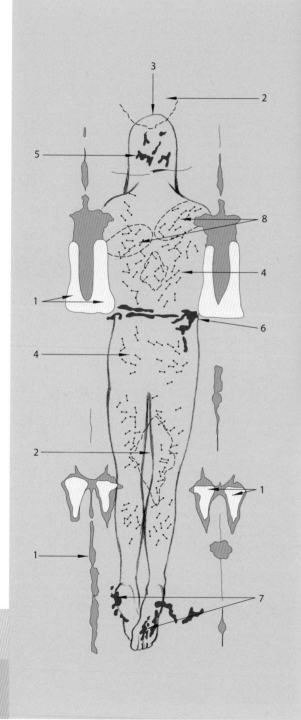

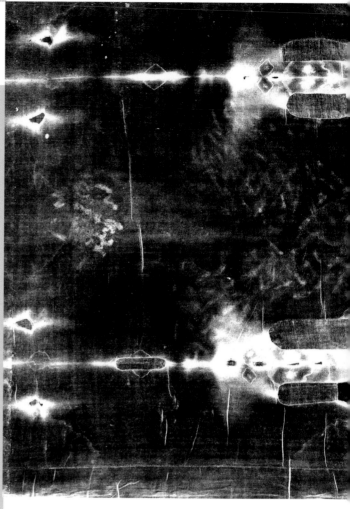

SHROUD IMPRINT
BACK

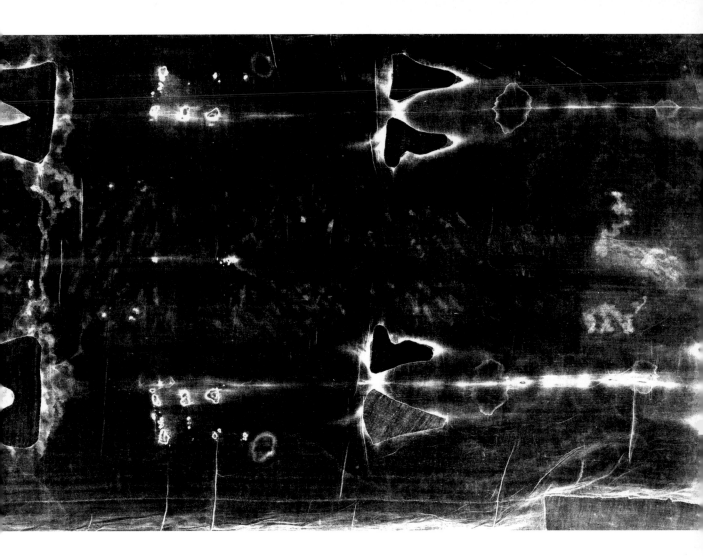

BACK OF THE TURIN SHROUD IMAGE

The following details can be observed:

1. Burn marks resulting from the 1532 fire

2. Staining caused by water used to
   extinguish the fire

3. Image of a male figure

4. Injuries sustained as a result of scourging

5. Bloodstains caused by lacerations

6. Combined blood and water stains flowing
   from pierced side

7. Bloodstains caused by nailing of the soles
   of the feet

8. Areas of abrasion caused by dragging
   a large angular object

COMPARE
page ▶ 253

THE MYSTERY OF THE SLANTED BEAM:
WAS CHRIST LAME?

CHRIST'S CROSS was made up of a vertical beam (*stipes*) and a horizontal one (*patibulum*). In Eastern icons—initially Greek, then Bulgarian and Russian—however, another element became popular in depictions of the crucifixion. This was the small beam under the feet (*suppedaneum*), which was nailed not perpendicularly to the Cross, but at a slanted angle.

The existence of this small beam isn't verified by historical sources or by medical analyses. According to doctors, if Christ had rested His feet on the beam, His agony would have lasted much longer, since His whole weight would not have been dragging Him down.

Where, then, did this Eastern practice of depicting the Cross come from? Some art historians believe that Christ was partly crippled and that His left leg was shorter than His right. This belief is based on iconic depictions in which Christ's body is in an S shape, called a "Byzantine contortion", as if He were in fact lame. There are also numerous ancient icons from the East that depict the baby Jesus with deformed feet. Similarly, the motif of a limping Messiah appears in numerous Eastern catechisms of the Christian Church.

The question remains, however, of how Christ's followers in the East came to regard Him as crippled. None of the Gospels mentions that Jesus had a limp. One logical explanation has to do with the image imprinted on the Turin Shroud: if we examine the cloth from behind, we can clearly see that the figure's right leg is longer than the left.

Was Christ really crippled? Doctors who examined the shroud posited the theory that as a result of the injuries sustained while carrying the Cross, Christ ended up with a dislocated hip and a deformed shoulder. Furthermore, when His feet were nailed to the Cross, first the right leg was nailed and then the left leg was twisted over it and secured. When Christ's body was removed from the Cross and rigor mortis had set in, it would have looked as if His legs were deformed, His hip elevated, and His shoulder lowered. This exact image was preserved on the Turin Shroud. Christians in the East, where the shroud was kept for 12 centuries, were most likely mistaken, therefore, in thinking that Christ was deformed from birth.

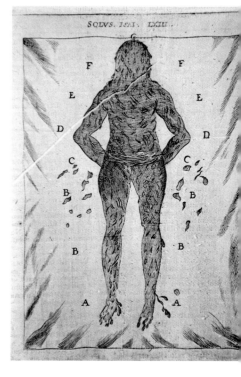

BOOK ILLUSTRATION from Archbishop Alfonso Paleotti's 1606 work. The image shows Christ with one leg longer than the other.

50

of Christ that became prevalent within the Church. According to Vignon, the Mandylion fulfilled that role of master icon.

The Turin Shroud was next photographed—using much more sophisticated equipment—by Giuseppe Enri in May 1931. The quality of these photographs was, unsurprisingly, much better than those of Secondo Pia. It was concluded that the shroud depicted an image like a photographic negative and that making it would have required production techniques that could not have existed before the nineteenth century.

At the first sindonology conference, which took place in Turin in the summer of 1939, the most important presentation came from two forensic specialists, Ruggero Romanese and Giovanni Judica-Cordiglia. Independently of each other, both scientists found that the image on the shroud was of a man who had died in extreme agony. They also dismissed the notion that the image could have been painted in the Middle Ages. A French surgeon, Pierre Barbet, arrived at a similar conclusion by proving that the shroud's imprint accurately showed all the anatomical and

THE TRUCK that arrived at the Royal Palace in Turin in early October 1978 was carrying almost 2.5 tons of scientific equipment, used by the American team to carry out tests on the shroud.

The Turin Shroud

51

✛

physiological traits of a dying man, which would not have been known to people living in previous centuries.

Some decades passed before the next series of tests were conducted upon the Turin Shroud. These took place after four archbishops of Turin—Michele Pellegrino, Anastasio Ballestrero, Giovanni Saldarini, and Severino Poletto—were appointed cardinals. It was their decision to invite a number of distinguished scientists to carry out experiments on the famous relic. This period marked the start of a new era in sindonology, characterized by a series of extraordinary discoveries.

The director of the Ghent Institute of Textile Technology, Professor Gilbert Raes, has claimed that the thread from which the shroud was woven came from the Middle East and that fabrics of this kind were already being used at the start of the Christian era. More specifically, according to the French writer Daniel Raffard de Brienne, the shroud was probably woven using a Jewish loom, since the linen material exhibited traces of cotton fiber but no traces of wool. This suggests that the weaver who manufactured the shroud wove it on a loom that used only fibers originating from plants; a separate loom would have been employed for work with ▶

WEAVER'S LOOM used in ancient times in Palestine. The Turin Shroud would have been produced on such a loom.

BARRIE SCHWORTZ, photographer from Arizona, currently travels all over the world giving lectures on the Turin Shroud.

AMERICAN SCIENTISTS Barrie Schwortz and Ray Rogers while carrying out tests on the relic in the Royal Palace, Turin.

JEWISH INVESTIGATIONS
INTO THE AUTHENTICITY OF THE TURIN SHROUD

IN 1977 JEWISH AMERICAN photographer Barrie Schwortz—a specialist in imaging, programming, and digital technology—joined a team of American scientists who together formed the Shroud of Turin Research Project (STURP). The team has conducted the most rigorous series of tests on the relic to date.

The notion that the shroud's image could have been painted was dismissed at the very outset, recalls Schwortz, due to the lack of any pigmentation or coloring. The theory that the image could be a photograph was likewise ignored, since the cloth didn't bear any traces of ionized silver. Schwortz states, "As a photographer, I have a decent understanding of the technology involved, as well as issues concerning focal lengths and lighting. I came to the conclusion that the image could not have been made by hand, and was created in a way that we are unable to duplicate. For someone such as myself, who has behind him a considerable amount of professional experience in photography, the image on the shroud makes a powerful impression even to this day. I have spent 30 years watching various attempts—made by scientists and skeptics alike—to reproduce the shroud's image. Nobody has been able to do so while retaining all of the relic's physical and chemical properties."

It took 18 years for Schwortz to become convinced of the Turin Shroud's authenticity. The decisive factor was a conversation with Alan Adler, another Jewish sindonologist. Adler was able to explain why, despite the amount of time that had passed, traces of blood found on the shroud retained their red coloring instead of turning brown, as might be expected. If a person is is tortured and not given anything to drink, his red blood cells burst and his liver releases a chemical compound called bilirubin. When this substance enters the bloodstream, it causes the blood to retain its red color permanently. "This evidence was like the missing part of the puzzle", recalls Schwortz. "After that conversation, it seemed as if every obstacle that had prevented me from believing the shroud to be authentic had been removed."

Today, Schwortz has no doubt that the Turin Shroud is a record of Christ's Passion. All the evidence found on the burial cloth confirms the details of Christ's death as related in the Gospels. Schwortz also states that the evidence collected from tests conducted on the shroud would not have been obtainable a hundred years ago; only in the last half century or so has the necessary technology been developed to examine the relic adequately. Schwortz is keen to point out, however, that despite this advance in technology, the more tests that are carried out on the shroud, the more enigmatic it becomes.

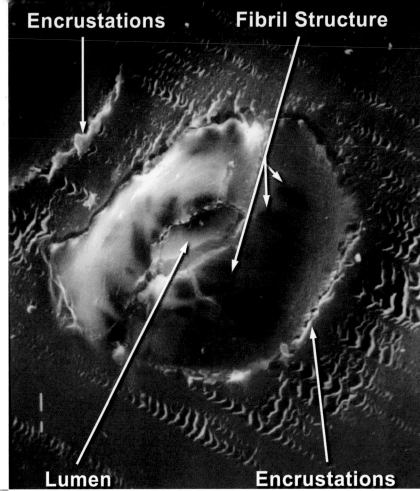

Encrustations   **Fibril Structure**

Lumen   **Encrustations**

VERTICAL CROSS-SECTION of the Turin Shroud's fabric, magnified 3650 times. The photograph was taken by Prof. Gilbert Raes of the Ghent Institute of Textile Technology. The "Encrustations" represent the coloring apparent in the imprinted image. The photo clearly shows that they do not penetrate the fabric's internal structure, and are a surface phenomenon.

LINEN THREAD from the Turin Shroud. Photo taken using 56x enlargement.

fibers originating from animals. Using separate looms was requrired by Jewish religious laws, which banned the mingling of plant and animal products, even in the manufacture of clothing and textiles. In 2002 the Swiss textile conservationist Mechthild Flury-Lemberg discovered that the shroud's stitching pattern was identical to that of burial clothes found in tombs at the Jewish fortress of Masada, dating back to the first century A.D.

Similarly, Pasadena-based scientists Jean Lorre and Donald Lynn concluded that the shroud's image could not be a painting, as there was no evidence of directional strokes or even the faintest trace of pigmentation. Italian scientists Giovanni Tamburelli and Nello Balossino discovered that the image has a three-dimensional character, such as cannot be found on any painting in the world. In their opinion, the image was made as a result of the direct imprint of a three-dimensional shape, specifically a dead body. According to French scientist Arnaud-Aaron Upinsky, "It's scientifically impossible for the Turin Shroud to have been painted by an artist. The image is like a photograph, produced using a camera. And a unique one at that: not only is it able to capture a negative image, but it can also reproduce a monochrome three-dimensional effect, which appears

LEFT: Netting placed on top of the Turin Shroud in order to divide it into
10-square-centimeter segments.

RIGHT: Vacuum tube used by Prof. Giovanni Riggi while carrying out tests on the shroud.

on the surface as a result of cellulose dehydration and is achieved through varying the pressure of the imprint."

No painter from the Middle Ages or earlier could have produced the shroud, since in that time the rules of perspective had not yet been established. Likewise, people did not possess sufficient anatomical knowledge to outline precisely—without a single mistake—all the details of the human form.

Significantly, testing on the Turin Shroud has revealed the presence of both red blood cells and skin cells. The Italian doctor Pierluigi Bollone has even identified the blood group as AB. This is the rarest of all blood groups, found in only 4 to 5 percent of the world's population. It occurs more frequently among Jews, however, accounting for 18 percent of the Jewish population.

Analysts have also remarked upon the shroud's image in relation to apparent blood traces. It turns out that there is no evidence of coloring or shading underneath the stains of blood, meaning that the bloodstains were the first to be imprinted on the shroud, with the imprint of a human figure occuring later.

After examining the properties of the blood found on the shroud, particularly concerning the presence of bilirubin, American chemist Alan D. Adler came to the conclusion that the blood traces were left by someone who died under traumatic circumstances, most likely as a result of intense suffering.

ALAN D. ADLER,
American chemist
and hematologist
of Jewish
ancestry, one
of the shroud's
analysts.

55
✠

THE SHROUD'S INSCRIPTIONS

ITALIAN SINDONOLOGIST Pietro Ugolotti was the first to discover graphic signs on the surface of the Turin Shroud. Using color filters with enlarged photographs of the shroud, he was able to discern the inscription NAZARENU above the figure's left brow.

Professor Aldo Marastoni—Italian paleographer, papyrologist, and priest—confirmed the presence of writing on the relic when he identified several loosely arranged symbols, reminiscent of Semitic, Greek, and Latin letters. He was able to decipher three letters from the Hebrew alphabet—*tav*, *vav*, and *yod*—as well as a full stop, above the figure's right brow. According to Marastoni, these symbols were not rendered directly on the shroud's surface. Rather, they were most likely painted on a separate object, specifically a so-called hood of shame, a type of headband, which was then imprinted on the shroud. Two other specialists in Hebrew studies—Roberto Messina and Carlo Orecchia—have deciphered the imprinted inscription to read "King of the Jews".

Marastoni also discovered a double imprint of letters in the middle of the figure's forehead, appearing in two lines. The upper line reads IBER, and the lower line reads IB. These letters, Marastoni claims, were inscribed on a headband that shifted slightly, causing a double imprint. The letters IBER and IB are indicative of the name Tiberius, the Roman emperor at the time of Christ's death. It is highly likely, therefore, that this headband bore the *titulus damnationis*, or sentence, of the condemned person.

More inscriptions were found in due course. The letters INNECE appear in three places on the shroud and have been reinterpreted by Marastoni as IN NECEM, meaning "to death". The words appear on the right and left sides of the figure's face and under the chin. Marastoni claims that the inscription originally appeared on three pieces of wood, used to create a special support (*furca*) around the head. He also discovered the word NEAZARE on the right side of the head, which he believes might also have appeared on the wooden support.

In 1982, the French monk R.P. Dubois deciphered the Greek letters P E Z O on the right side of the figure's face; these in his opinion could together form the words "I testify".

An important new phase in the reading of inscriptions on the Turin Shroud took place in the years 1997 and 1998 under the leadership of André Marion, a professor at the Optics Institute in Orsay. Using modern scanning equipment and microdensitometers, Marion was able to confirm the existence of those inscriptions already discovered, as well as some new ones, including the word IESOUS (Jesus) below the figure's chin.

In 2009, Barbara Frale (a medievalist working in the Vatican Archives) claimed that the shroud's inscriptions were an imprint of Christ's burial certificate. In those days, people sentenced to death were often buried in mass graves, and their bodies were given over to their families only after a year. The practice of burying convicted persons together with a document of identification became an easy way of finding the correct bodily remains after a year had gone by. Based on the reconstruction of the shroud's partially preserved inscriptions, experts have concluded that Christ's death certificate might have read as follows: "In the sixteenth year of the rule of Caesar Tiberius, Jesus of Nazareth, taken down at dusk following sentencing to death by a Roman judge, after Roman authorities found him guilty, is sent to burial with the stipulation that his body may be returned to his family only after a whole year has passed. Signed by [no signature has been preserved]."

There is no definitive consensus among sindonologists regarding the origins of the shroud's inscriptions. Maria Grazia Siliato and Marcel Alonso claim they were written on a so-called *exactor mortis*, or a piece of material in the shape of the letter U, which was fastened to a dead body to aid its identification. Gregory Kaplan, on the other hand, believes the words may be the imprints of seals left by priests and Pharisees acting as sentries, as related in St. Matthew's Gospel. Other scholars suggest that the graphic symbols found on the shroud could be the imprints of amulets and phylacteries. Although the case for interpreting the inscriptions' exact origins remains open, paleographers have dismissed the notion that they could have been forged during the Middle Ages, since the shapes of the letters suggest a specifically Roman calligraphic style. The word INNECE, for instance, was written in a particular type of script that was used in the first century A.D. but ceased to be used halfway through the second century.

1

PROF. ANDRÉ MARION used modern scanning equipment to discover two U-shaped geometric shapes – one nestled within the other – surrounding the dead individual's face. In his opinion these are traces of frames that bore the inscriptions.

INSCRIPTIONS ON THE TURIN SHROUD, which were deciphered thanks to the advanced photographic technology used by Prof. André Marion of the Optics Institute in Orsay:

1. (O)PSE KIA(THO) – "taken down at dusk"
2. PEZO – "I certify"
3. INNECE(M) – "to death"
4. (T)IB(ERIUS) – "Tiberius"
5. NNAZARENNOS – "Nazarene"
6. (I)ESOU(S) – "Jesus"

COMPARE

page ▶ 189

▶ **Other important discoveries have come in the field of botany.** In 1973 and 1978, Swiss biologist and criminologist Max Frei-Sulzer (a Protestant known for his critical outlook on relics) spent time extracting test samples of pollen grains found on the shroud. From this, he was able to identify as many as 58 plant species whose pollen grains had been deposited on the relic. Among those, only 17 species accounted for plants growing in Europe, with the remaining 41 pointing to plant types that are more prevalent in Asia and Africa. Frei-Sulzer discovered that only one geographical region in the world boasted 38 of those 41 plant species, and that was Judea.

The Israeli botanist Professor Avinoam Danin, of the University of Jerusalem, has conducted other palynological tests on the shroud. Regarded as a world authority on Palestinian plant matter, Danin confirmed Frei-Sulzer's results and discovered furthermore that three plants whose pollen grains were found on the shroud were in fact

THE ROCK ROSE (*Cistus creticus*) grows only in the Holy Land. Its pollen grains were among those found on the Turin Shroud.

THE POPPY ANEMONE (*Anemone coronaria*), called *calanit* in Hebrew. Its pollen grains were among those discovered on the Turin Shroud.

The Turin Shroud

58

THE CAROB TREE, (*Ceratonia siliqua*), also known as St. John's-bread. Its pollen grains were among those discovered on the Turin Shroud.

EXPERT SINDONOLOGISTS: Max Frei-Sulzer of Switzerland, Luigi Gonella of Italy, and John Jackson of the USA during tests carried out on the shroud in 1978.

THE SPINY THISTLE known as (*Gundelia tournefortii*) is endemic to the Holy Land. According to Prof. Alan Wangher, the Crown of Thorns was made from this plant.

endemic to the Holy Land. These are the rock rose (*Cistus creticus*), the bushy bean caper plant (*Zygophyllum dumosum*), and a certain kind of tumbleweed or thistle (*Gundelia tournefortii*). All of these blossom in the spring and do not grow anywhere in the world other than in Judea.

With the use of polarizing filters, the American professor Alan Wangher discovered in turn outlines of flowers and plants surrounding the image on the shroud. These came about, Wangher claims, through a phenomenon known as "corona discharge"; an electrical discharge that can occur on statically charged surfaces. Based on his findings, Wangher created a "floral map" of the Turin Shroud. Interestingly, the *Gundelia tournefortii* occupies a significant portion of this floral map; almost half of the pollen grains found on the shroud by Danin are of this species. Wangher also discovered that a large proportion of the *Gundelia* pollen grains were concentrated around the head of the imprinted figure. This result seems to confirm the notion that the Crown of Thorns was made using spikes from the *Gundelia tournefortii* plant.

The Turin Shroud has likewise been examined by several medical teams, whose results have overlapped. Multiple lacerations to the head confirm that the imprinted figure must have been forced to wear a headpiece made of thorns. This must have been a source of great pain, given that there are as many as 150 pain receptors ▶

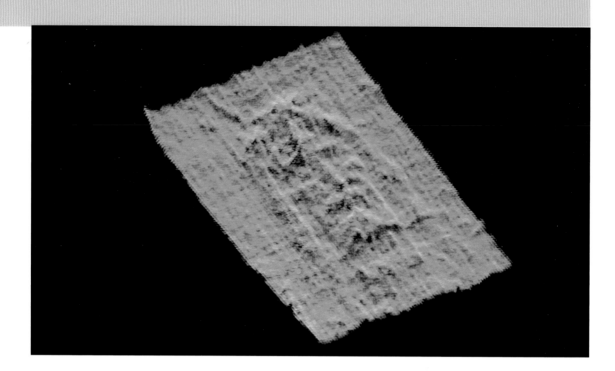

THE IMPOTENCE **OF MODERN SCIENCE**

IN 2009 LUIGI GARLASCHELLI, professor of chemistry at the University of Pavia in Italy, announced that over the space of a week he had completed a reproduction of the Turin Shroud using methods that would have been available during medieval times. It quickly turned out, however, that this was mere idle boasting. There were many differences between Garlaschelli's reproduction and the original relic, the main one concerning the process by which the shroud's image was made.

Microscopic testing has proved that the shroud's image was created as a result of the oxygenation and dehydration of the fibers found in the cloth's outermost threads. These protruding threads have an average diameter of just 10 to 20 microns and a maximum depth of 125 micrometers. Scientists have been unable to determine, however, what phenomenon caused the fibers to yellow and thereby create an image. One of the most frequently cited theories is that the image on the shroud was formed through contact with a human body that was able to emanate fumes or some kind of energy.

Dr. John Jackson, who has been studying the shroud since 1977, has remarked upon the shroud's unusual characteristics, including its remarkably high visual definition; a surface that lacks any evidence of pigmentation; molecular changes in the cellulose traces within the cloth that preserve the imprint; a saturation of the body's frontal imprint that corresponds to its relative distance from the surrounding cloth; the lack of an imprint showing the sides of the body; and the positioning of the front part of the body in such a way that is indicative of a person in a vertical position.

In Jackson's opinion, any theory that manages to explain adequately the provenance of all these characteristics requires a certain leap of faith. The American Janice Bennett summarizes Jackson's hypothesis: "First, the image of the body and the traces of blood came about through the cloth's direct contact with a human form. We reach this conclusion because the stains on the cloth are comprised solely of blood, while the image corresponds with that of a person lying on their back. Secondly, gravity was an important factor in the process, in the sense that whatever it was that created the image was able to do so only with the body in a vertical position. And finally, the shroud was positioned in two different ways, since the corresponding parts of the body and traces of blood that are visible on the shroud have clearly shifted in relation to each other. The bloodstains must have left their imprint directly upon initial contact with the cloth. However, at the point when the image of the body was formed, the shroud seemingly fell, so that the sides of the figure's face shifted by a few centimeters and overlapped with the pattern created by the bloodstains."

In other words, according to Jackson, the shroud was initially wrapped around a human body, which then, somehow, stopped providing a structural framework for the surrounding cloth, allowing for the cloth to fall. At this moment, the imprint was formed. Such a hypothesis would account for all the relic's unusual characteristics, but with two rather major ramifications: first of all, the body must have suddenly become "transparent" or, in other words, permeable to any physical objects surrounding it. Freed of a supporting framework, the cloth would have been able to fall. Secondly, at this moment the cloth must have somehow passed through the bodily form, resulting in its imprint. Jackson claims that such a phenomenon could be attributed to the emission of radiation, which might account for the image's high definition and three-dimensional aspect.

on the human head. The piercing thorns would also have torn blood vessels and irritated nerve endings, thereby compounding the pain.

There are likewise numerous contusions to be found on the figure's face. Above all, the face itself is not symmetrical, with the right side looking more damaged and swollen from what doctors have deemed a traumatic injury. These wounds appear not only on the face, but all over the body; as many as 600 wounds have been found on the skin's surface. Most of these are on the back and are as a result of scourging.

As documented by the poet Horace, scourging, or flogging, in Roman times was carried out with the use of a "horrible whip" (*horribile flagellum*). This whip consisted of a wooden handle and three ox-hide thongs. Each of these thongs was knotted with small balls of lead and bone fragments. The impact of such an instrument tore the skin, occasionally deeply lacerating the flesh.

Before the Second World War, Pierre Barbet had

already determined that the victim's body was nailed to the cross not at the palms but at the wrists. Later tests carried out by Pierluigi Baima Bollone, Lamberto Coppini, and Frank Zugibe have confirmed these results. The French medic Pierre Merat was able to confirm by means of reconstruction that if the body had been nailed at the palms, it would have eventually fallen from the cross. Specialists have claimed that if the shroud were a medieval forgery, the nail wounds would be found on the victim's palms, not on the wrists, since that was the way crucifixion

THREE-DIMENSIONAL IMAGE of Christ's face as seen on the Turin Shroud. The image was constructed in 1978 as part of tests lead by scientists Giovanni Tamburelli and Nello Balossino.

THE HANDS on the shroud, crossed over the lower abdomen. Nail wounds are visible on the wrists but not on the palms.

RECONSTRUCTION of the Crown of Thorns, based on analyses of the Turin Shroud.

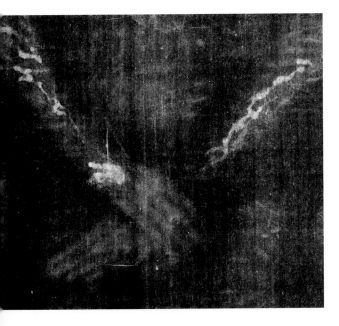

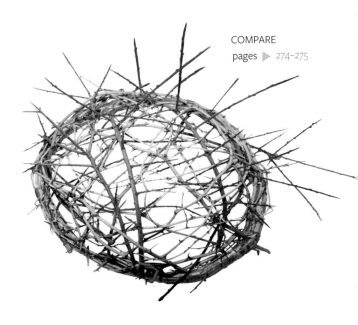

COMPARE
pages ▶ 274–275

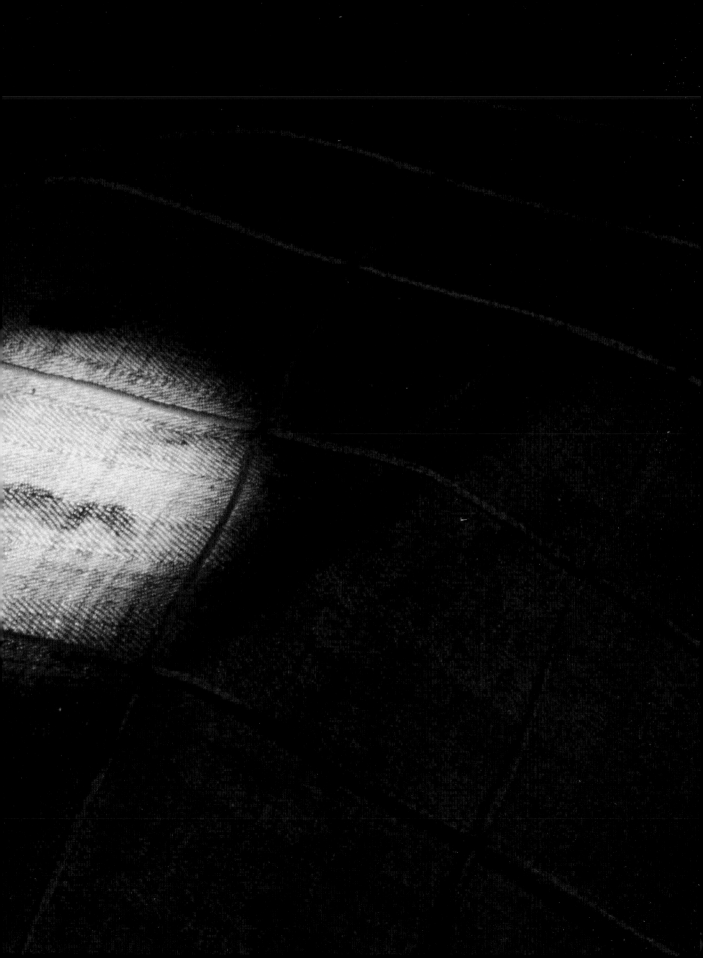

▶ was imagined at that time (as evidenced by numerous statues and pictures).

The next noteworthy analysis was conducted by American crystallographer Joseph Kohlbeck, who discovered mineral particles deposited around the feet of the shroud's imprinted figure. These particles testify to a large concentration of strontium, iron, and calcium carbonate, in the form of aragonite. Another mineralogist, Riccardo Levi-Setti of the University of Chicago, has observed that aragonite—a polymorphic variety of calcium carbonate—was used in building work in ancient Jerusalem. It's highly likely, therefore, that the shroud's figure had walked this city barefoot.

Following the analysis of high-definition photographs of the shroud's three-dimensional image, Italian scientists Pietro Ugolotti and Giovanni Tamburelli discovered—independently of each other—that a small coin, about 15 millimeters in diameter, had been placed in each of the victim's eye sockets. Shortly thereafter, the American Jesuit priest Francis L. Filas, professor of theology at Loyola University in Chicago, identified the coin that had been over the right eye. Made of bronze, it was minted in Judea under the Roman prefect Pontius Pilate between A.D. 26 and 36. In Greek, the coin was called a lepton; in Hebrew, a prutah. It was worth one-hundredth of a Greek drachma and was known as the "widow's penny". An analysis of the coin's imprinted inscription confirms that it dates from the sixteenth year of the reign of Caesar Tiberius. Since Tiberius came to power in A.D. 14, we can surmise that the coin was in circulation about A.D. 29 or 30. Later Father Filas identified the coin that had been placed over the left eye as another bronze lepton minted by Pilate during Tiberius' reign.

The dating of the coins coincides with the dating of

Christ's crucifixion. We know that He was sentenced to death during the time when Pilate was prefect of Judea, between A.D. 26 and 36. According to St. John's Gospel, Christ's execution took place on Friday, the fourteenth day of the month of Nisan in the Hebrew calendar. Between A.D. 26 and 36 the fourteenth day of Nisan fell on a Friday only twice: in A.D. 30 (April 7) and 33 (April 3). In both cases, this was the Friday preceding the holy festival of Passover.

BRONZE LEPTON minted during the rule of Pontius Pilate, Roman prefect of Judea. It appears from an image on the shroud that this coin had been placed on the crucified person's left eyelid.

THIS LEPTON had been placed over the right eyelid of the person on the Turin Shroud.

The Turin Shroud

64

✛

PREVIOUS PAGES: BEAM OF LIGHT illuminating a bloodstain on the forehead of the person on the Turin Shroud.

Two astronomers from Oxford University—Colin J. Humphreys and W.G. Waddington—have conducted analyses using as their starting point the New Testament accounts of Christ's death. St. Matthew's Gospel states that when Jesus died everything became dark, which previously had been interpreted to mean a solar eclipse. In the Acts of the Apostles, St. Peter proclaims that signs of the Messiah (including "the sun shall be turned to darkness and the moon into blood") have occurred. During a lunar eclipse, the moon can appear red as sunlight reaching the moon passes through the earth's atmosphere, thus the term "blood moon" can refer to a lunar eclipse. In dating previous solar and lunar eclipses, Humphreys and Waddington determined that on April 3, 33, a lunar eclipse was visible from Jeruslaem when the moon was rising and the sun was setting at 6:20 p.m. They concluded that the phenomenon recorded in the New Testatment was a lunar eclipse and that therefore the most most likely date of Christ's death was April 3, 33.

It's of great significance that all the tests that have been conducted on the Turin Shroud over the last few decades have reinforced the circumstances of Christ's death as described in the Gospels. All the tests have corresponded with the possibilty that the relic is indeed the authentic burial cloth of Christ—all of them but one. Radiocarbon dating tests were performed in 1988 on three places, in an attempt to determine the shroud's age. Tests in Zurich and inTucson, Arizona, concluded that the relic was made between 1262 and 1312, and a laboratory in Oxford dated it between 1353 and 1384.

From its inception, many scientists have noted that the method of carbon dating has its flaws, particularly if the carbon test samples are not actually representative of the material being dated. In other words, the test sample of radioisotope carbon 14 has to come from the same period as the test subject. If a material becomes contaminated with 14C particles 500 years after it was made, then tests would indicate that it is 500 years younger than it really is. Fabrics can become contaminated in this way much more easily than other materials, since they are able to absorb liquids containing traces ▶

PROF. BRUNO FABBIANI presents the results of his tests on the Turin Shroud to Grzegorz Górny and Fr. Bohdan Dutko.

65

THE MYSTERY OF THE **DISAPPEARING BODY**

ITALIAN SCIENTIST GINO ZANINOTTI has reconstructed the way in which Christ was laid in the tomb, based on analyses of the Turin Shroud and the Gospels. He focused specifically on how Jesus was wrapped in the burial cloths and how His body was able to leave this linen "cocoon".

According to physicists, the imprint was made as a result of the mysterious emanation of some form of energy within the cocoon. This eruption of energy caused a sort of "burning" of the fabric's surface and left marks that cannot be washed off or removed.

Based on the analysis of blood traces and its ability to gel, hematologists have concluded that the man's body must have been wrapped in the burial cloths two and a half hours after his death.

He could not have remained in them for longer than 36 hours, however, since the cloths bear no trace of bodily decay.

While examining the shroud, scientists claimed that at the moment of radiation, which caused the imprint on the cloth, the body must also have moved through the linen fabric,

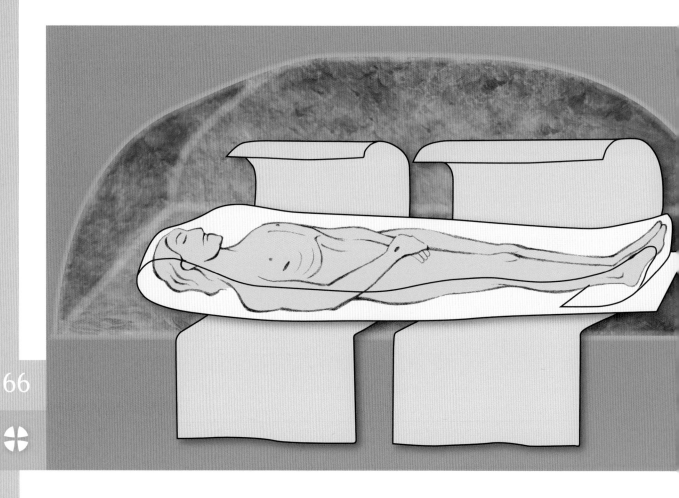

leaving its structure intact. Without anything solid to hold it up, the cocoon shape then collapsed. It was this view of the undisturbed burial cloths that St. John saw, causing him to "see and believe" (cf. Jn 20:8).

This is the best hypothesis modern science can construct. Still, however, there is no accounting for the origin of this eruption of energy, which created the most incredible image in human history.

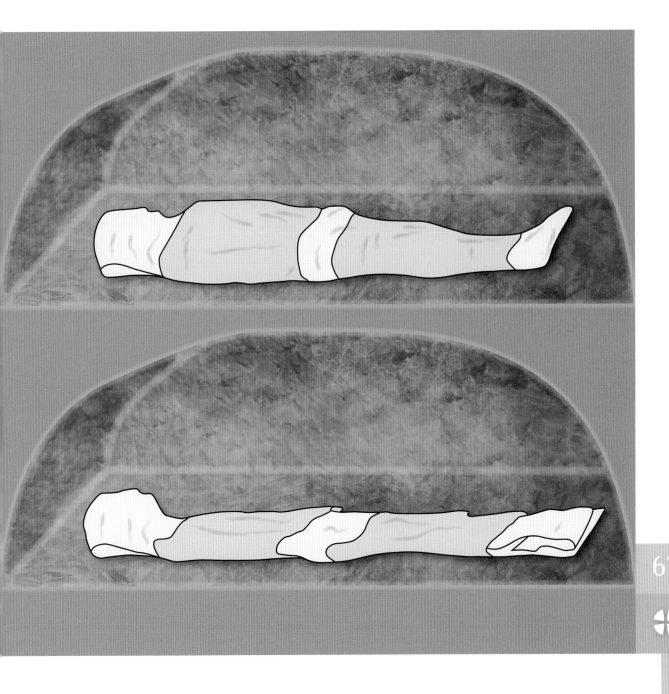

MARK EVANS, American microphotography specialist, takes a photo of the Turin Shroud.

of carbon. Furthermore, a fabric's thread contains numerous bacteria, fungi, and molds, which can absorb naturally occurring radioisotope carbon in the atmosphere. For the dating to be precise, a test subject must therefore be thoroughly cleaned of all later accretions and traces, which could otherwise influence the test's outcome. In the case of woven materials this is especially difficult, since they don't have a smooth surface and carbon molecules are able to embed themselves deep within the fabrics' structure. There is a known example of an Egyptian mummy that underwent testing in Manchester and turned out to be a thousand years older than the bandages in which it was wrapped. The test was flawed in this case because the bandages had absorbed a great deal more atmospheric 14C than the remains. In this context, it is possible to surmise that the fire in Chambéry in 1532 could have greatly increased the amount of radiocarbon in the shroud's fabric, thereby potentially negating future carbon dating tests.

There are in fact numerous examples of carbon dating in which results were incorrect by several thousand years. Such was the case when tests were conducted on mammoth fur, Barbados coral, and the shells of supposedly prehistoric snails.

Likewise, those laboratories that conducted tests on the relic have their history of spectacular errors in carbon dating. In Zurich, a 50-year-old tablecloth was judged to be 350 years old; in Oxford, an 11-year-old painting was believed to be 1200 years old; and in Turin, a Viking horn was judged to have been produced as recently as 2006.

In recent years scientists Joseph Marino and Sue Benford in 2000, Orazio Petrosillo in 2002, and Raymond Rogers in 2005 have each questioned the credibility of the carbon dating tests. They claim that the shroud's samples were actually taken from the patches sewn to the cloth in the fourteenth century.

Similarly, the majority of sindonologists are inclined to believe that a specific age cannot be determined using carbon dating, especially since it contradicts every other result obtained through historical, iconographical, biochemical, photographic, medical, and botanical analyses.

To this day the greatest mystery regarding the shroud is how a man's image could have become imprinted on the cloth. In spite of many detailed tests, modern science cannot explain the process by which this image was produced. Some scientists suppose that the image could have resulted from the emanation of a form of energy. Some believe that the imprint could have been caused by radiation (at an intensity of 1,013 electrons per square centimeter). This radiation must have been emitted vertically, then diffused and absorbed into the air. Although numerous attempts have been made, no one has been able to produce a copy of the shroud that retains all of its characteristics. Modern science, it would seem, does not have the means necessary to replicate this extraordinary and unique object.

The most recent results of tests on the Turin Shroud were published in December 2011 by the Italian National Agency for New Technologies, Energy and Sustainable Economic Development (ENEA). After five years of testing, they have concluded that no known method or technique existed before the twenty-first century that could have been used to produce the image depicted on the Shroud of Turin. The depth of the image's coloring is just 200 nanometers—the width of one of the material's microscopic cell walls. Scientists believe that a similar effect can be achieved only by using an ultraviolet laser. Modern science has admitted, therefore, that it is dealing with an image that one can indeed describe as *acheiropoietos*—"made without human hand".

FR. JOSÉ COTTINO, spokesman for Archbishop Anastasio Ballestrero, acted as a representative of the Turin Archdiocese during tests carried out on the Shroud in 1978.

The Turin Shroud

69

✛

HISTORY

TRUTH

TRADITION

PROOF

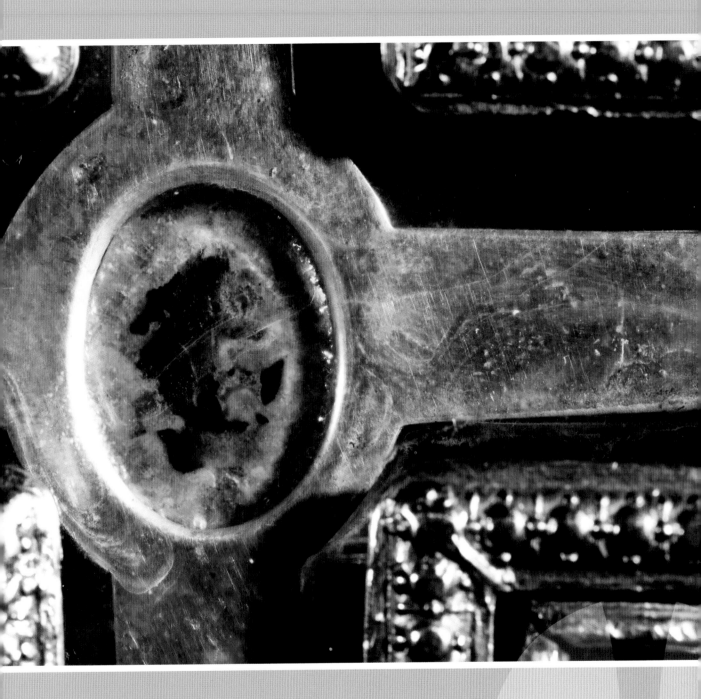

THE INSTRUMENT OF A **HORRIFYING DEATH**

THE TRUE CROSS

CHAPTER II

THE TRUE CROSS

In 1997 German historian Michael Hesemann stepped inside a Roman church and visited a chapel situated to the left of the nave, where he stood contemplating the religious icons on display. He smiled, knowing that he had thought of a way to prove the authenticity of Christianity's holiest relic—the True Cross. Upon entering the Roman Basilica of the Holy Cross in Jerusalem, Hesemann surely had no idea—much like Secondo Pia almost 100 years before him—of the sensational discoveries that would be made regarding the True Cross, and which he initiated.

THEOPHANU CROSS. Eleventh-century reliquary commissioned by Princess Theophanu, prioress of the convent in Essen. The fragment of the True Cross was placed behind a screen of mountain crystal from Egypt. Today, the staurotheke is kept in the treasury in Essen Cathedral.

**BALCONY ON
ST. HELENA'S
COLUMN**
in St. Peter's Basilica,
Rome—one of the
four pillars supporting
the church dome.

But why enter this particular basilica? In the fourth century A.D., this exact spot was the site of the Sessorium, the palatial home of the empress consort Flavia Iulia Helena Augusta, who was the wife of the emperor Constantius I and mother of Constantine the Great and is regarded as St. Helena by both Catholic and Orthodox Christians. Helena is largely credited with the discovery of the True Cross.

She renounced paganism about A.D. 312, as did her son, Constantine, who became the first Christian emperor. In 313 Constantine delivered his famous Edict of Milan, which granted religious freedom to all Christians, and his numerous legislative changes took their inspiration from gospel teachings. He banned gladiator fights, brought an end to death by crucifixion, made branding of the foreheads of slaves illegal, facilitated laws concerning their liberation, and made Sunday a holy day of rest. In Rome, he initiated plans to build eight Christian churches. In 314 he wrote to one of his bishops stating that God had entrusted him with the mission of uniting the Church and reconciling warring Christians. That same year, at a synod in Arles, Constantine condemned ▶

THE HOLY DISCOVERER

THE DAUGHTER OF AN INNKEEPER, Flavia Iulia Helena (A.D. 255–328) married a Roman legion officer named Constantius Chlorus. She bore him only one son, Constantine. Constantius rose steadily through military and political ranks, reaching a point where further advancement depended on abandoning his family. He divorced Helena and married Theodora, the daughter of Emperor Maximian. The marriage allowed him to become Caesar of Rome in 293, acquiring the imperial title of Augustus in 305.

Constantius died while fighting in Britain in 306, at which point his son Constantine was declared the new emperor. That same year, Constantine gave his mother the title of empress, and she converted to Christianity most likely around 312, under the influence of her pious son. Persuaded by him, she set out in 325 for the Holy Land, where she discovered the True Cross. Helena became renowned for her generosity to the poor and her care for prisoners and exiles.

She died on August 18, 330, and is regarded as a saint in the Catholic and Orthodox churches. She is considered an "Equal to the Apostles" in the Orthodox churches, as is her son, who is likewise part of the company of Orthodox saints.

In Eastern iconography, St. Helena is often depicted in imperial garments with a crown on her head or in rich vestments with a white veil. She always holds a cross, often with Constantine at her side. In Western art she is often shown holding a cross and three nails, along with a model of a church. Helena is the patron saint of dyers and needle and nail manufacturers, among others.

ST. HELENA. 1) Sculpture in St. Peter's Basilica, Rome, 2) Reliquary of the empress's skull in St. Peter's Cathedral, Trier, 3) Depiction on the Vilnius Calvary.

THE CHAPEL
of the Invention
of the Cross is
found on the
lowest level of the
Church of the Holy
Sepulchre,
Jerusalem. It
commemorates
St. Helena's
discovery of the
relics in A.D. 325.

the schismatic church of the Donatists. Eleven years later, he invited all the Christian bishops to what became known as the First Council of Nicaea, where he attempted to unite them all under one creed and to attain consensus in the Church.

At that time, Nicaea (present-day Iznik, in Turkey) was an important town and the site of two ecumenical councils. Between 1204 and 1261 it was the capital of the Byzantine Empire (or the Eastern Roman Empire). It was at the first of these two councils, in 325, that Constantine met Bishop Macarius of Jerusalem, who told the Roman emperor of a tradition, kept alive by Christians living in Jerusalem, that material evidence of Christ's crucifixion was buried somewhere under the city.

Jerusalem had been completely destroyed in A.D. 70, when Titus quelled the Jewish rebellion. Soldiers of the Twelfth Legion also razed the Temple of Jerusalem. A second rebellion broke out in 132, after the emperor Hadrian stated that he would rebuild Jerusalem but as a Hellenistic city called Colonia Aelia Capitolina, with temples dedicated to Jupiter, Juno, and Minerva. The city was once again razed and the Jews expelled from Judea. The region was then renamed

PREVIOUS PAGES:

The dome of St. Peter's Basilica in Rome is supported by four columns. Each of these pillars represents one of the four most important relics that were housed in the church treasury after it was built. The columns show St. Helena (the True Cross), St. Veronica (the Veil), St. Andrew (the saint's skull), and St. Longinus (the Spear).

Syria Palaestina. Aelia Capitolina, on the other hand, revealed a topographical and architectural layout that was in no way reminiscent of the old Jerusalem.

Despite these changes, however, the memory of Christ's Passion and its material vestiges lived on in the memory of the early Christians. This might have been influenced by Jesus' so-called brothers James and Simon, who were at the head of the Christian community in Jerusalem. The second name of the city's last Judeo-Christian bishop, Judas Cyriacus, also means "related to the Lord".

Upon hearing all these stories, Constantine decided to seek out those lost relics, excavate the place of Christ's torture and crucifixion, and build a Christian church on the site. He sent Helena to Jerusalem with the mission of finding the instruments of Christ's crucifixion. Her journey to the Holy Land has been documented by a number of fourth- and fifth-century historians, including Eusebius of Caesarea, Rufus of Aquileia, Theodoret of Cyprus, Sozomen of Gaza, Socrates Scholasticus, Gelasius of Cyzicus, and Alexander of Cyprus. Each of their accounts describes how the emperor's mother generously gave alms to the poor, released prisoners, freed slaves, and allowed exiles to return to their homes.

CHURCH OF THE HOLY SEPULCHRE was built by Constantine the Great over three important sites: the place of Christ's crucifixion, His burial, and the finding of the True Cross. St. Helena's biographer, Jan Drijvers, believes that "the church was erected in Jerusalem because of the Cross' discovery, and not because of the tomb's discovery."

The True Cross

79

Helena was supervising the excavation in Jerusalem when workers unearthed three wooden crosses and three nails. They were hidden in an ancient cistern not far from Golgotha, or the Place of the Skull, where Jesus had been crucified. The site of the discovery is perhaps not so surprising if Jewish customs surrounding burial are taken into account: everything that came into contact with a dead body was regarded as unclean and could not be kept within the city walls, especially during the Passover. The three crosses, which obviously had had direct contact with the dead, were, therefore, disposed of in the cistern that lay outside the city walls.

Helena and her workers quickly surmised that they had unearthed none other than Christ's Cross, as well as those of the two thieves crucified on either side of Him. In his *Life of Constantine* (written between A.D. 338 and 340), Eusebius of Caesarea cites a letter written by the emperor to Bishop Macarius. Constantine writes that Helena had been successful in finding "evidence of Christ's holy Passion, which had lain hidden for so long". The date of the discovery—September 14—is celebrated in the Church as the Feast of the Exultation of the Holy Cross.

While still in Jerusalem, Helena divided the Cross into three fragments: the first was left in Jerusalem, the second she took to Rome, and the third she passed on to her son to take to Constantinople, the new capital he was in the process of building.

RELIQUARY OF THE TRUE CROSS found in the Church of the Holy Sepulchre in Jerusalem. A fragment of the Cross is visible close up, where the arms intersect.

While browsing various historical sources, Michael Hesemann pondered one question in particular: How did Helena know the crosses came from Golgotha, and—moreover—how could she have been certain which one belonged to Jesus Christ? A large number of early Christian writers maintain that the Cross could be identified because of the miraculous role it played in healing a woman with an incurable illness. Only two people disagreed. The first was St. Ambrose, bishop of Milan, who, while delivering a eulogy at the funeral of Emperor Theodosius I in February 395, claimed that the crosses could be identified only thanks to the *titulus*, the wooden tablet that bore the inscription of the convict's name. This was later verified in a homily given by St. John Chrysostom, then bishop of Constantinople.

The standard cross comprised two parts: the vertical beam (*stipes*) measured between 3 and 4 meters long, while the horizontal beam (*patibulum*) typically ▶

A BRUTAL EXECUTION

DEATH BY CRUCIFIXION was never written into Jewish law. The practice was introduced by the Romans and was regarded as one of the most degrading forms of punishment. Cicero called it "the cruelest and most hideous form of torture", while Josephus referred to it as "the most tragic of deaths". Crucifixion was so cruel that a Roman citizen could not be executed in this manner. Instead, the sentence was reserved for slaves and noncitizen criminals or rebels. It was often used to suppress political uprisings, such as Spartacus' slave rebellion.

Medical doctor Truman Davis writes the following with regard to how the body reacts to crucifixion: "As the arms weaken, powerful spasms begin to attack the muscles, resulting in deep, unabated pain. Along with the spasms comes the inability to lift oneself. As a result of hanging from the arms, the muscles around the rib cage and intercostal muscles become paralyzed. Air can be breathed in, but it cannot be exhaled. Jesus would have strained to lift Himself, if only so that He could take a few short breaths. Eventually, carbon dioxide builds up in the lungs and in the blood and the spasms become slightly less intense. Jesus would have lifted Himself up spasmodically in order to breathe in life-giving oxygen."

The crucified victim begins to lose air. Blood slowly ceases to flow to the brain and heart. One way of prolonging life—despite the resulting pain— is to lift oneself up and take in oxygen so that blood is able to flow through the top half of the body. Every attempt to pull oneself up using the arms or legs results in the nail wounds tearing apart and becoming deeper. Every breath taken in the attempt to stay alive causes such pain that the body falls back down, utterly spent. Soon, however, the victim begins to suffocate again and has to raise himself to take in more air.

In most cases the executioner would opt to speed up the process by breaking the victim's legs, below the knees. The victim would no longer be able to lift himself and would die either by asphyxiation or by coronary insufficiency. Both of the thieves crucified on either side of Christ had their legs broken. Jesus was spared this act when the soldiers saw He was already dead.

THE CRUCIFIED CONVICT could not hang from the cross without moving. He had to struggle for every breath of air just to prolong his life by a few seconds.

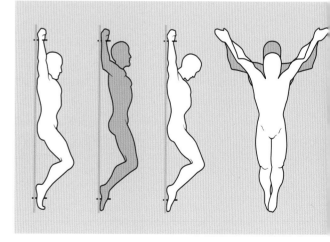

COMPARE
page ▶ 126

82

third element was often nailed above the head of
his crime. Thanks to St. John's Gospel, we know
head read, "Jesus of Nazareth, King of the Jews"
orum), hence many crucifixes bear the initials

that the Cross's authenticity could not be deter-
either the vertical or the horizontal beam. Even if
ces of wood were over 2,000 years old, this would
the notion that they were part of the True Cross.
ferent regarding the titulus, however. We know
that Christ's particular inscription was unique;
her Jesus of Nazareth who also claimed to be the
same spring. Furthermore, St. Matthew writes
was written in three languages. Conclusive proof,
ore come from examining the titulus.

divided up the titulus. This was standard practice at
e not preserved for the benefit of future scholarly
rious presence of the divine (*numinosum*) that was
gment. In accordance with the principle that a part
, relics were often divided up in the belief that each
amount of sacred power as had existed in the relic's

theological distinction between two acts of faith:
red service only to God; *dulia* venerated holy peo-
eld in particularly high esteem, since they acted as
cal evidence of the supernatural events for which

thanks to God.

The titulus was divided in half: the left half remained in Jerusalem, and the
right was taken to Rome under Helena's care. Upon her return to Rome, Helena
decided to convert part of the Sessorium in which she resided into a chapel

GOLDEN CROSS from Florence Cathedral. The seventeenth-century staurotheke contains the True Cross relic, which found its way to Florence in 1454 – one year after the Turks invaded Constantinople.

CATHEDRAL OF SANTA MARIA DEL FIORE in Florence, home to the staurotheke containing a fragment of the True Cross. The cathedral was in construction for almost 600 years – from 1296 to 1887.

dedicated to housing the relics she had brought back. These included one of the three nails, a fragment of the Cross, and half of the titulus. Helena also ordered sacks of earth to be brought back from Golgotha and scattered over the floor of the chapel.

After Helena's death, Constantine offered the Sessorium palace to the bishop of Rome. The palace was rededicated as the Basilica of the Holy Cross and has remained a place of worship ever since. It has been rebuilt and renamed (Hierusalem, Eleniana, Basilica Sessoriana) numerous times over the centuries, but the most important relics have always remained unmoved. Since Rome had been invaded and plundered on several occasions (by Goths, Vandals, Saracens, and Normans, among others), the titulus needed safe hiding. It was most likely under Valentinian II's rule that it was hidden within the walls above the chapel's altar. A brick marked its location with the words *titulus Crucis*.

The relic was retrieved from its hiding place in 1143, when Gherardo Caccianemici (who later became Pope Lucius II) decided to rebuild the basilica. The titulus was walled up once again after the building work had been finished, but this time it was placed above the arch of triumph in the Chapel of St. Helena.

The relic was unearthed once again almost 350 years later, in 1496, during renovation work started by the Cardinal Mendoza, the Spanish archbishop of Toledo. When the rebuilding was completed, it was decided that, rather than being hidden again, the titulus would be put on public display. As a result, the Church of the Holy Cross quickly became one of the most popular pilgrimage sites in Rome.

Only once did the titulus find itself in threatening circumstances—namely, when French armies occupied the city in 1798. Numerous churches were pillaged and destroyed, and an attempt to seize the basilica's relics was averted because they had been hidden elsewhere. The French commandeered the reliquaries instead, and it was only in 1803 that the relics themselves were returned to the basilica and stored in new reliquaries provided by the Spanish princess of Villahermosa.

In time, the titulus fell into obscurity, due in large part to ideas born of the Enlightenment, which reduced the devotion to relics to mere superstition. In 1997, when Michael Hesemann decided to examine the titulus, the relic came back to prominence. Hesemann believed that his tests could confirm one of three possible hypotheses: the relic was a forgery dating back to Helena's time, it was a medieval ▶

DOME OF FILIPPO BRUNELLESCHI

in Florence Cathedral. The architect won the commission to build the dome following a competition in 1418.

TREASURY IN ST. MARK'S BASILICA, which contains numerous relics looted in Constantinople, among them some of the largest known fragments of the True Cross: the cross of Empress Irene and the cross of Emperor Constantine.

THE RIALTO BRIDGE over Venice's Grand Canal was built from 1588 to 1591. In earlier years, the bridge was made of wood, not of stone. It collapsed twice, however—in 1444 and 1524—under the weight of crowds observing the parade of gondolas.

VENICE

DURING THE MIDDLE AGES, the Venetian Republic was the powerhouse of the Mediterranean Basin. It controlled the sea's eastern region, including the Adriatic coast, the Aegean Sea, Crete, Cyprus, Corfu, and a host of other islands. It had a monopoly on the silk and spice trade. It often came into conflict with other ruling powers, among them the Muslim Turks, who wished to rival the Venetian sphere of influence in the region. It even quarreled with the papacy, prompting Pope Julius II in 1509 to form an alliance called the League of Cambrai, which opposed the Venetian Republic.

For several centuries, the republic's main rival for regional domination was the Byzantine Empire. In 1204 the Venetians capitalized on their imperial rival's weakness, and under the initiative of the Venetian doge Enrico Dandolo, the Fourth Crusade altered course from the Holy Land and made straight for Constantinople. The Byzantine capital was looted and plundered, with the Venetians ending up the largest beneficiaries. The republic acquired countless riches, including numerous relics.

In the thirteenth century, Europe was inundated with holy objects stolen during the Fourth Crusade. Their main point of distribution was Venice, although some relics remained in the city. Among them were two large fragments of the True Cross, known as the Cross of Empress Irene and the Cross of Emperor Constantine. Today they are kept in St. Mark's Basilica.

RELIQUARY of the True Cross in the ancient cemetery chapel by Pisa Cathedral.

reproduction, or it was in fact the original tablet that had once been nailed to Christ's Cross.

As mentioned, the titulus was divided in half soon after it was discovered. The oldest surviving pilgrimage account from the Holy Land confirms the existence of the left half in Jerusalem. The Spanish pilgrim Egeria writes of her experience visiting the Church of the Holy Sepulchre in A.D. 383 and venerating the relic. In the fifth century, Socrates Scholasticus described the relic as "a board, containing different symbols written by Pilate, stating that Christ, King of the Jews, had been

crucified". Other accounts likewise confirm that the board was inscribed with the words *Rex Iudaeorum* (King of the Jews). Antonino di Piacenza writes about his visit to the Holy Land in 570 and how he "saw, held, and kissed" the relic, which, he adds, was "made of the wood of a walnut tree". Sozomen of Gaza, who in his youth had met some of the workers who actually discovered the crosses, writes that the titulus bore inscriptions in Hebrew, Greek, and Latin. In terms of ordering, this is only slightly different from St. John's account, which claims the inscriptions were in Hebrew, Latin, and Greek. No accounts exist from later years, and most historians surmise that the relic must have disappeared entirely in 614, when the Persians invaded Jerusalem.

Only the right half of the titulus has survived and to this day is housed in Rome, in the Church of the Holy Cross. The board bears the inscription stating that the sentenced person was Jesus of Nazareth. Tests have confirmed that the board was broken along its left side, cutting the inscribed markings in two. It measures 25 centimeters in length, which suggests that its total length was around half

ANCIENT CEMETERY by Pisa Cathedral. Soil from Jerusalem was specially imported to the cemetery, so that rich citizens could be buried in the same earth over which Christ once walked.

The True Cross

89

a meter. Other archaeological findings seem to verify this assumption, with the average tablet measuring about 50 centimeters.

Traces of whitewash have been found on the surface of the relic and black paint has been discovered within the recesses of the carved letters, which tallies with the methods used to make a typical titulus in Roman times. According to archaeologists Maria Siliato and Werner Eck, "First the board was whitewashed, and then the sentence was inscribed using black or red lettering. Very occasionally, the letters were also shaped using wire."

The Italian botanist Professor Elio Corona has identified the wood of the titulus: very old walnut (*Juglans regia*), which grows throughout the Near East and the eastern Mediterranean. This accords with Antonino di Piacenza's account from 570.

While all these details make a favorable case for the relic's authenticity, there's not quite enough evidence to make a conclusive judgment. Hesemann could not, unfortunately, conduct any dendrological tests on the wood, as the sample was too small to be dated accurately. He decided, therefore, to conduct paleographic tests that examine the actual writing itself (paleographers are able to pinpoint the time and place of an artifact's origin based on the style of writing it exhibits).

The inscription on the titulus comprises three lines of text. The first line is in Hebrew, the second in Greek, and the third in Latin. Interestingly, the Greek and Latin texts are written from right to left—thereby imitating the direction in which the Hebrew text is written. Both Greek and Latin versions use an abbreviated form of Jesus' name: IS in Greek, I in Latin. This sort of shorthand was characteristic of Roman inscriptions, particularly in the case of a common name. Two thousand years ago Jesus was a popular name in Judea. Indeed, in *The Jewish War* (c. 75) by the historian Titus Flavius Josephus, the name crops up fourteen times. For a convict with a common name, his place of origin was a more important distinguishing feature; in the case of Jesus this was *Nazarenus*.

In both the Greek and Latin lines, the first letters of a third word have also been preserved: in the Greek, the letter *B*; in the Latin, the letter *R*. In his Gospel, St. John identified the third word as king, which in Greek is *basileus* and in Latin is *rex*. Of course, we cannot be sure that the letters represent the start of those words, as the phrase is broken off.

Hesemann passed the inscription on to several renowned paleographers, not revealing its source. The Hebrew text was given to two Jewish specialists: Professor ▶

RELIQUARY OF THE CROSS in Venice, owned by the Sovereign Military Order Hospitaller of St. John of Jerusalem. The order was founded during the Crusades, and its members, known as the Knights of Malta, played an important role in the founding of hospitals while protecting Europe from Muslim invaders.

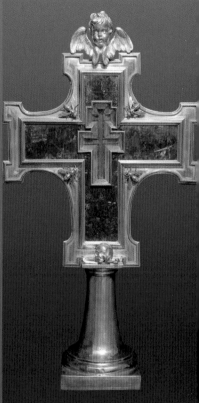

FRANCISCAN
Fr. Jerzy Kraj,
director of
the Christian
Information
Center in
Jerusalem,
together
with Grzegorz
Górny and his
wife, Angelika
Korszyńska-Górny.

THE PILGRIMAGE PHENOMENON

FROM THE EARLY MIDDLE AGES, churches that acquired relics associated with Christ quickly attained a holy status. Pilgrims would journey to these holy places to pray before the relics and receive indulgences. The oldest pilgrims' journals date back to the fourth century and concern the Holy Land, where devotees could see with their own eyes relics associated with the Passion of Christ. In time, as relics were dispersed throughout Europe, a dense network of pilgrimage routes developed all over the continent.

Goethe believed that European collective consciousness developed as a result of pilgrimages. These journeys allowed European Christians to broaden their horizons, develop their knowledge of their contemporaries in other lands, and become part of the religious culture of Christendom.

For centuries, pilgrimages were the only way in which people could experience the traditions, languages, and customs of other nations while discovering the things that link people together. Hospitals were founded along pilgrimage routes, a nascent travel culture began to develop, hotels appeared, and an increasing number of roads and bridges were built.

Visiting the relics preserved in such cities as Jerusalem, Rome, Aachen, and Trier shaped the worldview of many devout Europeans. Thanks to pilgrimages, Europe to a large extent became a community of the faithful.

Hannah Eshel and Dr. Gabriel Barkay, who examined the text independently of each other. Both of them theorized that this "Jewish style of writing" (slanted lettering with long "tails") was characteristic of the later Second Temple period, or the first century A.D. This style of writing was still in use two centuries later, prompting Eshel and Barkay to conclude that the inscription probably dates from a period between the first and third centuries.

Professor Carsten Peter Thiede of Ben-Gurion University in Beersheba and Dr. Leah di Segni of the Hebrew University of Jerusalem were responsible for examining the Greek portion of the inscription. The most striking part of the text for them was the style in which the letter *alpha* and the ligature *omicron-upsilon* (*a* and *ou*) were written. In their opinion, the text dated back to the first century.

These findings were confirmed by two other Jewish paleographers, Israel Roll and Ben Isaac of Tel Aviv University. They dated the Latin text to the early Roman Empire, or the first century A.D. The two specialists noticed the stylistic similarity between this sample and another inscription of the same period, found on an altar dedicated to the emperor Tiberius by Pontius Pilate. Italian archaeologists discovered the altar in 1961 in Caesarea.

THE INSCRIPTIONS on the *titulus* are written in three languages: Hebrew, Greek, and Latin—in a different order from that given by St. John in his Gospel (Hebrew, Latin, Greek). If the relic were a medieval forgery, its makers would have referred to biblical descriptions and copied the order of languages found in the Gospel.

TITULUS DAMNATIONIS of Jesus of Nazareth, found today in the Basilica of the Holy Cross in Jerusalem. It is 25 cm long, 14 cm wide, 2.6 cm thick, and weighs 687 grams.

CABINET in the Basilica of the Holy Cross in Jerusalem where all the relics imported to Rome by St. Helena can be found: the horizontal beam of the Good Thief's cross, a particle of the Holy Cross, the Holy Nail, and the *titulus damnationis*.

A year later, the aforementioned Professor Thiede published a book on the subject. In it he wrote that "the style of writing [found on the titulus] is startling. Whoever produced it could not have been a copyist or a counterfeiter." Thiede strongly contested the assertion that the titulus could be fake, dating back to late antiquity or the Middle Ages. No counterfeiter from either of those periods would have had sufficient knowledge of Hebrew, Greek, and Latin writing styles common throughout the Near East during the first century. Neither would he have abbreviated the name Jesus. Lastly, any forgery would most likely have followed the language ordering given by St. John in his Gospel.

Hesemann believes that his discovery has much wider consequences: "If one can claim with a great degree of certainty that the *titulus Crucis* does date back to Christ's time, then we could also verify the circumstances of its discovery and, indirectly, the authenticity of the three crosses and nails. We could also suggest that numerous relics associated with the True Cross, found today in various European cathedrals, are in fact genuine—or at least that those relics traceable to Rome, Constantinople, and Jerusalem are genuine."

As mentioned, Helena divided the True Cross into three parts. Soon each of those parts was divided up, and fragments were sent to even the most far-flung of Christian churches and places of worship. Almost every parish wanted to possess evidence of

Christ's suffering. We know from archaeological excavations that in the fourth century parts of the Cross were being housed in churches in Ravenna and the North African towns of Tixter and Cape Matifu. We also know that a number of bishops of Jerusalem bestowed fragments of the Cross on their closest friends. John II, for instance, passed on small fragments to St. Paulinus of Nola and Sulpicius Severus, whom he wrote that "within the smallest fragment can be found the True Cross' entire power". Certain Church Fathers, such as St. Gregory of Nyssa and St. John Chrysostom, have written that some Christians took to mounting fragments of the relic in gold and wearing them around their necks. No wonder, then, that in one of his catechetical lectures St. Cyril of Jerusalem declared that "wood from the True Cross" could be found not only in his basilica but also "in every corner of the globe".

Several decades later, what had once been a great source of pride for the Church Fathers invited accusation against Catholics in general. At the start of the sixteenth century, Erasmus of Rotterdam stated that "even a cargo ship would be too small to transport the numerous fragments of the True Cross, found scattered throughout the world". In a similar vein, Martin Luther guessed that "one could build a whole house using all the parts of the True Cross found scattered throughout the world". In their opinion, most relics of the Cross were forgeries.

The nineteenth-century French architect Charles Rohault de Fleury—a longtime researcher of Christian relics—decided to test the validity of these assertions, publishing his findings in 1870. He estimated that the Cross' total volume measured about 36,000 cubic centimeters, while the total volume of the Cross' scattered fragments was barely 4,000 cubic centimeters. This evidence suggested that all the known and official fragments of the relic actually amounted to less than one-ninth of the Cross' original volume. Critics may have rightly pointed to the sheer number of places boasting some part of the True Cross, but it's worth remembering that these were often just tiny fragments, sometimes mere splinters, of the original.

The authenticity of a particular fragment can be determined by testing the type of wood (the True Cross was made of black pine—*Pinus negra*), as well as by documenting its origin from one of three places: Rome, Constantinople, or Jerusalem. During the reign of Constantine, these were the three cities that had the large parts of the Cross before they were divided into smaller pieces.

Many pilgrims' accounts of the piece that St. Helena left in Jerusalem have survived; these state that the relic was venerated in the Church of the Holy Sepulchre. According to various reports, the relic was made up of one vertical and one horizontal beam. Devotees were allowed to kiss the Cross, although some pilgrims often took

The True Cross

96

TRUE CROSS FRAGMENT within a staurotheke in the parish church of St. Anthony the Great in Castel Sant'Elia, Italy. The relic is made up of two bits of wood joined in a cross.

RELIQUARY OF THE TRUE CROSS in the Sanctuary of Santa Maria ad Rupes in Castel Sant'Elia. Today, the sanctuary is run by a group of Michaelite Fathers from Poland.

the opportunity to bite a little bit off and take it with them. To prevent this sort of practice, a special position was created, known as a *staurophylax* ("custodian of the Cross"), who was charged with overseeing the relic's safety.

In the fifth century, the post of staurophylax was occupied for a time by the Galician St. Turibius—a friend of Pope Leo I and of Juvenal, patriarch and sometime bishop of Jerusalem. When he became bishop of Astorga, Turibius left the Holy Land and returned to Spain, where he died in 476. It is believed that he brought back with him a large piece of the True Cross, which today is kept in the Monastery of Santo Toribio de Liébana in Cantabria. The relic's presence at the monastery, however, has been documented only since the ninth century. While for many centuries it was regarded as a large piece of the original Cross, tests conducted at the Special School of Forestry in Madrid in 1958 confirmed that the fragment was made not of black pine, but of an ancient piece of Mediterranean cypress (*Cupressus sempervirens*), thus invalidating its authenticity.

In the year 614 the Persians invaded Jerusalem under the leadership of Shah Khosrau II. They not only took the city but also massacred its citizens, killing tens of thousands of people. They pillaged and destroyed numerous temples and ▶

GROTTO IN MONTE GARGANO, in the Sanctuary of St. Michael the Archangel. According to tradition, the battle between St. Michael and Lucifer took place in this very cave. Today, the shrine is a favored place among Italian exorcists. Inside is a main chapel beside a side chapel containing a reliquary of the True Cross.

churches and seized the True Cross, which they took back to the Persian capital of Ctesiphon. The bishop of Jerusalem, Zacharias, was also taken as a prisoner.

The Byzantine emperor Heraclius felt threatened by Khosrau, who not only had invaded Antioch, Damascus, Jerusalem, and Alexandria but also had launched three attacks on Constantinople itself. Heraclius even considered abandoning Constantinople and founding a new capital in Africa, before the patriarch Sergius managed to change his mind. He also persuaded the emperor to wage a holy war against the Persian infidels who had stolen Christianity's most cherished relic.

In 627, the Byzantine armies routed the Persian forces near Nineveh, and Heraclius entered the shah's palace in Dastgerd, located just 30 kilometers from Ctesiphon. The exhausted Persians were in no state to resist. Khosrau was toppled and killed by his own son, who succeeded him as Kavadh II and who started negotiations with the Byzantines. As a result, the True Cross was returned to the Christians in May 628. In September of the same year, the relic was placed in the Hagia Sophia in Constantinople.

SANTO TORIBIO DE LIÉBANA is the longest continuously running monastery in Spain. The baroque chapel, an eighteenth-century extension, houses the relic long considered the largest fragment of the Jerusalem segment of the True Cross.

The True Cross

After the winter, Heraclius decided to deliver the stolen relic personally to Jerusalem. We know from various chroniclers that on May 3, 629, the Byzantine ruler entered the holy city barefoot, without a crown, and dressed only in white linen underclothes. Before him he carried the same Cross that six centuries earlier Christ Himself had dragged. Bishop Zacharias, who had been freed from the Persians, accompanied the emperor.

In Jerusalem there was great joy among the Christians over the return of the True Cross and their bishop, but their joy did not last long. In 638 the recently united Muslim Arab tribes invaded the city. Initially the new occupying powers were tolerant with regard to the Christians. The caliph Umar signed a treaty with the patriarch Sophronius I, guaranteeing that Christian places of worship in Jerusalem would be protected in accordance with principles of the Islamic faith. This changed, however, when al-Hakim became caliph and began persecuting the Christian population. On October 18, 1009, he ordered that the Church of the Holy Sepulchre be demolished and the remains of Christ's tomb be destroyed.

The politics of repression begun by the Fatimid caliph produced an angry reaction among Christians in Europe. Calls to free the holy city from the hands of its pagan

NUMEROUS PILGRIMS traveling to Santo Toribio de Liébana take advantage of being able to kiss a relic, which medieval sources tell us is the left arm of the True Cross, together with a visible nail hole.

GILDED RELIQUARY made of solid silver, dating from the seventeenth century, and kept in the Santo Toribio de Liébana monastery. The reliquary has an opening that allows devotees to touch and to kiss the wood inside. Scientists claim it is around 2,000 years old and made of Mediterranean cyprus, which grows in Palestine but is not believed to be the type of wood that was used to make Christ's Cross.

captors met with increasing support, resulting eventually in the First Crusade. This ended successfully when the Crusaders occupied Jerusalem on July 15, 1099. The Latin Kingdom of Jerusalem's first leader, Godfrey of Bouillon, ordered the building of a new Church of the Holy Sepulchre. The Crusaders hoped that the True Cross would form the focus of the newly rebuilt church. It turned out, however, that the city possessed only four rather small fragments of the Cross. In 638, when the Arabs were closing in on the Holy Land, Patriarch Sophronius I had divided the Cross into 19 pieces, fearful that it would otherwise be destroyed by the invading Muslims. He sent three pieces to Constantinople and three more to Antioch. Georgia and Cyprus each received two pieces, and Alexandria, Ashqelon, Edessa, Damascus, and Crete were each sent one piece.

SANCTUARY OF THE CROSS in the Basilica of the Holy Cross in Jerusalem, Rome. A chapel was built inside the church in 1930, by the Italian architect Florestano di Fausto, to house the relics of the True Cross, including the titulus damnationis, a Holy Nail, two thorns from the Crown of Thorns, and a piece of the horizontal beam from the cross of the Good Thief.

In later years, the remaining four pieces in Jerusalem were divided into even smaller fragments. The Crusaders' Kingdom of Jerusalem was struggling financially and began to trade relics as a means to support itself. Thus fragments of the Cross found their way to numerous European cities. Two rather substantial fragments ended up in the town of Wienerwald, Austria; the first was delivered by St. Leopold III, margrave of Austria, and the second by his grandson Leopold V.

The Latin kings of Jerusalem sent to Europe emissaries bearing fragments of the Cross. These men used the relics to impart blessings in order to obtain alms in support of the Crusaders. Occasionally an emissary would be set upon and robbed. Such was the fate of the canon Conrad of Bavaria, who was attacked by men hired by Conrad II, count of Dachau. The count's successors later gave the relic to a monastery in Scheyern. As a result, the Bavarian abbey became one of the most important pilgrimage sites in medieval Germany.

Despite its initial success, however, the Latin Kingdom of Jerusalem did not last even until the end of the century. On July 4, 1187, the Crusader forces were defeated at

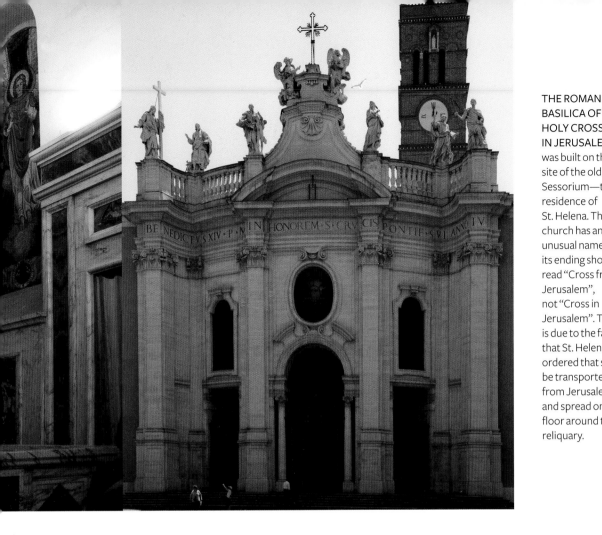

the Battle of Hattin, near the Sea of Galilee, by Saladin's forces. During the battle, the Saracens managed to seize the True Cross relic, which was being carried as a standard by the bishop of Bethlehem. The loss of their holy standard broke the morale of the Christian soldiers. The Muslim victors sent the relic to Damascus. Five years later, they refused an attempt made by the queen of Georgia to buy the relic. After that, there is no evidence of what happened to this particular piece of the True Cross.

Saladin occupied Jerusalem on October 2, 1187. Only a few small fragments of the original Cross remained in the city. The largest of them—measuring around 11.5 centimeters—is found today in St. James Cathedral in the Old Town's Armenian Quarter.

The second of the three original pieces of the True Cross, which St. Helena had divided and distributed, found its way to Rome. It was housed in the Sessorium (later rebuilt as the Basilica of the Holy Cross in Jerusalem) together with the right half of the titulus. It remained there for several centuries until 1629, when Pope Urban VIII ordered the relic to be rehoused in the newly built St. Peter's Basilica in the Vatican. It was placed

MONSTRANCE RELIQUARY from 1778. A small fragment of the True Cross was fitted between two mountain crystals, and was displayed every year on August 14 in the Church of St. John in Essen, Germany. Today it is kept in the treasury of the Essen Cathedral.

TWO CROSS FRAGMENTS in a reliquary in the Church of Divine Providence on Mount Calvary. The wood particles were moved from Assisi to Poland in 1847.

in a small chapel built in the column of St. Helena—one of four pillars supporting the church's dome. In later years, numerous popes would offer small bits of the relic to various people or communities.

Today the basilica houses just three fragments of the original Cross, which are kept in a reliquary dating from 1803. Both the right half of the titulus and a horizontal beam of one of the three crosses discovered by St. Helena are exhibited together with the fragments. The beam, labeled as "part of the cross belonging to the good thief" (*pars crucis boni latronis*), allows us to imagine the size of Christ's Cross by comparison.

The third piece of the original Cross was sent by St. Helena to the new Byzantine capital of Constantinople, whose official founding was celebrated on May 11, 330. The city's central point was a public forum known as the Augusteum, in the middle of which—and surrounded by four triumphal arches—stood a milestone called the Milion. Every point in the Byzantine Empire was measured in terms of its distance from the Milion, which constituted its center. A cupola was built above the milestone, upon which a large fragment of the True Cross was placed. This was in accordance with Constantine's vision that Christ's Cross should symbolize the center of the world.

A larger part of the Cross, however, was stored in the imperial treasury. Later, Byzantine emperors gave small pieces of the relic to various influential people ▶

RELIQUARY IN STRZELNO, which boasts Poland's largest collection of relics pertaining to saints, blesseds, and martyrs. It even contains relics of the first Christians from the catacombs in Rome. The relics include the remains of the Apostles Peter, James, Philip, and Bartholomew, as well as St. Agnes and St. Benedict of Nursia. Their authenticity cannot be confirmed, so we have to rely on the certificates issued by seventeenth- and eighteenth-century Italian bishops. The relic of the True Cross can be found in a monstrance reliquary above the tabernacle.

THE RELIQUARY ALTAR
IN STRZELNO

THE TOWN OF STRZELNO in the Kuyavian-Pomeranian province of Poland boasts an originally Romanesque church, which was consecrated in 1216 to the Holy Trinity. While the church itself has been rebuilt numerous times, its main attractions—columns that depict personifications of vice and virtue—still stand after hundreds of years. For centuries, the church has attracted pilgrims from all over Europe who come to venerate the True Cross relic, which is housed in a special altar along with the remains of 658 martyrs and saints.

The baroque altar was built in 1743, although the Gothic crucifix that occupies its central position dates back to the fourteenth century. The altar represents a magnificent frame for many relics, but the most prized among them is a fragment of the True Cross. Its authenticity was verified on August 30, 1729, by Archbishop of Milan Dennis Modino and was given the wax seal of approval by the papal nuncio, Bishop Baccario. The relic is housed in a small silver casket with crystal windows on each side.

FOURTEENTH-CENTURY CRUCIFIX forming part of the Holy Cross altar in Strzelno. Its miraculous properties are documented as early as 1461.

107

THE HOLY CROSS MONASTERY is the oldest sanctuary in Poland. The Benedictines and Jan Długosz both attribute the abbey's founding to King Bolesław I Chrobry, in 1006. It was built on the second highest peak in the Świętokrzyskie Mountains, namely Łysa Góra (Bald Mountain).

THE SANCTUARY OF THE HOLY CROSS is not lacking in pilgrims seeking blessing through holy relics.

SILVER RELIQUARY in the shape of an oval sun, funded by the seventeenth-century Holy Cross abbot Stanisław Sierakowski.

on whose support they relied. For instance, in 569, the Byzantine emperor Justin II offered a small fragment of the relic to the daughter of one of the three kings of Thuringia, St. Radegund, who founded a nunnery in Poitiers. Similarly, Constantine VIII passed on another fragment to Mangold I von Werd, a German count who bestowed it on an abbey in Donauwörth. We also know that parts of the Constantinople relic found their way to St. Peter's Basilica in Rome, to a monastery atop Mount Athos, and to a cathedral in Esztergom, Hungary.

According to Benedictine tradition, as well as Jan Długosz's documented history, it was from Hungary that a fragment of the True Cross eventually made its way to Poland. It was meant to be a gift from the Hungarian prince St. Emeric to the Benedictine monastery built at the summit of Bald Mountain. To this day, the relic is kept in a special golden case in the monastery's Oleśnicki Chapel. Recent tests have confirmed that the fragment is made of black pine—the same wood as the Cross on which Christ was crucified.

One fragment of the Constantinople Cross ended up in a nunnery in Essen, which in the tenth and eleventh centuries was experiencing its greatest period of prosperity. The Ottonian and Salian dynasties ruled the Holy Roman Empire, and three successive prioresses in Essen between 971 and 1058—namely, the princesses Matilda, Sofia, and Theophanu—were all descended from these ruling

families. Using their family connections, they were able to obtain for the monastery numerous precious relics, including a fragment of the True Cross. This was embedded in Egyptian mountain crystal and kept within a golden, jewel-encrusted reliquary. Today devotees can visit Theophanu's Cross in the treasury at Essen Cathedral.

For the next few centuries, Constantinople was famed throughout the Christian world as a fabulously rich city, full of splendor and paved with gold. Crusader and historian Geoffroi de Villehardouin wrote of the time he spent in the city: "The relics go without saying: there were as many in that city as there are throughout the rest of the world." Constantinople's wealth, however, soon became the envy of many Western European princes. In 1204, the Fourth Crusade (led by the Franks and the Venetians) made for the Byzantine capital instead of the Holy Land. The city was captured on April 13 and totally plundered by the crusading knights. The invasion remains a sore point between Catholic and Orthodox Christians even to this day.

The following can be found in a medieval chronicle from Cologne: "The captured city yielded priceless treasures, hugely expensive precious stones, as well as a piece of the True Cross. Brought over from Jerusalem by St. Helena, it was decorated with gold and precious stones and held in the highest regard. The bishops there present divided up the relic and distributed it among the crusading knights; later, after their return home, these fragments found their way to numerous churches and monasteries."

No wonder, then, that after 1204 dozens of holy relics—among them fragments of the True Cross—began to appear in numerous Western European towns, particularly in France and in Flanders. These included the towns of Angers, Baugé, Corbie, Lille, Limburg, Maastricht, Mettlach, and Trier. Often these fragments would be further divided and sent on to other places of worship. The place from which many such relics were distributed was Venice. Various pilgrims' accounts give the impression that Venice was less like a town and more like a giant reliquary. Today St. Mark's Basilica is home to one of the largest existing pieces of the True Cross, measuring over 42 centimeters in length. This relic, named for the Byzantine empress Irene, is numbered among the many spoils following the invasion of Constantinople.

Christians treated fragments of the True Cross with great reverence. They made expensive reliquaries for them known as *staurothekes* (from the Greek,

THE RELIC OF THE HOLY CROSS sanctuary was always kept in a cross-shaped reliquary with two sets of horizontal arms. This was influenced by the relic's Hungarian origins. After Pope Sylvester II made St. Stephen I of Hungary apostolic king in the year 1000, the Hungarian ruler began using a double-cross seal, following the example set by archbishops. From that point on, Hungarian monarchs would always use the same seal.

SEVENTEENTH-CENTURY FRESCOES in the Oleśnicki family chapel, Holy Cross Monastery, depict how the relics found their way to Poland from Hungary. St. Stephen's son, Prince St. Emeric, was supposed to have played a key role in their delivery.

stauro, meaning "stake", "beam", or "cross", and *theka*, meaning "packaging" or "casing"). The staurothekes came in various shapes, such as crosses, panels, or triptychs (three-part panels with hinged doors) and were often embellished with enamel, encrusted with precious stones, and covered in gold. Many of these reliquaries were masterpieces of gold craftsmanship. Examples include the staurothekes found in Limburg Cathedral, the Church of St. Eucharius and St. Matthias in Trier (which is based on the Limburg model), the panel from Floreffe (currently kept in the Louvre), and the triptych in the Marienstern Abbey in the former Lusatia.

Two of the oldest staurothekes in Poland, most likely of Byzantine origin, can be found in the royal treasury at Wawel Castle in Kraków and in the Museum of the First Piast in Lednica. Some reliquaries have disappeared, such as the Byzantine-Venetian staurotheke stolen by the Germans in 1939 from the Collegiate Church in Tum. The so-called Palatine Cross, or the coronation relic of the Polish ▶

TRAVEL RELIQUARIES in which relics were transported from place to place. Since the objects often fell victim to looting, they were transported in secrecy, using inconspicuous containers, so as not to attract the attention of robbers.

PRECIOUS **CONTAINERS**

CHRISTIANS HAVE ALWAYS TREATED fragments of the True Cross with great respect. As a sign of that veneration they would keep the fragments in staurothekes (from the Greek words *stauros*, meaning "stake", "beam" or "cross", and *theka*, meaning "container" or "packaging").

The most common sort of staurotheke was a wooden box coated in enamel, encrusted with precious stones, and layered with gold or silver. It usually had a cross-shaped interior, in which the relic was kept behind a glass screen.

Another popular type of reliquary for fragments of the True Cross was cross-shaped and made of precious metals and encrusted with jewels. The fragment was placed behind a glass or crystal screen at the cross's central point, where the vertical and horizontal beams met. Sometimes the screen was circular, making the staurotheke look like a monstrance.

The practice of making staurothekes originated in the Byzantine Empire. To this day, these reliquaries are considered masterpieces in jewel and gold work, although in the Middle Ages they were regarded as much less valuable than the fragments they contained. Today, the reverse is true, and reliquaries seem to generate much more interest than the relics themselves.

RELIQUARY OF THE HOLY CROSS at the Jasna Góra Monastery in Częstochowa, offered to the Pauline monks in 1744 by Maria Josepha of Austria, wife of Polish King Augustus III the Saxon. The relic itself was a gift from Pope Clement XI to Maria Josepha's mother, Princess Wilhelmina Amalia of Brunswick, wife of Holy Roman Emperor Joseph I. The reliquary was made in Vienna in 1703.

▶ kings (first used for the accession of Władysław II Jagiełło), can be found today in Notre Dame Cathedral. It was taken to France, along with a number of other items from the royal treasury, by Jan Kazimierz after his abdication in 1668. Before his death, he bequeathed the treasures to his sister-in-law Anne Gonzaga, who in turn passed them on to the Benedictine monastery in Saint-Germain-des-Prés. From there, they found their way to Notre Dame.

Following the Fourth Crusade, Western Europe was inundated with Byzantine relics. Not surprisingly, there was a concurrent increase in the number of forgeries and reproductions. Among them were a large number of fake cross fragments, which were categorized with several other Passion relics under the name of *arma Christi*. The Church, therefore, introduced more stringent rules in determining a relic's authenticity, and other relics (such as the supposed blood of Christ and milk of Mary) were discredited altogether. Since so many high-ranking Catholic officials strongly opposed the trade of relics, a ban on the practice was introduced during the Fourth Council of the Lateran in 1215. The edict stated that no Christian could buy or sell relics (*sacras reliquias vendere nefas est*), under punishment of excommunication. Despite this warning, the edict was often ignored.

To this day, the origins of numerous fragments of the True Cross have not been confirmed. We know, for instance, that the emperor Charlemagne was an avid collector of relics and owned numerous fragments of the Cross. He wore one fragment around his neck in a small reliquary made of gold, mountain crystal, and precious stones. Historians, however, cannot determine the origin of that particular fragment with any certainty. Some believe it was a gift from Pope Leo III, others that it was a present from a patriarch of Jerusalem. In time it became the possession of successive Holy Roman emperors.

One of them, Charles IV of the House of Luxembourg, was a particularly devout worshipper of relics. He had been raised on stories about the knights of the Round Table and the fabled castle of Munsalvaesche, which was supposed to contain the Holy Grail. Upon becoming emperor, he decided to realize his childhood dreams by building a stronghold and filling it with holy relics. In the fourteenth century he ordered the building of Karlštejn Castle, not far from Prague, and housed in it many holy objects imported from all over Europe. Karlštejn was one of the most heavily fortified castles in the whole empire and became known as the "fortress of the Holy Grail". A chapel was built at the castle's center, and Charles always entered it barefoot as a sign of respect. Some surviving frescoes depict the emperor in prayer.

THE CHAPEL OF THE HOLY CROSS in the Great Tower at Karlštejn Castle acted as the treasury for the relics collected by Holy Roman Emperor Charles IV. It was without doubt the most closely guarded place in the whole Empire – its entrance was approached through four large doors, which had a total of 19 locks.

Every so often, Charles would organize a public viewing (*den svatosti*) of his relics in the main square of Prague's New Town. Like so many others, his fragment of the True Cross was divided into smaller pieces and placed in new reliquaries; two of the most well-known examples can be found today in the treasury at St. Vitus Cathedral in Prague and at the Hofburg Palace in Vienna. Recent tests on the Viennese fragment of the Cross have confirmed that it is made of black pine.

The practice of collecting holy objects was typical of the late medieval period. Some churches competed with each other to attract pilgrims; by visiting these privileged places of worship, pilgrims could obtain religious indulgences (the remission of punishment in purgatory). The Reichenau Monastery near Wittenberg, for instance, claimed to have 18,970 relics, mainly the remains of saints and holy persons. Rivaling this collection was that of the archbishop of Brandenburg, which was kept in his St. Mary Magdalene Chapel in Halle and boasted 42 bodies of various saints. The most significant collections of any Polish church were found in St. Vincent's in Wrocław (over 1,500 relics) and in the Church of the Holy Trinity in Strzelno (658 relics). The most valuable object in these collections was most often a fragment of the True Cross. The altar of the church in Strzelno, for example, acts as a reliquary for the bones of various saints and several tiny pieces of the Cross.

Medieval Europe also witnessed the rising popularity of Stations of the Cross. These consisted of shrines that portrayed certain moments in the Lord's Passion. The shrines were laid out according to the *Via Dolorosa* (Way of the Cross) in Jerusalem. The of first of these was built between 1405 and 1420 near Cordova, Spain, under the initiative of the Dominican monk Alvarez. Similar examples began to appear in Germany soon afterward: the nuns of the convent in Villingen,

THE EMPEROR AND HIS FAIRY-TALE PALACE

CHARLES IV OF THE HOUSE OF LUXEMBOURG was king of Bohemia and Holy Roman emperor. During his reign, he moved his imperial capital to Prague, the city in which he was born, died, and enjoyed spending most of his time. Over the course of 30 years, he turned it into one of the most important political and cultural centers in Europe. In 1348, Charles instituted Central Europe's first university in Prague, which to this day bears his name (Charles University).

That same year, he commenced building the large Gothic castle of Karlštejn, modeling it on the mythical castle of Munsalvaesche, which was said to contain the Holy Grail. Charles stored the relics he had acquired from all over Europe in his fortress, which also served as a treasury for royal insignia, jewels, and important documents. During the Hussite Wars the Czech crown jewels were brought from Prague to Karlštejn, where they remained for almost 200 years.

The heart of the castle was the Chapel of the Holy Cross, located in the Great Tower, whose walls are 7 meters thick. More than 2,000 precious gems adorn the chapel's interior, along with 130 artworks painted by Charles' court painter, Theodoric. Only bishops and archbishops were granted access to the chapel, while women were banned from entering the Great Tower altogether. If there were one place in the entire empire that could be called the "holy of holies", then, according to Charles IV, the chapel at Karlštejn Castle would have been it.

116

Baden-Württemberg, opened a very detailed Way of the Cross that precisely matched the topographical layout of the route taken by Christ.

In Poland the most well-known Stations of the Cross are in Kalwaria Zebrzydowska, Kalwaria Kodeńska, Kalwaria Pacławska, Kalwaria Wileńska, and Góra Kalwaria, some of which boast relics of the True Cross. Kalwaria Wileńska, built on the outskirts of Vilnius (modern-day Lithuania) in the 1660s, is one such example. The Stations of the Cross ended at a hilltop, upon which was built the Calvary Church of the Holy Cross. Inside the church was a reliquary containing a fragment of Christ's Cross. The relic was stolen in 1960 and remained missing for over 40 years. It was returned in 2002 after the thief, a Belarusian, finally admitted to the crime.

Although we live in a secularized world, relics still have the power to arouse our emotions and our curiosity. The history of the largest piece of the True Cross to have found its way to Poland is perhaps testament to that fact. From Constantinople it was brought to Lublin in the fifteenth century and had remained there until July 1991, when the relic was stolen from the Dominican Church of St. Stanislaus, Bishop and Martyr; it has not been seen since.

CHURCH OF THE INVENTION OF THE HOLY CROSS was a central point of the Vilnius Calvary.

RELIQUARY from the Vilnius Calvary with a fragment of the True Cross, granted by Pope Pius VI (1755—1799) to the Vilnius Dominican monks.

VILNIUS CALVARY was founded as a votive offering in thanksgiving for the routing of the Russian Army from Vilnius in 1661.

DISCOVERY

TRUTH

MORE PRECIOUS **THAN A ROYAL DIADEM**

THE HOLY NAILS

THE HOLY NAILS

Which of the several dozen nails preserved in various churches throughout the world are the ones with which Christ was crucified? At the start of the twenty-first century, and following his earlier work on the True Cross, German historian Michael Hesemann resolved to find the answer to this question.

We know from historical sources that nails were among the instruments of Christ's Passion (*arma Christi*). Specifically, they were used to nail Christ's body to the Cross. In 1868, German art historian Franz Xaver Kraus published a list of 36 places in Europe purporting to own relics regarded as the Holy Nails. There was no doubt among everyone who came across this list that not all the relics listed could be authentic. But how to determine which are genuine?

RELIQUARY OF THE HOLY NAIL (1040–1045) belonged to Princess Theophanu. On Good Friday it was hidden in a replica of Christ's tomb and brought out again on Easter morning. Today it is kept in the treasury at Essen Cathedral.

PRAY CODEX, a twelfth-century manuscript kept in Budapest. One of its illustrations shows the resurrected Christ holding a cross on whose arm three nails are visible.

After researching numerous sources, including archaeological findings, Hesemann concluded that there must originally have been three nails. Two were nailed through Christ's hands and one through His feet. This is confirmed by some of the oldest sources available, describing how St. Helena discovered the True Cross. Chroniclers state that in A.D. 325 Helena found not only three crosses in Jerusalem (belonging to Christ and the two thieves), but also three nails.

There is the possibility that more than three nails were unearthed, for example, those that were used to crucify the two thieves, those that joined the cross' upright beam with the crossbeam, or those that secured the titulus. Contemporary writers don't comment on these, however, since from a Christian point of view, the most important nails were those that directly pierced the flesh of the Savior.

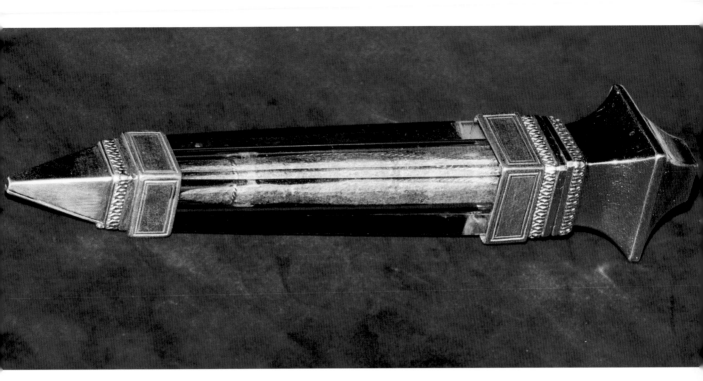

RELIQUARY OF THE HOLY NAIL KEPT in the Notre Dame Cathedral treasury, Paris. Experts believe it is slightly too small to be deemed an authentic relic.

They are held in the highest regard, as Christians believe that they are blessed with the blood of Christ.

Since Hesemann knew that St. Helena had discovered three nails, he decided to examine every so-called Holy Nail in Europe and to determine whether its documented history could be used to trace its origin back to the Holy Land.

The next task was to compare the venerated objects with genuine arti-facts—excavated nails that the Romans used to crucify prisoners. Israeli archaeologists found these nails, which dated back to the Second Temple period, when in 1968 they excavated four tombs in the ancient settlement of Giv'at ha-Mivtar (an area in modern-day northern Jerusalem). One of the tombs contained the body of a young man who had been crucified. His name was Yehohanan ben Hagkol—John, son of Ezekiel. According to archaeologists, he was put to death by Roman occupants of the city sometime between A.D. 6 and 65. His feet were placed one on top of the other and pierced with a nail.

OSSUARY inscribed with Yehohanan ben Hagkol, in which archaeologists discovered the foot of a man pierced with a nail. According to Israeli anthropologist Nicu Haas, the nail would have measured 16 centimeters and pierced both feet. On the other hand, two other Israeli scientists— Joseph Zias and Eliezer Sekeles—believe the nail was only 11.5 centimeters in length and pierced only the right foot.

COMPARE
page ▶ 82

The Holy Nails

The discovery in Giv'at ha-Mivtar provided archaeologists with a model of the sort of nails the Romans used in crucifixions. It was most likely a carpenter's nail, quadrangular in shape, measuring around 16 centimeters long and 0.9 centimeters wide at its thickest point. It was usually used to secure large pieces of wood and occasionally used in executions.

Initial comparisons between the Giv'at ha-Mivtar nails and some of the nail relics suggested that a portion of the latter could not be authentic. For instance, the nail kept in the Hapsburg treasury in the Hofburg Palace in Vienna turned out to be a fake, as it measured 18 centimeters and was made of silver. Some relics, such as those venerated in Arras and Paris, were too small to pierce a human hand or foot. There are three explanations that might account for these relics: these objects are forgeries; they include a part of the original nail, which was sawn off and melted into a nail shape; or they are so-called third-class relics, which came into contact with the original relic.

All of this begs the question, then, of which relics can be regarded as authentic. Some of the oldest sources on the subject tell us that Helena took one of the three original nails back to Rome and gave two to her son, Constantine, who took them to the empire's newly built capital of Constantinople. In her private chapel at the Sessorium palace, the nail that Helena brought back to the Eternal City was used to join a fragment of the True Cross with a piece of the titulus, as well as with a piece of the supposed cross of the Good Thief. Over time, Helena's private chapel was rebuilt to become the Basilica of the Holy Cross in Jerusalem.

Church chronicles tell us that since the fourth century, the Holy Cross Basilica has been home to a relic of the Holy Nail (*Santo Chiodo*). For centuries, the nail served as a model for numerous replicas, some of which were

✢

HOLY NAIL
from the Basilica of the Holy Cross in Jerusalem, Rome, brought from the Holy Land by St. Helena. It has been preserved almost entirely intact to this day.

MODERN RECONSTRUCTION of the sort of nail that was used in crucifixions in Christ's time, based on archaeological discoveries made at Giv'at ha-Mivtar.

The Holy Nails

SANTA MARIA DELLA SCALA HOSPITAL is located in the center of Siena, across the piazza from the cathedral dedicated to Most Holy Mary of the Assumption. Today it houses one of the largest museum complexes in Tuscany.

third-class relics. Hesemann compared this nail with the Giv'at ha-Mivtar example and found that they are very similar. The Holy Cross relic is also quadrangular and 0.9 centimeters thick, but it's only 11.5 centimeters long, whereas the more recently excavated nail measures 16 centimeters. Closer inspection of the Holy Cross nail revealed that it is missing the original head. Archaeologists surmise that it could have broken off when the nail was removed from the wooden cross. The nail is also missing its tip, and signs of sawing suggest that small parts of the nail had been cut off. These sawn-off fragments were likely melted together with other metals to make replicas. Thus, although a number of the Holy Nails venerated today might not be wholly authentic, they may contain material taken from an original. Unfortunately, it is impossible to determine which of these nails contain any particles from the nail Helena brought back to Rome. Hesemann concluded that at least the relic in Holy Cross Basilica was probably one of the nails from Christ's Cross. It is possible, after all, to trace its uninterrupted history from the present day all the way back to St. Helena.

So what of the other two nails,

which ended up in Constantinople? We know for certain that for centuries one of them was the property of the Byzantine imperial dynasty. In 1354 Pietro di Giunta Torrigiani, a Venetian merchant trading in Constantinople, bought some of the relics from the imperial treasury, including one of the Holy Nails.

He sought help from Bishop Piero di Tommaso Soderini, the papal nuncio in Constantinople, who provided a four-man team to confirm the relics' authenticity. Definitive confirmation, however, came from the empress consort Irene Asanina, who was then residing in the convent of Hagia Martha. She admitted that the treasures had once belonged to her but that she had sold them out of necessity when her husband, the Byzantine emperor John VI, abdicated. Pope Innocent VI consequently expressed an interest in acquiring the Holy Nail.

Somewhat unexpectedly, however, the rector at the Santa Maria della Scala hospital in Siena, Andrea di Grazia, warned the pope against making the purchase and instead made an offer of his own. Since canon law forbade the trade of relics, Torrigiani and Soderini signed a deed of donation to the hospital. In return for offering the precious relic, the hospital handsomely rewarded Torrigiani.

Santa Maria della Scala was not just a medical establishment, but also a home for pilgrims and orphans, a welfare office, a bank, and a museum. As a rich institution it held considerable sway over the life of the town. No wonder, ▶

HOLY NAIL RELIQUARY kept in Siena since 1559. The citizens of Siena obtained the relic instead of Pope Innocent VI, who desperately wanted to buy it.

The Holy Nails

127

SANTA MARIA DELLA SCALA

SANTA MARIA DELLA SCALA
in Siena was one of the oldest and largest hospitals in Europe. From as early as the eleventh century, the cathedral's canons set up a shelter for sick and weary pilgrims opposite the church. Initially, the hospital stood as an independent institution, before eventually being linked with other municipal authorities. Countless donations made by rich townspeople soon turned the establishment into the city's largest and most influential property. Among its donors were St. Catherine and St. Bernardine of Siena. While the hospital treasury accumulated numerous donated works of art, the institution itself also served as a pilgrim shelter, orphanage, welfare office, bank, and museum.

Midway through the fourteenth century, the hospital authorities decided to make Siena an important pilgrimage site. With this aim in mind, the Holy Nail was brought from Constantinople and housed in a newly built chapel. The hospital itself was full of artworks, and the rooms in which the sick lay were filled with paintings by Tuscan artists. The Santa Maria della Scala operated in this way for over nine centuries. It was closed only in 1995, whereupon a museum was opened in its place, on Siena's cathedral piazza.

SANTA MARIA DELLA SCALA HOSPITAL.
The sick lay beneath frescoes painted by Domenico di Bartolo from 1440 to 1444, depicting acts of kindness toward the needy.

then, that it was able to make a better offer than the pope, who was at that time residing in Avignon.

In 1359 a large ceremonial procession marked the arrival of the Holy Nail in Siena. From that moment on, it became the town's most popular pilgrimage attraction. A new chapel was even built to house the relic—the Cappella del Manto, or Manto Chapel. Public displays of relics were organized in the chapel every year, especially on March 25, a tradition that continues to this day.

Is the nail in the Santa Maria della Scala genuine?

Hesemann is inclined to believe that it is, given its similarity to the nail found at Giv'at ha-Mivtar and to the nail kept in the Basilica of the Holy Cross. Like those two, the relic in Siena is also quadrangular, although somewhat thinner due to apparent sawing. It's 15 centimeters long, although its tip is partially broken off. Significantly, its history can be traced all the way back to Constantinople.

It's worth noting that as part of the transactions made by Torrigiani, another, much smaller nail from the imperial palace found its way to the Apennine Peninsula. According to tradition, it was supposedly nailed through the titulus bearing the convict's sentence. To this day it's preserved in the Tuscan town of Colle di Val d'Elsa. No tests have been carried out on the relic, however, so its authenticity is still unverified.

CATHEDRAL IN COLLE VAL D'ELSA, Tuscany, which houses the nail bought in Constantinople in 1357.

The fate of the third Holy Nail is slightly more difficult to determine. There is much evidence to suggest that it was divided up into smaller fragments. In the fifth century, Theodoret of Cyrus wrote that under St. Helena's initiative, part of the nail was embedded in the emperor Constantine's helmet to protect his head in battle, and another part was melted into his horse's harness. This was not just for protection, however; it also coincided with the prophecy made in the book of Zechariah, which states, "In that day, 'Holiness to the Lord' shall be engraved on the bells of the horses" (Zech 14:20). This version of events was confirmed by St. Ambrose, who likewise read into their symbolic meaning. The nail fragment in the emperor's helmet was a sign of the good news, and its presence in the horse's reins represented "fair restraint instead of illegitimate rule".

Today there are two places where the emperor's harness—supposedly containing a fragment of the Holy Nail—is venerated: Milan and Carpentras. During the later period of the Roman Empire, Milan was one of the most important Roman metropolises. The emperor Theodosius I died there in his palace in 395. He is regarded by historians as the last emperor to have ruled over both

CHAPEL OF THE HOLY NAIL in Colle Val d'Elsa. The decorative tabernacle with its inscription dedicated to the relic was sculpted by the Italian Mino da Fiesole (1429–1484).

NAIL in Colle Val d'Elsa. It was supposed to have nailed the titulus damnationis to Christ's Cross.

The Holy Nails

131

✠

PILGRIM IN MILAN CATHEDRAL praying before the crucifix of St. Charles Borromeo. This was the cross the Milanese archbishop carried during the penitential procession in 1576, asking God for an end to the plague epidemic.

eastern and western halves of the Roman Empire. In accordance with his dying wishes, Theodosius' imperial insignia remained in Milan under the care of his friend and bishop, St. Ambrose. The emperor's inheritance included the imperial harness, preserved in the Church of St. Thecla.

It was almost a thousand years after the death of Theodosius', in 1389, that the next piece of documentation appeared concerning the Holy Nail. The source in question speaks of a relic that "for the longest time" had been preserved in St. Thecla's, in the former diocese of St. Ambrose. In 1461 the harness was moved in a ceremonial procession to Milan's cathedral, where, beginning in 1489, it was exhibited to the public every year on May 3.

The Holy Nail (*Santo Chiodo*) enjoyed remarkable popularity among devotees, but a new era in its history began in 1566, when Charles Borromeo became archbishop of Milan. Borromeo was one of the architects of the Council of Trent and a leading figure of the Counter-Reformation. When a plague hit the city in 1576, the archbishop did not lock himself up in his palace for fear of contracting the disease; instead, he went out every day and visited the sick, praying with them and offering the sacraments. He also organized three penitential processions to ▶

CATHEDRAL OF THE NATIVITY OF MARY in Milan, which houses a relic of the Holy Nail (*Santo Chiodo*), is one of the largest churches in the world (157 meters long and 109 meters wide). The cathedral took over 400 years to build.

EVERY YEAR ON SEPTEMBER 14,
the Feast of the Exultation of the
Cross, the Holy Nail is elevated
on a moving sixteenth-century
reliquary in Milan Cathedral, which
is filled with pilgrims.

SANTO CHIODO. The cross-shaped reliquary contains a bridle believed to be part of Constantine's imperial harness. Under St. Helena's recommendation, the harness was fitted with a nail fragment from Jesus' Cross.

FOLLOWING PAGES: INTERIOR OF MILAN Cathedral—the largest Gothic church in the world. In the presbytery, at a height of 42 meters (right under the cathedral vaulting), hangs the reliquary of the Holy Nail.

pray for an end to the epidemic; these involved carrying the reliquary containing the Holy Nail through the streets of Milan. Borromeo himself walked through the streets like a man convicted: his feet were bare, and he wore just one garment and tied a cord around his neck. In his arms he carried a cross, specially made for the occasion. When the plague ended, it was seen as an intervention by divine providence.

A year later, on May 3, 1577, Milan's citizens organized an act of "raising up" (quite literally) the Holy Nail, in thanks for saving the town. Under the archbishop's supervision, a special mechanism was built to elevate him and the relic, and it remains one of the greatest feats of baroque engineering. The lift was constructed in the shape of an elaborate cloud, with a purple canopy and angelic figures; like an elevator it raised the archbishop and the relic upward to a height of 42 meters—right up into the cathedral's vault, where the relic was hung.

Every year thereafter, the relic was brought down by the archbishop of Milan, who carried it in a procession through the city streets. Afterward, the relic was returned to its place of honor in the cathedral. This tradition ceased in the second half of the twentieth century, however, around the time of the Second Vatican Council. Today the Holy Nail is lowered, displayed in the cathedral, and then raised again in honor of the Feast of the Exultation of the Cross on September 14. Local legend maintains that Leonardo da Vinci built the mechanical lift dubbed the *nivola* ("cloud"), but a quick check of dates reveals that Leonardo died 58 years before its construction.

The Milanese relic is a piece of twisted iron, about 30 centimeters long and weighing 700 grams. The shape is reminiscent of a horse's bridle. There is no guarantee, however, that this is the imperial harness with the embedded Holy Nail, especially since another relic, also considered to be Constantine's harness, is venerated in the French town of Carpentras.

As mentioned, the imperial harness was kept in Milan following the death of Theodosius in 395. Historical sources inform us that midway through the sixth century, Pope Vigilius struck a deal with the Byzantine emperor Justinian, offering him a relic to seal the agreement. Justinian chose the harness fitted with the Holy Nail fragment. We do not know whether the relic was removed in its entirety from the Church of St. Thecla or whether a part of it was sawn off. We do know, however, that the relic was 17 centimeters long and that it was offered to the Byzantine emperor in the presence of the patriarch of Constantinople and the bishop of Caesarea.

From as early as the sixth century, Byzantine sources, including inventory lists of objects in the imperial treasury, make reference to a holy harness kept at the palace in Constantinople. The French stole it from there during the Fourth Crusade in 1204, and it ended up in the hands of a papal nuncio who took it personally to Rome. It remained in the Eternal City for the next hundred years, until the time of Pope Clement V. In 1309 Clement moved the Holy See (effectively the papal court) from Rome to Avignon, taking with him a number of relics, including Constantine's harness and the Holy Nail.

The Avignon Papacy came to an end in 1377, when Pope Gregory XI moved his court back to Rome, but not all the relics that Clement had originally brought with him to Avignon were returned by Gregory. The imperial harness remained in the small town of Carpentras, and in 1451, Pope Nicholas V decided that the relic would stay there for good. It was destroyed during the French Revolution, but a replica made in 1872 is visited to this day.

Before it was destroyed, the French harness was never examined in such a way that could have determined whether it bore an authentic fragment of one of the Holy Nails. Tests have been conducted, however, on the helmet, or diadem. that Constantine wore.

We know from the writings of Theodoret of Cyrus that under Helena's influence, a fragment of the Holy Nail was embedded in the emperor's helmet. While delivering Emperor Theodosius' eulogy, St. Ambrose stated that "emperors had greater respect for the nail from Christ's Cross than for their own diadem." Some historians take this to mean that Constantine's headpiece—adorned with a precious relic—was not a helmet but a crown. For almost a thousand years, however, no one ever encountered either.

In the sixteenth century Church authorities in the Italian town of Monza began to claim that they possessed a crown in their cathedral that was fitted with a nail from Constantine's harness. Soon, Monza became a popular pilgrimage site. Tests conducted on the relic in the last century, however, do not back up this version of events. Significantly, a metal band found on the inside of the crown was revealed to be made of silver.

Historians are quick to stress that this is indicative of a very valuable piece of imperial insignia, especially since the Holy Roman emperor Charles V and Napoleon Bonaparte were crowned with it (in 1530 and 1804, respectively). Scientists believe that the *Corona Ferrea* in Monza is in fact the legendary crown of the Lombards, worn by the likes of Charlemagne (774), Otto I (951),

THE BRIDLE FRAGMENT of Emperor Constantine was kept in Carpentras, and was destroyed by French revolutionaries. The imperial harness remains part of the town's coat of arms.

The Holy Nails

140

✥

Henry IV (1081), and Frederick I Barbarossa (1155). In any case, it is definitely not a relic of Christ.

Since the third of the Holy Nails was divided in pieces, there is a chance that those fragments were melted into or mounted onto other objects. The possibility can't be discounted, but it would require very thorough and time-consuming testing. Even then, experts believe that a unanimous verdict is by no means guaranteed. If a fragment of the original Holy Nail was sawn off and melted into another nail, there is practically no way this can be verified.

By way of conclusion, it's worth summarizing the most well-known relics that are venerated as Holy Nails, even though we have no way of telling whether they contain fragments of the originals. One nail, 9 centimeters long, is kept in the cathedral treasury at Notre Dame. Another, preserved in Trier, measures 15 centimeters, has a missing head and a partially broken tip, and can be dated back to 980. For centuries, people have venerated the spike of a nail found in St. Stephen's Cathedral in Toul, in the French region of Lorraine. Two more nails can be found in the cathedral treasuries at Cologne and Essen, although these days it is their artful reliquaries that attract greater interest, being made entirely of gold.

In Poland there is only one relic purported to be a nail from Christ's Cross. Pope Martin V gave it to King Władysław II Jagiełło as a gift in 1425. Today, it is kept in a radiant monstrance in the treasury at Wawel Castle.

RELIQUARIES OF THE HOLY NAIL:

1) Found in the treasury at Essen Cathedral. However, experts do not believe that this is one of the original nails from Golgotha.

2-3) Found in Wawel Cathedral, Kraków. King Władysław Jagiełło was supposed to have received the Holy Nail from the pope. The relic itself is a 1.5-centimeter fragment sawn from a larger nail. The fragment has been incorporated into a replica a based on the original Holy Nail, separated by a metal plate.

The Holy Nails

141

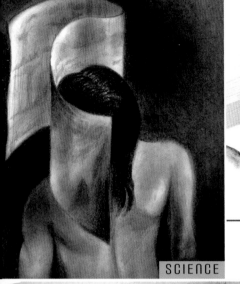

SCIENCE

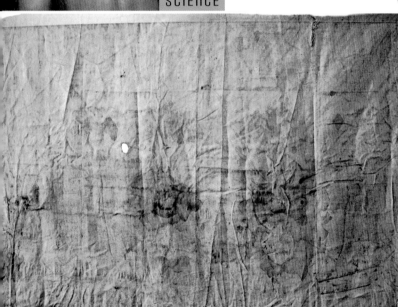

HISTORY

761
Oviedo
636
Toledo
Sevilla
616

711
Monsacro

616
Cartagena

Mediterranean

614
Alexandria

Black Sea

Sea

Jerusalem
33

0   500   1000
kilometers

THE SUDARIUM
OF OVIEDO

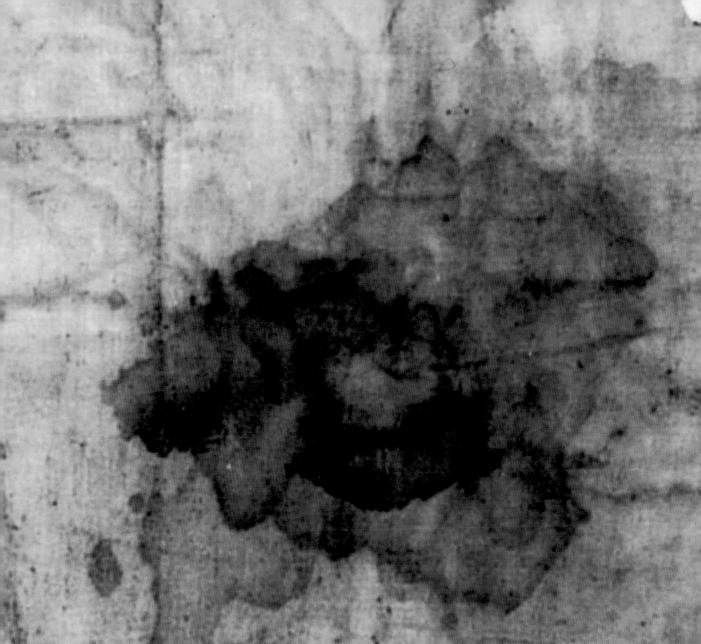

CLOSE-UP OF THE SUDARIUM
with blood that flowed from the
nose and lips.

METHOD
USED to wrap
the veil around
Christ's head.

CHAPTER IV

THE SUDARIUM OF OVIEDO

An unusual investigation got underway
in Spain on December 8, 1989.
Dr. José Delfin Villalain Blanco
and engineer Guillermo Heras Moreno
led a team of about forty scientists—
specialists in such fields as criminology,
hematology, palynology, mathematics,
computer science, and polarized imaging.
These experts had solved numerous crimes
in Spain. This time they were confronted
with a rather different task:

THE SUDARIUM'S JOURNEY from Jerusalem to Oviedo.

145

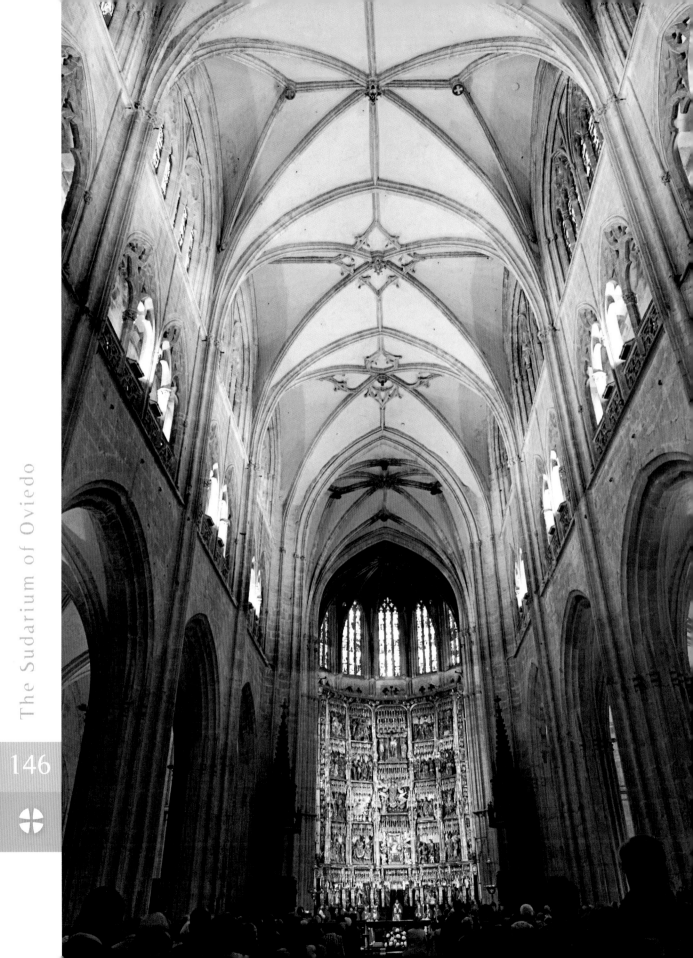

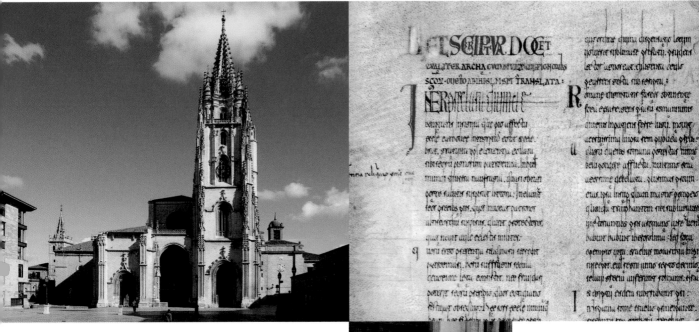

OVIEDO CATHEDRAL, which, according to a 1465 chronicle by Don Diego de Granada, was the site of numerous relics, among them the remains of numerous saints.

LAST WILL AND TESTAMENT OF KING ALFONSO II, dated November 16, 812, is the oldest document mentioning the Sudarium of Oviedo.

to determine the origins of the Sudarium of Oviedo, considered by Catholics to be one of the burial cloths of Christ.

In their accounts of Jesus' Resurrection, the four evangelists refer to different kinds of burial cloths, including the *sindon* (sheet or shroud), *sudarion* (scarf or kerchief), and *othonion* (canvas or cloth). The author of the most detailed account is St. John. Unlike the other three Gospel writers, he was at the empty tomb on Easter morning. He writes the following: "Peter therefore went out with the other disciple, and they went toward to the tomb. They both ran together, but the other disciple outran Peter and came to the tomb first. And he, stooping down and looking in, saw the linen cloths lying there; yet he did not go in. Then Simon Peter came, following him, and went into the tomb; and he saw the linen cloths lying there, and the handkerchief that had ▷

PILGRIMS from South America arrive in Oviedo for a public showing of the relic.

The Sudarium of Oviedo

147

✠

THE SUDARIUM
OF OVIEDO,
the veil wrapped
around Christ's
head following
His death on the
Cross..

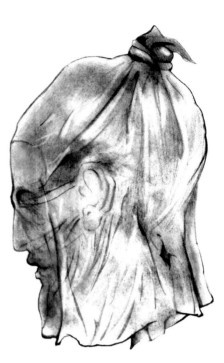

THE VEIL WAS PLACED around Jesus' head while He was still on the Cross, soon after His death. In keeping with Jewish burial customs, every drop of blood had to be buried with the body. The veil was used in particular to stop the flow of blood from the lips and nose.

COMPARE
page ▶ 158

been on His head, not lying with the linen cloths, but folded together in a place by itself. Then the other disciple, who came to the tomb first, went in also, and he saw and believed" (Jn 20:3–8).

Paraphrasing this excerpt from St. John's Gospel, the early-fifth-century Greek epic poet Nonnus of Panopolis writes: "When Simon Peter came after him, he immediately entered the tomb. He saw the linen cloths lying on the bare ground, and a garment that covered His head, with a knot on the upper corner of the part covering the hair. In Syrian it is called a sudarion. It was not together with the other burial cloths, but was folded and placed in another place."

Several early Christian writings, such as the life of St. Nino of Georgia or the Gospel commentaries of Nestorian Bishop Izodada of Merv, tell us that St. Peter was the sudarium's first owner. In reality, however, the relic's history is unknown throughout the six centuries after Christ. Historians are inclined to believe that it was preserved in the Holy Land, probably hidden, although there are no pilgrims' accounts concerning the relic. The sudarium resurfaced only at the start of the seventh century.

Using various medieval manuscripts, it's possible to trace how the sudarium found its way to Spain from the Holy Land. When the Persians invaded Jerusalem in 614, the relic was transported to Alexandria. Two years later, the Persian armies occupied Alexandria, and the Christian authorities were forced to move the sacred cloth to another location. It was transported by sea to Cartagena, on the Iberian Peninsula, and thereafter to Seville, ending up in Toledo, which was at that time

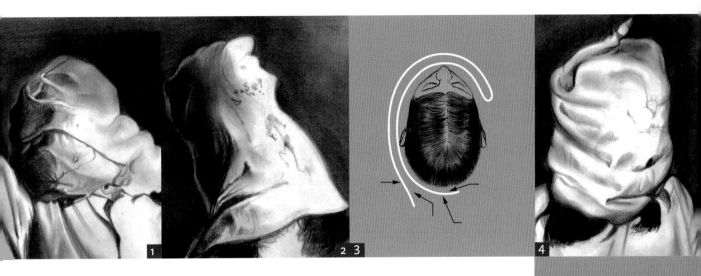

the main Christian center in Spain. The sudarium was kept in Toledo for 75 years, from 636 to 711, when the Muslims invaded the Iberian Peninsula. Many Christians escaped to the north, taking with them a chest full of relics from Toledo and burying it near the peak of Monsacro, in the region of Asturias. It remained there for nearly half a century, until it was unearthed in 761. The recovered sudarium was then moved to the cathedral treasury in the regional capital of Oviedo.

The relic remained in Oviedo from that moment on, and its history in that time has been well documented. Oviedo Cathedral soon became an important pilgrimage site in Europe, influenced by the fact that it lies on the pilgrimage route to Santiago de Compostela (the Way of St. James). Although pilgrims were not allowed to set eyes on the relic, they must have delighted in being able to touch and kiss the chest in which it was hidden. The chest itself was opened very rarely. One such occasion was March 13, 1075, when Alfonso VI and his retinue came to Toledo to see the sudarium. It was next opened 640 years later, in 1715, at the request of King Philip V. In time, the relic was removed from its chest more frequently and sometimes even for public display. Eventually it became traditional to display the relic three times a year: on the Feast of the Exultation of the Cross (September 14), on the Feast of St. Matthew (September 21), and on Good Friday.

The sudarium came close to being completely destroyed on October 12, 1934, when left-wing terrorists planted dynamite in the crypt of St. Leocadia in Oviedo Cathedral. The explosion was so powerful that the Holy Chamber (*Cámara Santa*), in which the relics were kept, was almost obliterated. Numerous works of ▶

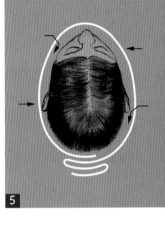

METHODS OF WEARING THE VEIL
Illustrations 1-3 show how the veil was worn while the body was vertical (1 – front view, 2 – back view, 3 – vertical projection). The veil wasn't wrapped tightly around the head since the right cheek was rested on the shoulder. Illustrations 4-5 show how the head was wrapped when the body was laid horizontally (4 – front view, 5 – horizontal projection).

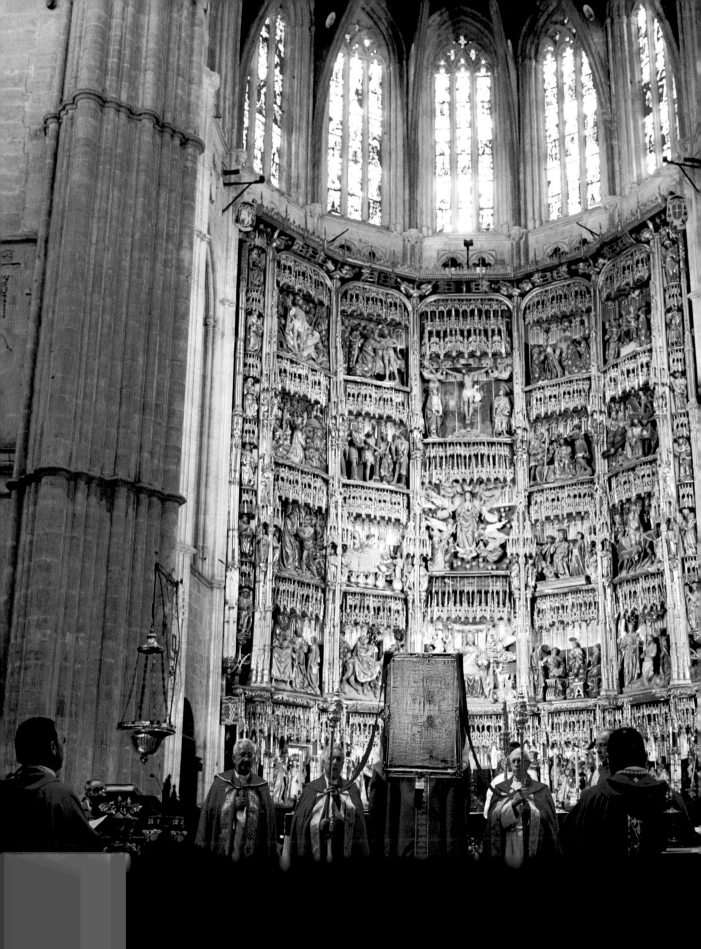

ABRIOSE.ESTE.ARCO.AÑO.DIç.29

ARCHBISHOP
JESUS SANZ
MONTES
blesses the
cathedral
congregation
with the
Sudarium relic on
September 21, 2011.

The Sudarium of Oviedo

153

▶ art were destroyed. "Only remnants of the Holy Chest remain", wrote Maximiliano Arboleya, the church deacon, in a letter to a friend. He added, however, that "the holy Sudarium, which was among the first of the relics to be recovered, is in good condition." The crypt was restored in 1942 (the final stone in its vaulting was laid by General Franco), and the relic can be found there today.

THE VEIL FROM OVIEDO was made from linen using a Z weave.

Such was the extent of the historical knowledge possessed by Blanco and Moreno's scientific team. The experts were confronted with a crumpled and stained linen cloth measuring 85.5 by 52.6 centimeters, still showing visible traces of blood. No image was visible on the fabric, just bloodstains that appeared symmetrically against the folds in the cloth. The scientists' one task was to determine the relic's authenticity.

THE OVIEDO RELIC is in very good condition, in part because linen is an unusually long-lasting material. The oldest preserved linen fabric is around seven thousand years old.

The initial impulse for conducting tests on the sudarium came in 1965, when Giulio Ricci, an Italian sindonologist and priest, first visited Oviedo. Ricci was on a quest to find examples of Christ's burial clothes other than the Turin Shroud. By comparing the bloodstains found on the Turin and Oviedo cloths, Ricci concluded that the sudarium might well be the scarf from Christ's tomb.

Scientists were able to determine that the scarf dates back to the time of the Roman Empire. The sort of weave and the use of a so-called Z twist suggested that

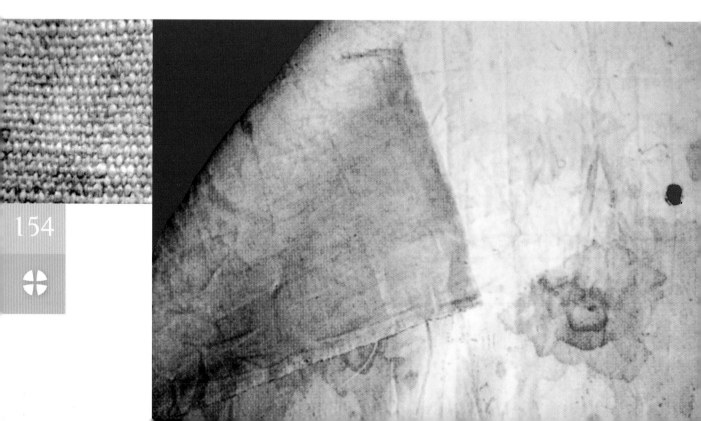

CÁMARA SANTA
in Oviedo
Cathedral was
built in the ninth
century by King
Alfonso II to form
a shelter for the
Sudarium and its
reliquary.

The Sudarium of Oviedo

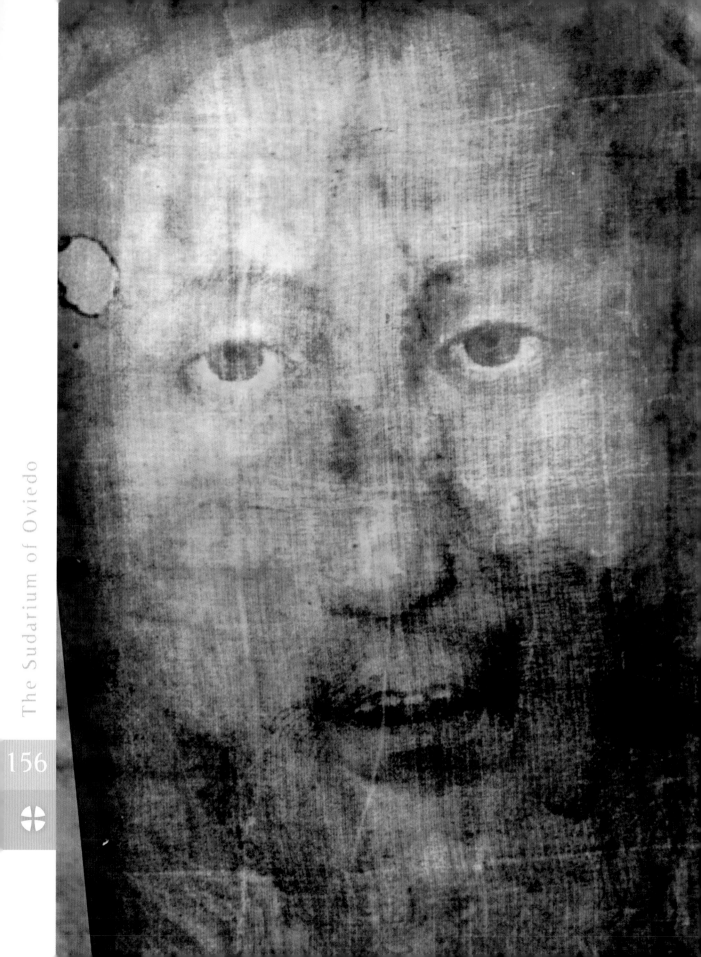

it must have been produced sometime between 400 B.C. and A.D. 500. This sort of linen was not made before this period or after it. The sudarium yielded some rather surprising results for the palynologists who examined it. They discovered 141 pollen grains and 10 fungus spores, of which 99 percent were endemic to the Mediterranean region and only 1 percent to the Atlantic region (this ratio seems consistent with relic's journey, as documented in medieval manuscripts).

The most significant finding, however, was that three of the plant species discovered on the sudarium are endemic to the Holy Land and grow only in Palestine. These are the terebinth (*Pistacia palaestina*), a species of tamarisk (*Tamarix hampeana*), and the "batha" oak (*Quercus*). All three species can be found within a radius of 20 kilometers of Jerusalem. All three blossom in the spring, which would coincide with the date of Christ's crucifixion, April 3, 33.

Scientists also discovered on the sudarium traces of myrrh

and aloe, substances used in the anointing of corpses to slow the rate of decomposition. This would tally with St. John's Gospel, which states that following the crucifixion Nicodemus brought myrrh and aloe with which to anoint Christ's body.

A criminological evaluation of the sudarium reveals that the scarf was wrapped around the head of an adult male who wore a beard and mustache and whose hair was tied at the back. He was already dead when the cloth was wrapped around him.

The stains on the cloth have been identified as traces of blood. The most visible and most concentrated of these traces outline the shape of a person's face. They are also arranged symmetrically, which suggests that the cloth was folded in half before

BY PLACING the Sudarium of Oviedo on two cloths— the Turin Shroud (above) and the Veil of Manoppello (left)—it becomes apparent that all the fabrics had been laid on the face of the same man.

THE TEREBINTH and the tamarind trees are endemic to the Holy Land. Their pollen grains were discovered on the Sudarium of Oviedo.

LOWER PART of the sudarium's largest stain, formed when the body was hanging vertically on the cross.

COMPARE
page ▶ 150

being wrapped around the head. The blood pattern shows that when the scarf was tied around the head, the body must have been in a vertical position, with the head itself bent down, 20 degrees to the right. The body was then laid horizontally, with the head angled slightly forward.

Hematological analyses have revealed that the traces of blood on the cloth are of two kinds. One kind was a result of pneumothorax (the presence of air in the space between the lungs and the chest wall), which allowed a mixture of body fluid and blood to settle in the chest cavity after death. The pneumothorax would have resulted from crucifixion and, more specifically, positional asphyxia. The stains roughly correspond with the position of the nose and mouth, from which the mixture would have emerged after death, indicating that the person was no longer alive when the scarf was wrapped around his head.

All the evidence suggests that a sudden discharge from the nose and mouth while the body was still on the cross created the stains. Scientists have located the exact stain that came about when the nose was squeezed in an attempt to staunch the flow of blood. This tallies with Jewish burial custom, which dictates that the soul is to be found in the blood and that therefore not a single drop of it should be wasted.

The mixture of blood and water brought about through pneumothorax brings to mind St. John's Gospel, which states that when a soldier pierced Jesus' side, "blood

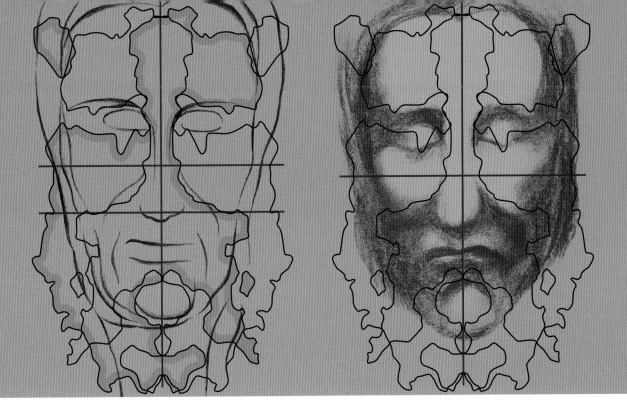

and water immediately flowed out". This description corresponds to the phenomenon of both body fluid and blood filling the air pocket in the chest cavity caused by pneumothorax.

The second kind of stains detected on the cloth were caused by live blood—in other words, blood that flowed from injuries sustained before death. The patterns suggest that the blood came from wounds caused by the Crown of Thorns, while the nature of the injuries themselves implies that they were made while the person was still alive and started bleeding about an hour before the sudarium was wrapped around his head.

Following numerous reconstructions and computer simulations, Professor Jorge Manuel Rodriguez was able to determine exactly how the sudarium was used. First it was folded in two and wrapped around the head of a person who was hanging in a vertical position. The head was not entirely covered, however; the right cheek remained bare because it was pressed against the right shoulder due to the position in which the head was leaning. Reconstructions show that the shoulder must have been slightly elevated, while the head would have been angled at 70 degrees to the front, and 20 degrees to the right.

This body positioning can be achieved only if the body is hanging up and the shoulders are stretched apart. Scientists have come to the conclusion that the body's feet must have been fixed to the cross; otherwise the person would have died after only 15 to 20 minutes. This is not long enough to account for the

COMPARISON OF BLOOD STAINS between the Sudarium of Oviedo and the Turin Shroud indicates an amazing correlation.

The Sudarium of Oviedo

159

CARRYING OF THE SUDARIUM
from the Cámara Santa to the cathedral's main altar. This takes place only three times a year, when the relic is shown to the public: the Feast of the Exultation of the Holy Cross (September 14), the Feast of St. Matthew (September 21), and Good Friday.

DRAPE COVERING THE SUDARIUM,
used three times a year during public showings of the relic.

volume of fluid that has been detected on the scarf. Later, when the body was being taken from the cross, someone used his left hand to stem the flow of blood and water from the person's nose and mouth.

When the body was eventually laid horizontally, the sudarium was removed and wrapped around the head again, this time using a different method. First of all, the cloth was no longer folded in half, but unrolled to its full size. And secondly, it was now wrapped around the whole head, covering it like a hood. Thirdly, to keep it from coming unwrapped, the cloth was fastened to the hair using sharp pins, leaving small perforations on the fabric. The head covering became cone shaped when it was tied at the top of the head.

The body was then turned over once again, in such a way that the face was pointing downward and leaning against someone's left palm. The stains on the fabric indicate that this may have lasted about 5 to 10 minutes. The corpse was then turned on its side; the cloth was removed from the head, and the body was anointed with myrrh and aloe. Scientists claim that after that, the cloth was not wrapped around the head again. In that case, it was not covering the face when the body was finally laid to rest.

Scientists have excluded the possibility that the Sudarium of Oviedo might be a fake for the simple reason that they have found no proof of that being the case. Forgeries were common during the Middle Ages when relics were in high demand, but people in that era simply didn't have sufficient knowledge of physiological and pathological processes of the human body to create the sort of patterns on the sudarium that have been detected recently using advanced technology. Likewise unbelievable is the notion that medieval forgers could have found the sort of pollen seeds known only to grow in the Holy Land, since that sort of knowledge was absolutely unavailable to them. All the tests conducted in Spain back up the hypothesis that the Sudarium of Oviedo is indeed a burial cloth of Jesus Christ.

These results have prompted other sindonologists, among them Dr. Alan Wangher, to conduct comparative studies of the Turin Shroud and the Sudarium of Oviedo. It turns out that the blood on both samples belonged to a male with AB blood type. The size of the nose imprint is identical on each sample, measuring eight centimeters long and two centimeters wide. Similarly, in both cases the right side of the nose appears swollen and bent slightly in that direction, and the right cheek exhibits a large wound. The bloodstains on both cloths are similar to each other in shape and arrangement, especially with regard to the live blood traces, which would have been brought on through injuries sustained before death. Scientists claim, therefore, that the Turin Shroud and the Sudarium of Oviedo almost certainly covered the same person. All the traces detected on both cloths are in accordance with the biblical narration of Christ's suffering, death, and burial.

The only tests that negate this theory are those that have been conducted using carbon dating. Based on findings in Tucson, Arizona, the sudarium dates back to sometime between A.D. 642 and 869, while tests carried out in Toronto claim the relic was produced between 653 and 786. As was mentioned in the chapter on the Turin Shroud, carbon dating is not renowned for its reliability. One example of this concerns the remains of a woman discovered in a peat bog in Lindow Moss, Great Britain. C14 testing revealed that the woman had been killed around A.D. 400. Meanwhile, police investigations and DNA testing confirmed that the woman was in fact Malika Rein-Bart, who was murdered by her husband in 1960. Such a huge discrepancy (over 1,500 years) resulted from the numerous kinds of carbon particles found in peat. For similar reasons, woven fabrics are very unsuited to carbon dating, since they easily absorb carbon particles.

American archaeologist Eugenia Louise Nitowski has claimed that "in every sort of test and in every scientific discipline, results are determined on the strength of the evidence available. Taking archaeology as an example, if we have 10 pieces of evidence, including one result achieved using carbon dating that doesn't fit in with the other nine results, then without hesitation that piece of evidence is considered anomalous and disregarded due to unaccountable contamination."

Sindonologist Mark Guscin draws attention to another significant point. If the results achieved by carbon dating are accurate, we would have to admit that during the Middle Ages, two highly refined forgeries were produced: the sudarium in the seventh or eighth century and the Turin Shroud hundreds of years later. The forgerers would have produced the fake relics in such a way, however, that the details on both (blood type, the size and arrangement of the wounds, the types of pollen seeds) were identical to each other. Such an operation would have been impossible, since the sudarium spent the entirety of the eighth century locked in a chest in Spain, and no one knew of its specific characteristics. Besides, determining blood groups, identifying pollen species, and photographing and scanning are all processes that were unavailable during the Middle Ages. Based on these arguments, we can justifiably disregard the theory that the sudarium is a fake and recognize it as an authentic relic.

THE MYSTERIOUS VESSEL

EVERY YEAR ON SEPTEMBER 21, the Feast of St. Matthew, the sudarium relic is displayed in Oviedo Cathedral. This is also the one day of the year when devotees are allowed access to a marble vessel preserved in an alcove in one of the church's walls. People line up to draw water from the vessel, which, according to tradition, is one of the 6 stone containers from the wedding at Cana, where Christ performed His first public miracle by turning water into wine. Throughout the rest of the year, the marble container is kept behind a set of wooden doors.

Historians have no clue as to how the vessel ended up in Oviedo and rather doubt its authenticity. The first source that refers to it appears very late, toward the end of the eleventh century. The vessel has also never been subjected to scientific tests. In any case, its proportions are quite impressive, measuring 71 centimeters high and 62 centimeters deep, with an external diameter of 92 centimeters and an internal diameter of 61 centimeters.

STONE VESSEL
venerated as the wine jar from
the wedding at Cana.

163

PILGRIMS IN OVIEDO pray and drink water from the stone vessel every year on September 21st.

TRADITION

MERCI
A LA
TUNIQUE
DE JESUS
S. J.

DISCOVERY

TRUTH

4,8 µ

0   10   20

HISTORY

VNICA · INCONSVTILIS · DOMINI · NOSTRI · JESV · C

30   40   50   60   70   80   90   cm

THE TUNIC
OF ARGENTEUIL

CHAPTER V

THE TUNIC OF ARGENTEUIL

A unique institution was founded in Paris in 2004 and was charged with the responsibility of determining the authenticity of various relics. Two French scientists led the mission. Their attention was drawn to one relic in particular, preserved in a small town just outside the capital. Professor André Marion, a physicist at the Optics Institute in Orsay and lecturer at the Paris-Sud University, and Professor Gérard Lucotte, a renowned geneticist credited with discovering the origins of DNA variations in the Y chromosome, together founded the Institute of Genetic Molecular Anthropology in Paris, where Lucotte also lectures.

PUBLIC SHOWING OF THE TUNIC of Argenteuil in 1984. The robe was placed on a mannequin and presented in a special wardrobe-like reliquary used for public showings.

LARGEST PRESERVED FRAGMENT
of the Tunic of Argenteuil – the robe's back.

Their chosen subject was a relic preserved for centuries in the Basilica of St. Denis in Argenteuil: a tunic that, according to Christian tradition, was worn by Christ. Marion and Lucotte decided to examine the tunic to determine whether it was a forgery or an authentic relic. Lucotte approached his work without any particular bias—he recalls how he lost his faith at the age of 16 following a lecture on Spinoza's *Ethics*. Yet, the scientists' discovery exceeded their wildest expectations.

We know from the Gospels that before His death,

Christ was mocked as the "King of the Jews": a crown of thorns was placed on His head and a purple robe thrown over His shoulders, and He was ridiculed and showered with abuse. St. Matthew writes that "after they had mocked Him, they took off the robe and put His own clothes on Him, and led Him to be crucified" (Mt 27:31). At the place of execution, the Roman soldiers removed Jesus' clothes and crucified Him. In his Gospel, St. John writes the following: "When the soldiers had crucified Jesus, they took His garments and divided them into four parts, one part for each soldier; also His tunic. But the tunic was without seam, woven in one piece from top to bottom, so they said to one another, 'Let us not tear it, but

MANNEQUIN
in wardrobe reliquary, used during public showings of the tunic.

DURING
a public showing of the relic in 1984, around 75,000 people came to Argenteuil to see the tunic.

ARGENTEUIL BASILICA.

Inside, the Chapel of the Holy Tunic contains an altar bearing a representation of three theological virtues: faith, hope, and love. The niche above the altar, which is made of four azure columns holding up a canopy in the form of a cupola, contains the reliquary of Christ's tunic.

cast lots for it to see whose it shall be.' This was to fulfill the Scripture, which says, 'They divided my garments among them, and for my clothing they cast lots.' So the soldiers did these things" (Jn 19:23–24). In this passage St. John refers to verse 18 of Psalm 22: "They divide my garments among themselves, and for my clothing they cast lots." What's more, the psalm begins with the words spoken by Christ on the Cross, namely, "My God, my God, why have You forsaken me?"

In those days, the typical dress of Jews living in Palestine was made up of several parts. These included underwear, a tunic worn under the clothes (*sadin*), a tunic or robe worn on top (*chetoneh*), and a coat or cloak (*simba*). While the external tunic was pleated and fairly wide and reached down to the feet, the tunic worn underneath was tighter and somewhat shorter, reaching down to the knee. It was this sort of tunic—woven in one piece and without a seam, as St. John describes—that was believed to have found its way to Argenteuil. But how did it get there?

In 1156, in a local Benedictine monastery an unusual discovery was made: an old garment together with two letters, one written in Latin, the other in French. The letters revealed that the garment was Christ's tunic, the very one for which the Roman soldiers had cast lots at Golgotha. On learning of the discovery, King Louis VII came all the way from Paris to worship the relic. From that moment on, Argenteuil became an important pilgrimage site in medieval France. ▶

croire...

BASILICA
OF ST. DENIS
in Argenteuil,
designed in a neo-
Romanesque style
by the nineteenth-
century French
architect Théodore
Ballu.

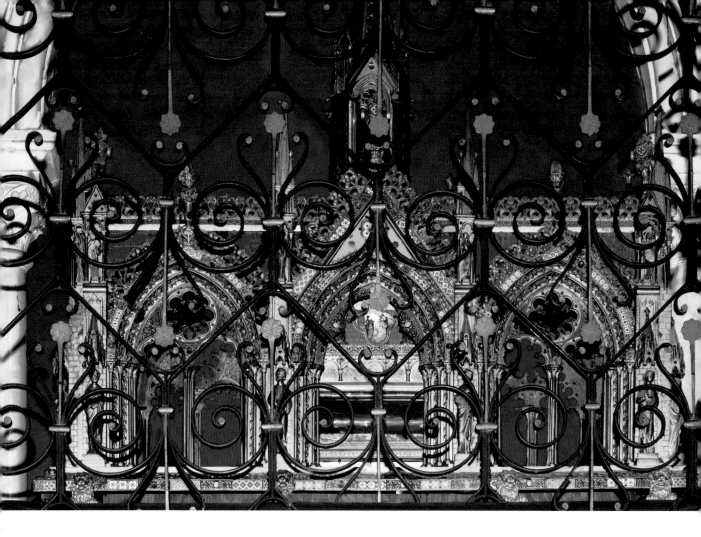

▷

The tunic's earlier history, like that of other relics belonging to Christ, is largely unknown. In its early years, Christianity was persecuted within the Roman Empire, and devotees of the fledgling faith had to conceal themselves and their rituals. No documentation therefore exists from this time regarding Christian relics. It is likely that friends of Jesus bought the tunic from the soldiers who had cast lots for it. For Christ's torturers, the bloodstained tunic was of no great value, whereas for Christ's followers it signified a priceless memory of their Messiah. The average executioner, recruited from among various mercenaries, earned an annual salary of about 225 denarii. Certainly, it would be of no great surprise if the executioner decided to make a little extra money by selling Christ's tunic to His disciples. They would have been prepared to pay any price to obtain the robe, which they believed possessed miraculous properties.

In the Gospels of St. Mark and St. Matthew we find stories in which the sick are cured just by touching Christ's garments. Old Christian legends state that following His Resurrection the tunic was placed under the care of St. Peter.

DECORATED RELIQUARY containing the Tunic of Argenteuil. It is reminiscent of a Gothic cathedral, with three portals and four spires.

FRESCO on the wall of the basilica, depicting Christ's tunic.

Historians also posit the theory that it became the property of the Christian community in Palestine.

The first historical reference to the tunic appears only at the end of the sixth century. Its author is St. Gregory of Tours, who produced the first biographical history of the Franks. In his work, *Glory of the Martyrs*, Gregory states the following: "The Gospel tells us of a tunic that covered the blessed body and for which lots were cast, since it was woven from one piece of material and without a seam. Thus the prophecy of David was fulfilled: 'They divide my garments among themselves, and for my clothing they cast lots.' But I could not keep silent about what I have heard from some people about this Tunic of the Immaculate Lamb. They say that it is still in the city of Galatia, in a church named for the Holy Archangels. This city is about 150 miles from Constantinople. In the church is a very obscure crypt where this garment was stored in a wooden box. Pious believers most assiduously adored this box that was justly deserving [of adoration because] it held this garment [that] was worthy both to touch and to clothe the body of the Lord."

175

PREVIOUS PAGE:
Fragment of
the Tunic of
Argenteuil, visible
through the
reliquary's glass
screen.

**EMPEROR
CHARLEMAGNE**
presents his
daughter
Theodrada,
prioress of
Argenteuil,
with a reliquary
containing
Christ's tunic.
Painting from
the nineteenth
century found in
Argenteuil Basilica.

To this day, historians are unable to agree upon the exact location of the ancient city of Galatia. Some experts believe it could have been the town of Germia, famed for its basilica venerating the archangels, but this is mere conjecture.

The next reference to the Holy Tunic is found in a chronicle dating from A.D. 610, written by an anonymous French historian whom future generations called Fredegar. He writes that in 590, a marble chest was discovered in Zafad, near Jerusalem, containing the "holy robe" of Christ—the same robe for which the Roman soldiers had cast lots. The relic was transported in a ceremonial procession back to Jerusalem.

This account has caused disagreement among historians. Some believe that Zafad is the town of Safed, which lies on the Sea of Galilee; others claim that the town in question is actually Jaffa, located by the Mediterranean Sea and the home of St. Peter from A.D. 36 to 44.

In 614, the Persians under Khosrau II invaded Jerusalem, pillaging numerous relics in the process. According to some scientists, the Holy Tunic may have been among those relics. Fourteen years later, after the Byzantine emperor Heraclius had defeated the Persian armies, the relic was returned to the Christians. Thereafter, the tunic was kept safe in the Boukoleon Palace in Constantinople.

No other historical sources exist that make reference to the Holy Tunic before its discovery in Argenteuil in 1156. We can only speculate about its circumstances

PAINTING ABOVE
THE ALTAR,
by the tabernacle
in the Chapel of
the Holy Tunic,
depicting an angel
bearing Jesus' robe.

before then. Even before examining the tunic, therefore, Lucotte and Marion had to admit that if this were a relic of Christ, then very little could be said about it regarding the first 12 centuries of its existence. It seemed to belong more to the world of fantasy and legend than to history.

On the basis of the letters that were found alongside the tunic, it is possible to reconstruct fairly accurately its whereabouts from the start of the eleventh century. These are tied with the emperor Charlemagne, who was known in his day to be an avid collector of relics. St. Angilbert, who served Charlemagne as a diplomat and abbot, wrote that the emperor "solicited the help of several legates to obtain relics from numerous countries, from as far as Jerusalem, Constantinople, and Rome". The emperor was said to have brought the tunic back from Rome following his coronation. One theory is that he received it in the form of a dowry from the Byzantine empress Irene. Pope Leo III planned the marriage in order to mend the rift that had existed for some time between Rome and Constantinople. A royal coup reduced the plans to nothing, however, and Irene was banished from the Byzantine capital. Charlemagne happily accepted the Holy Tunic, and before his death in 814 he bequeathed it to the Benedictine convent in Argenteuil, at which his daughter Theodrada was abbess.

Soon afterward, the Kingdom of the Franks fell to the Normans, who pillaged and laid waste to towns and countryside alike while following the Seine from its mouth further inland. They occupied Paris in 841 and destroyed the convent in Argenteuil four years later. Before the abbey was destroyed, however, the tunic was walled up in a special hiding place with the two letters accounting for its origins. It's highly likely that Theodrada herself hid the tunic before escaping from the oncoming Normans. She found a new home at the abbey in Schwarzach am Main, where she died around 848. Following her death, the tunic was forgotten.

The relic was discovered only by accident some 300 years later, in 1156. From that point, its history is comparatively well documented. Such chroniclers as Robert of Torigni, Roger of Wendover, Matthew Paris, and Bartholomew Cotton have all written about the relic. News of the tunic gradually spread throughout Europe, and pilgrims journeyed from the farthest corners of the continent to see it. King Louis IX came twice to see the tunic that Christ had worn on the Way of the Cross.

In 1534 the Holy Tunic was transported to Paris under the recommendation of King Francis I. During this time of the Reformation, one of the numerous disagreements between Catholics and Protestants had to do with relics. Lutherans and Calvinists were both strongly opposed to the veneration of any kind of relic—the remains of saints as well as relics belonging to Christ. Francis—a devout Catholic—decided to make a show of his faith by organizing a procession in Paris, which he himself led. The procession made its way through the city, showing off every relic linked with the Passion that was to be found in France at that time. Chroniclers related how people were gladdened to see those holy objects that so few had ever seen before. Among the relics on display were a fragment of the True Cross, the Crown of Thorns, the shaft of the spear that pierced Jesus' side, and the sponge that wetted His lips on the Cross. The procession's central spot, however, was occupied by the Tunic of Argenteuil.

Thirty-three years later, the tunic was almost destroyed. In 1567 Argenteuil fell under Protestant occupation. The following is an account of one eyewitness: "At dawn, taking advantage of the changing of the guard, the Huguenots edged toward the town under cover of nearby vineyards and homes, before attacking its weakest points. Upon entering the town, they set fire to some of the many remarkable shrines, including this worshipful church. They did this for a number of reasons, but mainly because of the tunic that was preserved inside."

In the words of a later abbot, Jacques Fouyn, the invaders "looted relics and other holy objects. However, during this awful destruction of the holy objects, which the Lord left to the impudence of His opposers, the Holy Tunic of Christ did not fall into their unclean hands and avoided their devastation, which is why it remains in the same place today."

The tunic was saved, having been safely hidden away before the Protestant occupation. The invaders attempted to extract its whereabouts from the abbot Lucas. He refused to reveal where the relic was hidden and was hanged from the window of his cell as punishment.

▶

Fin tragique de Marie Antoinette d'Autriche Reine de France, exécutée le 16. Octobre 1793.

THE FRENCH REVOLUTION:
A PERIOD OF DESTRUCTION

THE ITALIAN WRITER ROSA ALBERONI claims that the French Revolution was a war declared by the "cult of the Enlightenment" on Catholicism. The facts seem to speak for themselves: on November 10, 1793, Notre Dame Cathedral was transformed into a temple of rational thought. A replica of Mount Olympus, atop which stood a local prostitute wearing a white dress, an azure coat, and a red cap, was brought into the cathedral. When she sat on her throne, a hymn broke out in her honor, hailing her as the Goddess of Reason. Portraits of the new "saints", including Robespierre, Marat, and other revolutionary leaders, were hung up around the church. .

One month earlier, the National Convention abolished the Christian calendar and replaced it with a revolutionary calendar whose new year began on September 22, 1792—the day Louis XVI was arrested. Everything that could be associated with Christianity was destroyed: clergymen were murdered, the priesthood was abolished, religious symbols were removed, churches were demolished, cemeteries were desecrated, and observance of Sunday and other holy days was forbidden.

Relics associated with Christ also fell victim to revolutionary zeal. In 1793 a crowd stormed the Sainte-Chapelle and destroyed its interior. Several of the relics kept inside were lost; these included the fragment of the True Cross bought from Baldwin II (considered the largest piece of the relic in existence), the shaft of the Longinus Spear, a piece of burial shroud, and the sponge used to moisten Christ's lips on the Cross. In 1794 the Convention ordered the burning of the Shroud of Besançon, which had been venerated as one of Christ's burial cloths.

181

CROSS IN
ARGENTEUIL
BASILICA
erected to mark
the tunic's public
showing in 1984.

J.B. 1936

À L[...]
15 NOVEMBRE
J.F.

EN TOUCHANT
SEULEMENT
LA FRANGE
DE SON VÊTEMENT
J'AI ÉTÉ GUÉRIE

OSTENSION
DE 1934
15 MAI
M. HARMEGNIES

HOMMAGE À LA S[?]. TUNIQUE

GUÉRISON DE MA FILLE

JUILLET 1895

JOSEPH BERNIER

ZOUAVE PONTIFICAL

MERCI !
1895 MB

▷ When the religious wars came to an end, the abbey was rebuilt, and the Holy Tunic was returned to its place. This peace signaled a new era of holiness for the town of Argenteuil, with a new wave of European pilgrims flocking to see the precious relic. Among the pilgrims were King Henry III of France, Maria de' Medici, and Cardinal Richelieu. The abbey's chronicles relate how King Louis XIII came three times to pray before the tunic. When the monks offered to open the reliquary and to remove the robe for him to see, Louis declined, stating that he needed only to glimpse a tiny part of the relic in order to believe in the rest. His words have gone down in the abbey's history, and from that time many pilgrims have followed the king's example by worshipping in front of the closed reliquary. In 1613, Pope Paul V authorized the Brotherhood of the Holy Tunic, which gave thanks for the Holy Passion and veneration of the Tunic of Argenteuil.

With time, suspicions began to grow that the relic on display in Argenteuil was not in fact authentic. People began to doubt whether it actually escaped the plundering of the Huguenots and whether the monks had replaced it with a forgery. Indeed, the reliquary containing the tunic itself vanished during the religious wars, after which the robe was kept in a new container.

Since rumors on the subject began to grow ever stronger, a clerical investigation was proposed in 1647 by the French prelate Pierre du Cambout de Coislin.

VOTIVE OFFERINGS in Argenteuil Basilica, honoring Christ's tunic in thanksgiving for received graces.

CANDLE OFFERED by Pope Pius IX in 1854 in exchange for a 20-centimeter cutting of the tunic.

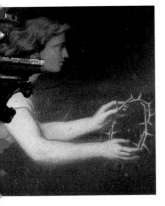

PAINTING in the Chapel of the Holy Tunic, found by the tabernacle above the altar, depicting an angel carrying the Crown of Thorns.

It's not known whether Coislin was the actual leader of the investigation or just its initiator, since he became an abbot at Argenteuil at the mere age of 7 and at 11 held the position of church canon in Paris. The investigation concluded that the tunic preserved at the abbey was the same as the one that was kept there before the Protestant invasion. The official declaration resulted in a new wave of pilgrims journeying to Argenteuil. In 1653, Pope Innocent X confirmed and blessed the devotion to the Argenteuil relic, although he did not make any definitive judgment as to the relic's authenticity.

In 1667 the first printed text on the subject of the tunic, written by the abbot Gabriel de Gaumont, appeared. He wrote that the tunic had diminished in size over the years, since monks and priests had torn off small parts of it to serve as miniature relics. The practice continued, and in 1680, the abbot Charles Petey de l'Hostallerie cut off a sizable piece and donated it to the neighboring abbey of St. Cornelius in Compiègne, where it can still be found today.

The most important academic work relating to the tunic was a treatise dating from 1677, written by the historian Gabriel Gerberon, who was also a Jansenist monk. The treatise appeared in eight editions over the next hundred years, and its findings are still cited in studies published today. In his work, Gerberon claimed there was irrefutable proof that the tunic had been preserved continuously in Argenteuil since the days of Charlemagne. Still, nobody could provide any evidence as to where it was kept during the previous eight centuries.

The next dangerous period to befall the Holy Tunic came about during the French Revolution. In 1790 the new revolutionary government of France abolished the monasteries, including the Benedictine monastery in Argenteuil. The tunic had to be transported to the local parish church, although it did not remain safe there for long.

On November 10, 1793, the National Convention passed more anti-Church laws, and everything that was linked with Christianity was destroyed. The encrusted gilded silver reliquary containing the tunic was confiscated on November 18, in accordance with the law that every parish was compelled to give up its treasures. The tunic itself, however, was removed prior to the reliquary's confiscation.

Meanwhile, disturbing news reached Argenteuil from Paris. A swarm of revolutionaries had forced its way into the royal chapel, the Sainte-Chapelle, destroying and plundering everything they found. A number of relics were lost, including a fragment of the True Cross kept in the Baldwin reliquary and the staff of the

THE BLESSED
VIRGIN MARY
holding her Son's
tunic. Painting
in Argenteuil
Basilica.

INSTRUMENTS
OF CHRIST'S
TORTURE
(arma Christi)
on a fresco in
the Basilica of St.
Denis.

Holy Spear. The abbot Ozet, former rector at Argenteuil, feared that the Holy
Tunic—which was then in his care—might meet a similar fate. He made a crucial
decision, therefore, to cut the tunic into pieces and hide each piece in a different
place. In this way, he hoped at least one piece would escape the turbulence of the
Revolution unscathed.

The abbot put his plan into effect at night, together with the sacristan, secretly
dividing up the tunic. They buried the two largest pieces in different places in the
garden of the presbytery, and they distributed the other pieces among some of
their most trusted parishioners. Soon afterward, Ozet was arrested by the revolutionaries and spent the next two years in prison. He was released after the most
antireligious period of the Revolution was over. On Ascension Day in 1795, the
abbot dug up the buried pieces of the tunic and collected the fragments that had
been distributed amongst his parishioners. Not all the fragments were returned,
however; a piece of about 5 square centimeters that had been entrusted to the
parish of Sucy-en-Brie had been destroyed. Four small fragments that had been
hidden away in Longpont-sur-Orge remained there and can be found today in the
town's Notre Dame Basilica. In 1854 Pope Pius IX requested a small fragment of
the relic and received a cutting 20 centimeters long. All of this meant that the
tunic could not be restored to its original form.

PLACING THE TUNIC of Argenteuil over the Turin Shroud shows a correlation in the patterning of the wounds on both cloths.

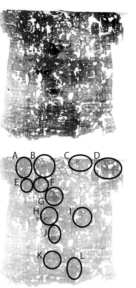

A COMPARISON OF THE FABRICS from Argenteuil and Longpont-sur-Orge reveals that they come from the same robe. The fragment from Longpont-sur-Orge was discovered after the French Revolution.

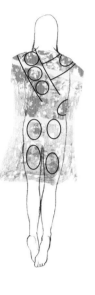

INFRARED PHOTOGRAPHS have revealed that the Tunic is almost entirely covered in blood.

BLOOD-STAIN PATTERNS on the tunic indicate that its owner must have cararied on his back a heavy, 20-centimeter-wide object, which abraded his skin from the left shoulder to the right hip.

188

Once the French Revolution and the Napoleonic Wars were over, the devotion to the tunic was revived. In 1865 it was transported to the newly built Basilica of St. Denis. Toward the end of the nineteenth century, the bishop of Versailles proposed that the tunic's various fragments be examined. Since it was in quite a bad state, the decision was made to have it reconstructed.

On April 26, 1892, the 20 fragments of the tunic were sewn together and lined with a reinforcing material. The restoration was made easier by the fact that the abbot had cut the tunic in such a way that its back was preserved in one piece, measuring 122 centimeters long by 110 centimeters wide. The abbot Jacquemot, however, who left a report on the tunic, wrote that there could be no certainty as to whether all the fragments were sewn in the correct places. Indeed, only the two largest parts of the relic could be matched to one another perfectly. Apart from the back of the tunic, this included a rectangular fragment measuring 60 by 40 centimeters. The remaining pieces were much smaller and were sewn together in a way that recreated the tunic's original shape.

The tests carried out on the tunic toward the end of the nineteenth century yielded some interesting results. The tunic was made of sheep's wool and had indeed been woven in one piece. Some stains, not visible to the naked eye, were discovered; samples taken from the fabric identified the stains as blood. Finally, it was confirmed that the dye used to color the tunic was the same as that used

on Coptic burial clothing in the second century. Tests conducted in the 1930s concluded that this dye was made from a mixture of madder and iron. It has been found in, among other places, first-century Christian tombs in Antinoopolis, Egypt.

Meanwhile, growing secularization in France resulted in a diminished interest in relics and in the Tunic of Argenteuil. With every passing year, fewer pilgrims traveled to the town. The tunic itself was put on public display less frequently. After 1894 it was exhibited only three times: in 1934, in 1984, and in 2000 (when devotees could look at the relic only through a glass screen set in the reliquary placed in front of the altar).

It seemed as if the relic would simply fade from public interest. It did, however, attract the attention of our two French scientists, who focused mainly on the tunic's largest piece. With the use of high-definition and infrared imaging, scanners, a microdensitometer, and a CCD digital camera, Marion was able to map out the patterning of the bloodstains on the tunic's back in 1997. Some of the wounds had been more scratched and abraded than others. The most bloodied areas were situated within a strip about 20 centimeters wide, measuring from the left shoulder, down through the middle of the back, to the right hip. A photographic analysis revealed that this long mark was probably made by a long and heavy object that pressed for some time against the back of the person wearing the tunic and scraped against his already wounded skin.

TEREBINTH, whose pollen grains were discovered on the Tunic of Argenteuil, is native to the Holy Land.

COMPARE
pages ▶ 58–59

The Tunic of Argenteuil

PROF. GÉRARD LUCOTTE, world-renowned geneticist working on the Tunic of Argenteuil, on a Parisian street with Countess Catherine de Thieulloy and Grzegorz Górny.

In 1998 scientists at the Optics Institute in Orsay decided to compare the blood-stain patterns on the Tunic of Argenteuil and on the Turin Shroud. They created realistic and rotational computerized geometric models of what the tunic would look like if worn by a man of the same physical stature and morphology as the man depicted on the shroud. The result was absolutely bewildering: it turned out that the bloodstains on the tunic were aligned exactly with the imprinted wounds visible on the shroud. Overlaying both images drove the scientists to the conclusion that both cloths were stained by the same bleeding man.

Could that man have been Jesus of Nazareth? It was confirmed that the tunic was produced using horizontal looms, whose width matched the proportions of those looms used in Christ's time. The weave, made using a so-called Z twist, indicates that the robe was probably made in the Near or Middle East. The fabric's dye was made of dyer's madder (*Rubia tinctorum*), which was in widespread use in ancient times around the Mediterranean Basin. The dyeing took place before the fabric was woven, and alum was used alongside the dye to dress the cloth. Both of these practices were common in the first century.

Because of these results, interest in the tunic steadily grew throughout the scientific community. In 2004, the Institute of Genetic Molecular Anthropology in Paris commenced tests

ANDRÉ MARION
(1945–2009) was
a professor at the
Optics Institute in
Orsay, an expert
sindonologist,
and the author of
*New Discoveries
Concerning the
Shroud of Turin* and
Jesus and Science.
Together with
Gérard Lucotte, he
wrote *The Tunic of
Argenteuil* and the
Turin Shroud in 2006.

on the relic. During restoration work one year earlier, the tunic was cleaned with a special vacuum cleaner. Scientists therefore decided to analyze the vacuumed particles. With the use of a scanning electron microscope (SEM), they discovered 115 pollen grains belonged to 18 plant species. The most frequently occurring types of pollen were from nettle (*Urtica fragilis*), with 41 grains, and Syrian mesquite (*Prosopis farcta*), with 13 grains. Most of the pollen grains belonged to species that had already been discovered on the Turin Shroud (six species) and the Sudarium of Oviedo (seven species). Among them were Lebanon cedar (*Cedrus libani*) and spreading pellitory (*Parietaria judaica*). The most significant discovery, however, was of two species endemic to Palestine: the terebinth (*Pistacia palaestina*) and the tamarisk (*Tamarix hampeana*). Their pollen grains have likewise been discovered on the Turin and Oviedo cloths.

Gérard Lucotte continued his analysis by turning to the bloodstains left on the tunic. For centuries they were invisible to the naked eye but were eventually detected using an electron microscope. Examining individual fibers in turn, Lucotte concluded that the robe was at one point entirely covered in blood. The flesh on the back of the person who wore it must have been utterly ravaged.

Numerous red blood cells were discovered on the cloth, attached to the fabric's fibers. Besides this, traces of urea—a constituent element of perspiration—were found among many groups of red blood cells. According to Lucotte, this points to a rare condition, known as hematidrosis, in which one sweats blood. The source of this condition is an extreme level of stress, which causes the organism to go into histaminic shock. The American anatomic pathologist Dr. Frederick Zugibe, who is familiar with this phenomenon, claims that it is brought on most often in the face of unavoidable death. This is another indicator that the tunic's owner could have been Christ. Indeed, St. Luke (who was also a doctor) wrote in his Gospel that while Jesus prayed in the Garden of Gethsemane, he sweat blood.

The next important observation Lucotte made had to do with the nature of the red blood cells (erythrocytes). These cells are usually disc-shaped with two concave (biconcave) sides. Many of the cells discovered on the tunic, however, were either spherical or with only one concave side (cup-shaped). This occurs when an organism is subjected to a great deal of trauma, such as prolonged agony.

Apart from red blood cells, Lucotte was also able to identify white blood cells (leukocytes) on the relic's fabric. Unlike red blood cells, leukocytes possess a cell nucleus containing chromosomes, which in turn contain strands of DNA, which carry the genetic information of a living organism. No two people on Earth have the same DNA, which is why it is regarded as molecular proof of a person's identity.

White blood cells are far more delicate and fragile in composition than their red counterparts. There are also about 500 times as many red cells as there are white cells in the human body, illustrating just how difficult it was to detect the presence of leukocytes on the tunic's fabric. Lucotte had to examine several thousand blood cells before he was able to identify just 10 well-preserved leukocytes. This then allowed him to conduct DNA tests using the cells' nuclei.

It has already been mentioned that the person who wore the tunic had type AB blood. This discovery was made in 1985 by a doctor of hematology from Saint-Prix who was sent a small sample of the blood found on the Holy Tunic. We know, too, that this was the blood type identified on the Turin Shroud and the Sudarium of Oviedo. Lucotte's DNA analysis also concluded that the person whose blood was found on the relic was male, possessing the XY chromosome.

It just so happened that Lucotte is regarded as one of the world's leading authorities on Y chromosome haplogroups; based on their composition, he is able to determine with a great degree of probability the ethnicity of any given male. He discovered that the male who wore the tunic carried the J2 haplogroup, which is defined by the 12f2 genetic marker and the equivalent M172 and M12 markers. The J2 haplogroup is found in greatest concentration throughout Jewish populations in the Middle East—of which Jesus Christ was obviously a part.

From all the tests conducted on the Holy Tunic of Argenteuil, only one result challenges its ancient origins. This was achieved using carbon dating tests, which took place in 2004 and 2005 under the initiative of the subprefect of Argenteuil, Jean-Pierre Maurice. A sample of the relic's fabric was tested twice using C14 radiocarbon particles. The first test, in 2004, concluded that the tunic dated back to between A.D. 530 and 650, and the second test, in 2005, placed the date between 670 and 880. Already, the variation in results points to the unreliable nature of carbon testing, as has been discussed with regard to the Turin Shroud.

Lucotte says the following with regard to the limitations of carbon dating: "There are many factors that can alter the results of tests using radiocarbon particles. Even scientists who carry out the tests admit that this method of dating only works properly when the test sample is actually representative of the material whose age one wishes to determine. In other words, the C14 particles in the test sample must come from the same era as the fabric as a whole. If at some point over the years the fabric became suffused with either older or younger carbon particles, then the tests would obviously be rendered inconclusive. In the case where older carbon particles are present, the fabric is dated as being older than it is, and the opposite is true if the fabric contains younger carbon particles."

Carbon dating can be particularly unreliable with fabrics, since they easily absorb fluids containing substances in which one can find traces of carbon, such as calcium carbonate (which occurs naturally as chalk, limestone, and marble) or organic materials. The presence of these carbon particles, which can become deeply embedded within the fabric,

LEFT: Red blood cell on the Tunic of Argenteuil, magnified 8000 times. Image taken using a scanning electron microscope.

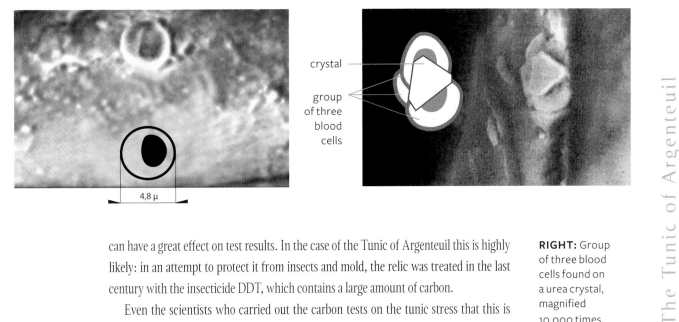

4,8 μ

crystal

group of three blood cells

can have a great effect on test results. In the case of the Tunic of Argenteuil this is highly likely: in an attempt to protect it from insects and mold, the relic was treated in the last century with the insecticide DDT, which contains a large amount of carbon.

Even the scientists who carried out the carbon tests on the tunic stress that this is a fallible method and that in determining a material's origins, one ought to take into account the results of other scientific methods. The tunic has undergone a large variety of tests, including an analysis of its woven fabric, the presence of pollen grains, the genetic composition of bloodstains found on the cloth, and comparative tests alongside the Turin Shroud. All these results, claims Lucotte, suggest strongly that the Holy Tunic of Argenteuil is an authentic garment once worn by Christ.

RIGHT: Group of three blood cells found on a urea crystal, magnified 10,000 times.

The Tunic of Argenteuil

193

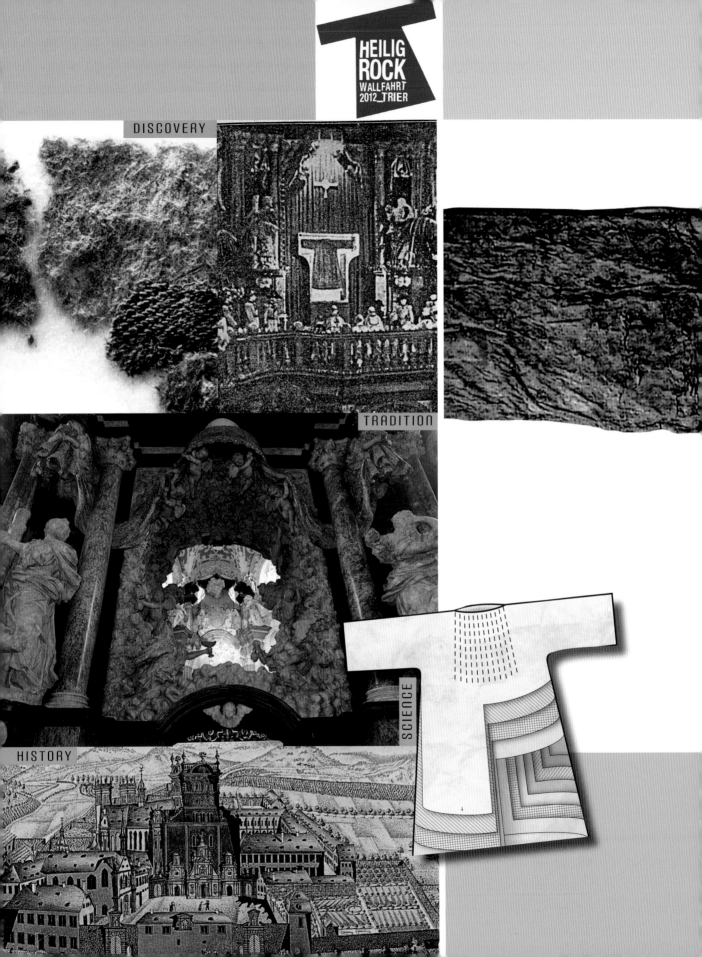

HEILIG
ROCK
WALLFAHRT
2012_TRIER

DISCOVERY

TRADITION

SCIENCE

HISTORY

THE HOLY COAT
OF TRIER

CHAPTER VI

THE HOLY COAT OF TRIER

Swiss-educated Mechthild Flury-Lemberg must have experienced a feeling like no other when examining the robe many believed to be the coat once worn by Jesus Christ. She was at that time the only scientist ever to have been granted the opportunity to conduct a thorough examination of the relic. While analyzing the woven fabric, she reminded herself of thehistory of this holy object. On April 14, 1512, a discovery was made that reverberated throughout the whole of Europe. Local tradition had maintained for centuries that a vestment once worn by Christ was hidden somewhere in the cathedral of Trier, Germany.

Trier · Berlin

GERMANY

197

HOLY COAT OF TRIER. Following reconstruction in 1891, the relic was shown to the public in 1891, 1933, 1959, 1996, and 2012.

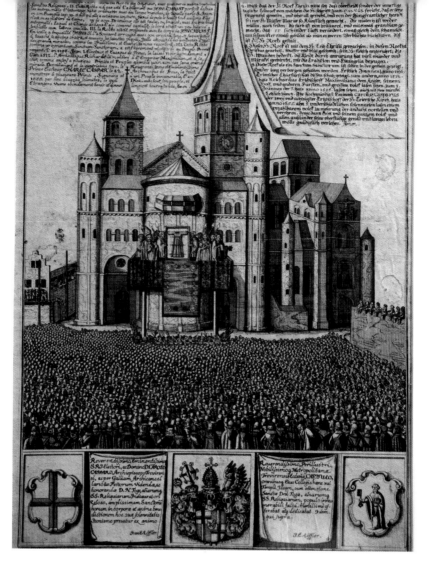

PUBLIC SHOWING of the coat in 1655, from a seventeenth-century German print.

ENTRANCE TO THE CHAPEL OF THE HOLY COAT, where the relic is kept. It is permanently hidden from visitors to the cathedral—only the reliquary is visible through a barred gate.

The robe was the subject of numerous legends, but nobody living had ever set eyes on it. Holy Roman Emperor Maximilian I decided to end this uncertainty about the relic's existence and ordered the bishop of Trier, Richard von Greiffenclau, to commence a search in St. Peter's Cathedral. And so the bishop and some of his canons began the task of searching for the lost relic. Eventually, they found a hollowed chamber beneath the cathedral floor—a secret crypt, containing three bolted chests.

On April 22, in the presence of Emperor Maximilian, the three reliquaries were opened. The first one contained the remains of St. Maternus of Cologne, the former bishop of Trier known as the Apostle of Alsace, who had died in 328. The second reliquary revealed a knife and a die. According to the cathedral clergy, the knife was possibly the one used by Christ at the Last Supper, and the die could have been used by the Roman soldiers who had cast lots for Christ's

seamless robe. The third reliquary excited the greatest amount of interest, however, as it contained a folded garment. Europe's most powerful ruler fell to his knees before it and gave thanks.

The relic was put on public display on May 3. Commentators wrote that in its first two weeks, the relic attracted more than a hundred thousand pilgrims. Trier soon became one of the most important pilgrimage sites in all of Europe. Since the robe was old and almost disintegrated in one's hands, the decision was made to restore it so that visitors and devotees could worship it in all its glory. To that end, the disintegrating fragments were glued onto a contemporary liturgical robe and hung up on a special hanger. In this way, the relic was presented to its adoring public, most often from the cathedral balcony. In 1515 Pope Leo X granted those who made a pilgrimage to Trier the same religious indulgences as were granted to pilgrims journeying to Rome.

Five years after the coat's discovery, the Reformation began in Germany. On October 31, 1517, the Augustinian monk Martin Luther nailed his *Ninety-Five Theses* to the door of the Wittenberg Castle church, thus opening a new chapter in the history of Christianity—the Protestant Reformation. Protestants criticized a number of Catholic traditions, including the selling of indulgences, the organizing of pilgrimages, and the veneration of relics. Luther himself scoffed at ▶

CHAPEL OF THE HOLY COAT, which occupies the central point of the presbytery in Trier Cathedral.

SKULL OF ST. HELENA, a gift from Holy Roman Emperor Charles IV, in the crypt of Trier Cathedral.

ST. PETER'S CATHEDRAL IN TRIER is the oldest bishop's church in Germany.

EMPEROR CHARLEMAGNE'S THRONE ROOM in the old imperial palace in Trier. Built in the fourth century, it is the largest surviving Roman hall (67 meters long, 27.2 meters wide and 33 meters high). Its interior was richly decorated with marble, mosaics and statues, while the floor and walls were heated with hot air produced by five stoves under a double floor. Today, the auditorium is the site of an evangelical church.

▶

THE LAST PUBLIC SHOWING of the Holy Coat of Trier took place between April 13 and May 13, 2012.

the recently discovered holy robe, asking, "What are the crooks in Trier up to now? What devil organized the world's largest bazaar here, selling countless miraculous tokens?"

The question of the relic's authenticity, denigrated so forcefully by Luther, is one that has been asked on numerous occasions over the last few hundred years. How was it possible that a robe belonging to Christ could be discovered 15 centuries after He was supposed to have worn it? How did the Palestinian garment find its way to Trier? The Protestants maintained that the robe was a medieval forgery, fashioned by

Catholic clergymen. Emperor Maximilian was the one most often accused of creating a fake robe; with it he supposedly planned to strengthen his imperial authority and legitimize his apparent ancestral lineage, which reached all the way back to Constantine the Great.

CROWDS OF PILGRIMS in Trier Cathedral, 2012.

Over the next few centuries, numerous historians attempted to find out how the Holy Coat could have made its way from Jerusalem to Germany. It is worth noting that the cathedral in Trier is the oldest church in Germany. It was built from A.D. 313 to 320 from part of a palace that had been bequeathed to the bishop Agritius by St. Helena. It was built under the order of Constantine himself, who decided to celebrate his 20 years of reign by constructing 4 huge churches: the Church of the Holy Sepulchre in Jerusalem, the Church of the Nativity in Bethlehem, St. Peter's Basilica in Rome, and the cathedral in Trier. The decision indicated just how important a role the city had in the Roman Empire. At that time Trier, known under its Latin name of *Augusta Treverorum*, was one of the three largest imperial metropolises: it was the unofficial Roman capital of Northern Europe and was dubbed the Rome of the North. The emperor Constantius and his wife Helena resided here, and their son, Constantine, held court here. Indeed, the latter's throne room has been preserved to this day.

Archaeological excavations carried out between 1965 and 1968 by Theodor Konrad Kempf proved that the church was always intended as a pilgrimage site. The German archaeologist claimed that within the church a special area had been set aside in which pilgrims could venerate the relic preserved there. A unique discovery was made during Kempf's excavations: Christian graffiti making supplications to Christ. Until then, ▷

THE HOLY COAT OF TRIER occupies a sacred place within a highly secularized German society.

205

THE BLACK GATE (*PORTA NIGRA*) in Trier is the oldest Roman defense fortification in Germany (dating back to the second century), as well as the largest town gate north of the Alps. It was built from blocks of gray sandstone linked together with lead-coated iron hooks instead of with mortar. Emperor Constantine and his mother, St. Helena, arrived in Trier through this gate.

the only similar kind of pictography known to exist was in the tomb of St. Peter, in the basilica in the Vatican. The graffiti suggests that the church in Trier was indeed a popular pilgrimage site for Christians.

In Kempf's opinion, the main reason to believe that the church in Trier was the site of an important relic has to do with an ivory tablet, dating from the fourth or fifth century, preserved in the cathedral treasury. It depicts a scene in which St. Helena is receiving a precious reliquary from two bishops. This takes place during a procession led by the emperor himself, with the gift on its way to a church under construction, visible in the background. According to art historians, this ivory tablet formed part of the front of the precious reliquary.

A great deal of doubt, however, arises from the fact that, until the ninth century, there was no single piece of written evidence that mentioned a holy garment preserved in Trier. Neither St. Ambrose, who was born in the city, nor St. Athanasius, who for some time lived there, makes any reference to the relic. Similarly, St. Helena's early biographers made no mention of Christ's coat being among the relics she discovered. It was only halfway through the ninth century that a French monk, Altmann of Hautvillers, wrote that Helena brought a chest full of relics back to Trier.

An anonymous author provided more details on this subject in a biography of Bishop Agritius, written between 1050 and 1072. The author writes that St. Helena returned from her trip to the Holy Land bearing several relics, which she donated to the bishop. Among the relics were the remains of St. Matthias, one of the Holy Nails, the knife that Christ used during the Last Supper, and the Holy

Coat. The author admitted that he did not actually see the relics with his own eyes, but rather relied on "truthful sources". It was only in 1805 that an anonymous monk who wrote a history of Trier in his work *Gesta Treverorum* left a description of the relics found in the cathedral. The list was extended, in fact, with the inclusion of such objects as St. Andrew's sandal, one of St. Peter's teeth, and the head of Pope St. Cornelius.

Historians were still curious to know why there was no mention of the relic between the fourth century (when it was to have arrived in Trier) and the eleventh century (when it received its first mention in Agritius' biography). Likewise a cause for doubt is the fact that after its first mention, almost 500 years went by before the Holy Coat received its first public showing in 1512.

One explanation for all this could have to do with Trier's history. At the time of the migration of the peoples, it was the most frequently invaded settlement in Germany. During the fifth and sixth centuries, it was pillaged six times—by the Vandals, the Franks, and the Huns. These were bloody invasions, with numerous buildings destroyed and entire populations murdered. In 883 Trier fell to the Vikings, who slaughtered the city's population and razed the settlement. No wonder, then, that under these circumstances, as the author of *Gesta Treverorum* writes, the city's clergy "hid and buried Trier's relics and any other holy objects". Since much of the city's population perished under attacks by the barbarians, it's quite likely that among the victims were those who had hidden the relics in the first place. Indeed, the invading hordes often targeted the Catholic clergy in particular. The Vikings, for instance, murdered every monk in the city's monastery.

CHRIST'S CRUCIFIXION.
Illumination on vellum (1380) owned by the archbishop of Trier, Kuno von Falkenstein. Christ's torturers can be seen at the foot of the Cross casting lots for His coat.

STATUE OF ST. HELENA
in Trier Cathedral. The empress is presented with her usual attributes: a cross in her right hand and three nails in her left.

The Holy Coat of Trier

209

✠

PILGRIMAGE MEMORIAL PLAQUE
from 1459, showing St. Helena, St. Matthias and Bishop Maternus with the Holy Coat of Trier.

SILVER MEDAL
from 1715. The reverse side shows St. Helena holding the robe from Trier.

210

For centuries thereafter, the relics became part of an oral tradition, but no one ever set eyes on them. Extensive building and renovation work took place on the destroyed cathedral throughout the tenth and eleventh centuries. During this rebuilding phase the hidden reliquary was discovered and the Holy Coat was mentioned in writing. A chronicle dating from 1121 stated that the robe was walled up within the new altar dedicated to St. Nicholas. Another source relates how the relic was processed out of the cathedral in 1196.

Following its discovery, the Holy Coat was not removed from its reliquary for public viewing for another five centuries. This was linked with the practice, common in the period between late antiquity and the Middle Ages, of walling up holy objects, and only occasionally displaying them. Legends about monks who went blind upon seeing the relic and pilgrims who died after touching it became popular among the townsfolk. These legends reflected the common belief that relics ought to be approached with a degree of fear and respect.

For the city's bishops, the mere fact that the relic was safe in their care was more important than how many times it was shown off in public. Only they were allowed to look upon Christ's holy robe. This is certainly evident given the number of fragments that the bishops offered as gifts to various rulers and hierarchs. In all likelihood, these fragments were scraps that had fallen off the robe. German historian Bernhard Schmitt has counted 13 places that were recipients of such fragments: Andechs, Bamberg, Bremen, Halle, Cologne, Lille, Mainz, Maria Laach, Petershausen, Weingarten, Weissenau, Windberg, and Wittenberg. Besides this, we know that in 1353 Trier's Archbishop Baldwin donated a piece of the relic to his cousin Emperor Charles IV, which to this day can be found in St. Vitus Cathedral in Prague. The emperor in turn offered the archbishop a gift: the skull of St. Helena, which he ordered to be transported from Rome.

In 1512 Bishop Richard von Greiffenclau did not express any interest in seeing the relic. Indeed, he did not even know exactly where it had been hidden. It was enough for him to know that the relic could be found somewhere in the cathedral. When Maximilian I requested to see the relic, the bishop initially resisted. Beginning in 1524, however, the Holy Coat was put on public display every seven years. The public exhibition was modeled on the example set by the bishops in Aachen with their own relics.

Because of religious conflicts that arose in Germany in the seventeenth century, the Holy Coat was exhibited less and less frequently. During the Thirty Years' War, the relic was transported initially to the fortress at Ehrenbreitstein, near ▷

**SARCOPHAGUS OF
ST. MATTHEW,**
the only Apostle whose
tomb lies north of the
Alps, in the Church of St.
Eucharius and St. Matthias
in Trier.

**CHURCH OF
ST. EUCHARIUS
AND ST. MATTHIAS,**
where the relic of the
True Cross is kept in
a thirteenth-century
staurotheke. The relic
was brought from
Constantinople by the
knight Heinrich von
Ulmen, after the Fourth
Crusade.

THE ROME OF THE NORTH

SITUATED ON THE BANKS OF THE MOSELLE RIVER, Trier is one of Germany's oldest cities. It was established in 16 B.C. after the Romans subdued the inhabiting Treveri tribe and founded a new settlement called Augusta Treverorum. Augustus made Trier the capital of the Roman province of Gallia Belgica. The town was also the official residence of Constantius I and his son Constantine the Great. The latter divided the empire into four prefectures (also known as tetrarchies): the East with Constantinople as its capital city, Italy with Milan as its capital, Illyricum with its capital Sirmium (modern-day Sremska Mitrovica), and Gaul with its capital Augusta Treverorum, where the empress Helena also had her palace.

Some of Trier's Roman monuments have survived to this day, including the second-century Black Gate (*Porta Nigra*), an amphitheater, an ancient bridge over the Moselle, the imperial thermal baths, and Constantine's throne hall. The city is also the oldest seat of a Christian bishop in Germany, with the Basilica of St. Peter dating back to between A.D. 310 and 320. Here is kept the relic of the Holy Coat of Christ, which according to legend was brought back from the Holy Land by St. Helena.

The Basilica of St. Eucharius and St. Matthias contains a relic of the True Cross, brought over from Constantinople by an imperial prefect. It is kept in a gold staurotheke, which was made by goldsmiths in Trier who modeled their design on the original Byzantine reliquary that was stolen by the German knight Heinrich von Ulmen during the Fourth Crusade and later donated to a convent in Stuben.

Pilgrims can visit the tomb of St. Matthias in the basilica's crypt. This is the only tomb of any of the Apostles that can be found north of the Alps.

Der Heilige Rock im Dome zu Trier

ausgestellt im heiligen Jahr

1933

Koblenz, and then to the treasury in Cologne. It was returned to Trier four years after the signing of the Peace of Westphalia, which brought the Thirty Years' War to an end.

During the years in which the Holy Roman Empire was at military odds with France, Trier, which lay close to the French border, was often under attack. Fearing that the Holy Coat could fall into the hands of the French, the city's bishops hid the relic every so often in Ehrenbreitstein Fortress. Between 1667 and 1810, the relic spent a total of 90 years hidden in the fortress. The longest continuous period in which the relic remained outside of Trier was from 1792 to 1810, around the time of the French Revolution and the Napoleonic Wars. It was moved initially to Würzburg, then to Bamberg, ending up eventually in Augsburg.

When the relic was finally returned to Trier in 1810, about 230,000 pilgrims came to see it. Five years later, the city was amalgamated into the Kingdom of Prussia, as decided at the Congress of Vienna. The Prussians were openly discriminatory toward Catholics, and during the nineteenth century the Holy Coat was displayed only twice: in 1844 and 1891. Both these events turned into Catholic demonstrations against the anticlerical state. Historians estimate that over half a million pilgrims journeyed to Trier in 1844, and around two million in 1891.

When the relic was next put on public display in 1933,

the occasion likewise turned into a protest against the regime in Berlin, this time against the Nazis. Just before the Second World War erupted, the Holy Coat was moved to Limburg, returning to Trier in 1944.

The relic's next public exhibition came 26 years later, when Germany was experiencing remarkable economic prosperity, as well as a period of religious revival. In 1959, about 1.8 million people came to see the relic in the space of 64 days. Similar circumstances were noted in 1996, when, despite increased secularism, about 700,000 pilgrims visited Trier during a period of 28 days.

A large number of pilgrims must have asked themselves about the relic's authenticity. Unfortunately, the Holy Coat has not been subjected to as many rigorous tests as the the Shroud of Turin, the Sudarium of Oviedo, or the Holy Tunic of Argenteuil. The only analysis to have been carried out was by Mechthild Flury-Lemberg in 1973 and 1974. As a master textile restorer, Flury-Lemberg focused her attention solely on the relic's cloth and did not concern herself with blood tests

The Holy Coat of Trier

213

✛

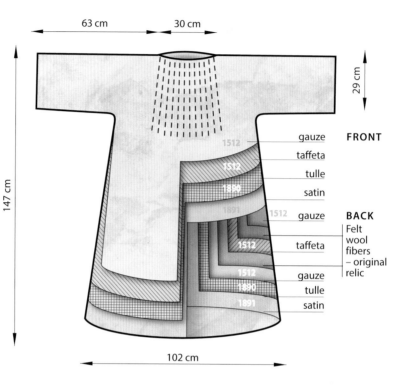

HORIZONTAL CROSS-SECTION of the robe, showing the Holy Coat's various layers of fabric.

or investigations into plant species detectable on the fabric. In spite of this, her findings throw interesting light on the relic's origins.

In Flury-Lemberg's opinion, the robe is made up of seven layers of fabric, glued together with rubber during the restoration work of 1891. The seven layers are as follows: a red-brown silk satin from 1891, a brown tulle from 1890, a delicate silk gauze from 1512, a felt wool-fiber layer, a greenish silk taffeta from 1512, another felt wool-fiber layer, and another silk gauze from 1512. The parts that make up the original relic, according to Flury-Lemberg, are those wool-fiber layers, which in reality are mere shreds of material that would easily disintegrate in one's hand. It turned out that centuries spent in a damp climate had reduced the relic's original fabric to its barest strands. What was left could only have been saved by the restoration work that took place in 1512 and again in 1891.

Flury-Lemberg's tests led her to conclude that the relic's oldest layers dated back to the early Roman Empire. She likewise dispelled the notion that it could be a medieval forgery. In her opinion, the fabric dates back to ancient times,

FELTED FIBERS of wool, which comprise the original part of the Holy Coat.

OFFICIAL LOGO commemorating the Holy Coat's public showing in 2012.

although it's impossible to say whether it comes from the first century or even as late as the fourth. While the evidence gathered by Flury-Lemberg does not conclusively prove the relic's authenticity, it certainly doesn't discount that possibility.

The case remains open, especially since during her tests Flury-Lemberg discovered the remains of several gold and green silk threads, originating in the Middle East, most likely from Syria. One of them dates back to the sixth century and others to around the turn of the ninth century. This suggests that the robe may have been venerated during the early Middle Ages in the eastern regions of the Roman Empire. Much of this, however, remains mere speculation.

In 1996, as part of its public exhibition, the bishop of Trier, Hermann Joseph Spital, declared the holy object to be a third-class relic. That is to say, the robe was not worn by Christ, but it did come into contact with the original garment. Historians dispute this judgment, however, since the practice of producing third-class relics began only during the Middle Ages, while the oldest parts of the Holy Coat date back to a much earlier period. Conclusive proof as to the relic's authenticity still lies before us.

215

TRADITION

TRUTH

DISCOVERY

HISTORY

705
Rome
1506?
1608?
Manoppello
Constatinople
Black Sea
574
Camulia
Edessa
Mediterranean Sea
Jerusalem
33

0   500   1000
kilometres

THE VEIL
OF MANOPPELLO

THE VEIL OF
MANOPPELLO
shows an imprint
of Christ's face.
Paul Badde writes
that however much
is gained from
photographing
the Turin Shroud is
lost with the Veil of
Manoppello. It turns
out that paintings
of the relic are more
faithful to the original
than photographs,
which flatten the
image. Indeed, the
imprint changes like
a rainbow, combining
the effects
of a hologram,
a photograph,
a painting,
and a drawing.

CHAPTER VII

THE VEIL OF MANOPPELLO

One of the most significant discoveries ever to have been made in the field of sindonology took place in a Trappist convent in Dahlem, Germany.
In January 1979 one of the convent's sisters, Blandina Paschalis Schlömer, found herself leafing through the December 1978 issue of the Catholic magazine *Das Zeichen Mariens*.

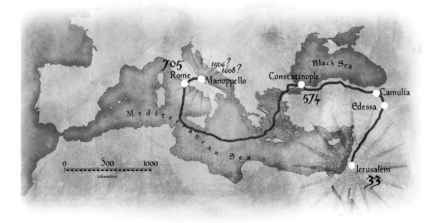

THE VEIL'S JOURNEY from Jerusalem to Manoppello.

THE RELIQUARY CONTAINING THE VEIL
is kept above the altar. It is accessible to
pilgrims, who can view the reliquary from both
sides—from the church's main nave and from
a special podium behind the altar.

NEW FACADE
of the Capuchin
church in
Manoppello,
constructed from
1960 to 1965. Fr.
Pio addressed his
Capuchin brothers
in 1963, saying that
"the Holy Face of
Manoppello is surely
the greatest miracle
we possess".

In it was an article by Renzo Allegri and Paul O. Schenker entitled "The Volto
Santo of Manoppello", in which the authors talked about an image of Christ that
was preserved in a small town in the Italian region of Abruzzo. A reproduction of
the image accompanied the article's text.

Sr. Blandina, herself a creator of icons, looks at images differently from the way
most people do and observes details that most people miss. From the moment she
gazed upon it, the image in the article grabbed her attention. It reminded her of
something, but she couldn't quite figure out what. Eventually, she realized that the
image in the article bore a striking resemblance to the depiction of Christ's face
imprinted on the Turin Shroud. No one besides her had noticed this similarity, but
Sr. Blandina remained steadfast in her conviction.

She spent the next few years investigating her theory. She gathered all the
information available about the Turin Shroud and the image from Manoppello, ▶

GERMAN TRAPPIST
Sr. Blandina Paschalis Schlömmer was the first to note the similarity between the faces on the Veil of Manoppello and the Turin Shroud. She moved into a hermitage not far from the church in Manoppello in 2003 and visits nearly every day to contemplate the image of Christ.

RELIQUARY OF THE HOLY VISAGE of Manoppello, dating from 1646, made by Nazzareno Jotti from solid silver, gold, and precious stones. The three figures on the stem represent faith, hope, and love. Beneath them is a plate with an effigy of St. Nicholas of Bari. The two figures on either side represent St. Michael (Archangel) and St. Francis of Assisi.

including folio reproductions of the depictions in high definition. Placing one on top of the other, she was amazed to find that the anatomical details, even the wounds, on both faces matched perfectly.

In 1984 Sr. Blandina sent a letter containing her research to one of Germany's most eminent sindonologists, a Jesuit by the name of Werner Bulst, who lived in Darmstadt. At the time, Bulst happened to be hosting a fellow sindonologist and Jesuit, Heinrich Pfeiffer, who was a lecturer in art history at the Pontifical Gregorian University in Rome.

Pfeiffer read through all the materials sent by Sr. Blandina and was convinced of the similarities between the images. On his return to Italy, he decided to travel to Manoppello to examine the image, preserved in a Capuchin church. Upon

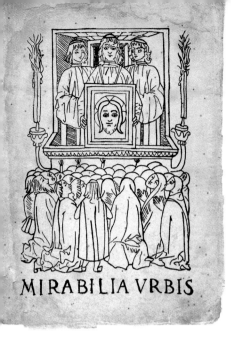

MIRABILIA VRBIS

PRESENTATION OF
THE VERONICA.
Contemporary
drawing based
on a medieval
manuscript.

entering the church and seeing the cloth above the main altar, he was no longer in any doubt: "Why, this is the lost 'Veronica' from St. Peter's Basilica in Rome!"

Every Catholic knows that one of the Stations of the Cross is a scene in which St. Veronica wipes Jesus' face with a cloth. According to legend an imprint of Christ's face was left on the cloth. There may well be some truth to this legend, as numerous sources make reference to the so-called veil of Veronica. For several centuries it was the most popular pilgrimage attraction in medieval Rome, drawing visitors from all over Europe. It was seen and written about by the likes of Petrarch, Dante, and St. Bridget of Sweden. Then all of a sudden, the relic vanished and became nothing more than a fantastical religious creation.

The oldest sources mentioning the veil date back to the sixth century. Back then it was more commonly known as the Shroud or Veil of Camulia, a town situated in modern-day Turkey. Camulia no longer exists, although it used to lie close to Edessa, where the Mandylion (later known as the Shroud of Turin) was supposed to have been kept. The depictions in both relics were referred to using the term *eikon acheiropoietos*, which means "icon made without human hand". Everyone who saw the image of Christ's face on the Veil of Camulia was convinced that it could not have been made by man. No one, however, could explain how the image came into being. The oldest Syrian source on the veil states that it was "drawn from water".

When and how the veil appeared in Camulia is not known. We do know, however, that the relic left the town in A.D. 574, when the emperor Justin II ordered that it be moved to Constantinople. There it acquired the role of imperial standard, or labarum, used only when the emperor stood at the head of his army. When Constantine the Great converted to Christianity, he ordered that a labarum be made bearing the sign Chi-Rho (the symbol for Christ's name—a letter P crossed with an X and a crown). Justin, however, preferred to use the holy veil. On most days it was kept hidden. Only the emperor could set eyes upon it, and then only once a year, following confession and the reception of Communion.

HANS MEMLING'S *St. Veronica*, from 1470. There are two theories that attempt to explain the origins of this name. One is based on the Greco-Roman conflation of the words *vera* (Latin, meaning "real") and *eikon* (Greek, meaning "image"). The other is based on the Greek expression *pheronike*, meaning "carrying victor"—from *phero* ("carry") and *nike* ("victory").

A MASTER ICON

TOWARD THE END OF THE TWENTIETH CENTURY, German art historian Hans Belting wrote a thesis stating that for centuries there must have existed an original, master icon upon which nearly every other depiction of Christ's face in the Christian world was based, both in the East and in the West. Significantly, Belting never came across the image imprinted upon the Veil of Manoppello.

An Austrian priest, Andreas Resch, decided to continue Belting's work. He compared the face on the veil with some of the world's oldest depictions of Christ, such as the Good Shepherd in the Catacombs of Priscilla, in Rome; the shepherd reading in the Catacombs of Aurelius; Christ and the disciples during the Last Supper in the Catacombs of Domitilla; Christ upon a throne in the Catacombs of Marcellinus and Peter; Christ in the Catacombs of Commodilla; and Christ with the Apostles in an apse of the St. Pudentiana Basilica in Rome.

It turns out that the proportions and facial details in these images are the same as those of the imprinted face on the Veil of Manoppello. Similar results were noted when Resch compared the Veronica image with several more recent paintings of Christ, including the Holy Faces of Novgorod and Genoa, both dating from the twelfth century, and the ninth-century Icon of the Holy Face in Laon. Based on his findings, Resch concluded that the model used for later depictions of Christ's face was indeed the Veil of Manoppello, venerated throughout its long history as the True Image, or *vera eikon*.

▷ The veil was taken out for military campaigns. Teofilaktos Simokattes wrote that during the Battle of Solachon in 586, the veil acted as divine inspiration for the Byzantine forces. Simokattes also wrote that the labarum was "created by God Himself and hadn't been woven or painted by man". In 622, the standard played a pivotal role in the war against the Persians, inspiring Heraclius' armies in battle against the armies of Khosrau II. The seventh-century Greek poet George Pisida wrote an account of the campaign, in which he called the veil's depiction a "master-portrait created by God". The relic continued to act as the imperial standard until the end of the seventh century.

Art historians have discerned a significant cultural phenomenon that coincided with the period in which the veil was transported to Constantinople. Until midway through the sixth century, Christ's visage in religious iconography had been influenced most evidently by depictions of young men from Greek mythology. From that point on, however, a radical change can be seen in the way Christ's image is presented. A canonical depiction is formed, based almost entirely on the images found on the Veil of Camulia and the Mandylion of Edessa.

FRENCH IMAGE made in Paris, dating from the nineteenth century, showing the Veil of St. Veronica. At the time, this was one of the most famous motifs in Christian iconography.

The Veil of Manoppello

227

✛

A dispute remains between art historians and sindonologists as to which of the two cloths was the definitive model influencing all other iconographical depictions of Christ. According to Austrian scientist Andreas Resch, it is more likely that the Veil of Camulia served as the prototype for other depictions. This is because the image on the veil was more clearly visible and detailed than the imprint found on the Mandylion, which by comparison was blurred and unclear, looking more like a photographic negative. Indeed, the image on the Mandylion was exposed in the fullest detail only in 1898, with the advent of photographic technology. Christ's face, modeled on the veil's depiction, started to appear on Byzantine coins, such as the solidus minted by Emperor Justinian II in 692.

The veil disappeared around the time Justinian was overthrown; his usurpers cut off his nose and sent him into exile. For the next 10 years, from 695 to 705, the deposed emperor gathered foreign support and prepared for his return. When he once again seized power, Justinian had his usurping predecessors (Leontius and Tiberius Apsimarus) brought in chains before him in the Hippodrome, whereupon he made a symbolic gesture of using them as footstools

SEVENTEENTH-CENTURY LITHOGRAPH of St. Veronica with the veil. Print made by French engraver Charles David (1600–1636).

The Veil of Manoppello

228

✛

EARLY TWENTIETH-CENTURY PRINT. The reverse bears the following inscription: "The signatory, Canon of the Basilica of St. Peter Prince of the Apostles in Rome, consciously assures and verifies those looking at the Image of the Face of Our Lord Jesus Christ, imprinted on white linen, in likeness of the image that was so miraculously created from the Most Blessed Perspiration on the Veil of St. Veronica, is of the same dimensions and size. He also verifies that this image was touched against the miraculous Veil of St. Veronica and rubbed against wood from the True Cross, as well as the spear that pierced Christ's side. These holy Relics are found in St. Peter's Basilica in the Vatican, in Rome, and are venerated by the Supreme Pastors, the most eminent dignitaries and all nations. Confirmed by stamp and seal: ... Father Marcin Pinciurek."

ST. PETER'S SQUARE IN ROME, whose central point is occupied by an Egyptian obelisk dating from the eighth century B.C. that was brought to Rome by Emperor Caligula and installed in the Circus of Nero. The obelisk is said to have witnessed the martyrdom of St. Peter and the first Christians.

before executing them. The period of Justinian's absence was so turbulent that the patriarch of Constantinople Kallinikos I decided to move the veil to safety in Rome, under the care of a Greek from Calabria, who in 705 became Pope John VII.

Sources tell us that the relic was housed in St. Peter's Basilica in Rome, in the Chapel of St. Veronica, built by the new pope. It was here that the relic actually acquired the nickname "the Veronica", the name being a combination of the Latin adjective *vera* ("real") and the Greek noun *eikon* ("image"). A legend grew regarding the veil's origins. A seventh-century author wrote that "Christ left an imprint of His most holy visage before death, at the time when his sweat turned to blood, which flowed to the ground." Later accounts developed the legend, stating that the cloth was handed to Christ by St. Veronica.

In 1197 Pope Celestine III ordered that the veil be placed in a specially built niche above an altar inside the old St. Peter's Basilica. His successor, Pope Innocent III, who moved the Holy See from the Lateran to the Vatican, became the first official promoter of

ST. PETER'S BASILICA is erected on the site where, supposedly, St. Peter was crucified and buried. Constantine built the first church here in A.D. 324. However, the old basilica was close to collapsing in the sixteenth century, prompting Pope Julius II to have it demolished and rebuilt.

the Veronica. In 1208 he instituted the annual tradition of parading the relic throughout the streets of Rome. Following the ceremonial procession, alms were given to the poor, with an upper limit of three denarii—enough to buy bread, meat, and wine.

The Veronica relic drew pilgrims like a magnet from all over the Christian world. It also proved to be Rome's largest source of income. Reproductions of the veil's image became widespread, with its artists forming their own exclusive guild. Numerous sources that record the experiences of those who came to see the relic have been preserved. Dante's "Image of Man" in *Paradiso* of *The Divine Comedy* is based on the Veronica.

Everyone who saw the veil's image, however, described it in a different way. St. Gertrude of Helfta claimed in the eighth century that it had a warm, golden, honey coloring. The following century, Julian of Norwich described it as "gloomy and sad". Martin Luther saw only a transparent bit of fabric and no

The Veil of Manoppello

231

✠

IN SUNLIGHT the Face of Manoppello becomes invisible. This is what Martin Luther experienced during his pilgrimage to Rome, prompting him to state that the Veronica relic was a fake, since it didn't bear an imprint of Christ's face.

face whatsoever, which confirmed his belief that the relic was fraudulent and the papacy was fooling its blinded devotees.

In 1506 Pope Julius II decided to rebuild the crumbling Basilica of St. Peter, which dated back to the days of Constantine the Great. The new basilica, which became the largest Christian church in the world, took 120 years to build and was consecrated in 1626 by Pope Urban VIII. There is much to suggest that the basilica in effect became a reliquary for the Veronica. The church's cornerstone was placed under one of the four large pillars supporting the cupola, specifically, the column of St. Veronica, in which the church's main repository was situated. The Latin inscription on St. Veronica's column reads, "Pope Urban VIII built and embellished this place in the Jubilee Year of 1625 for the fitting veneration of the Savior's majestic image as imprinted on the Veil of Veronica."

Following the completion of the new basilica, the role of Rome's most important relic actually diminished. It was put on public display very rarely, even during the rebuilding of the church: it appeared in 1533, 1535, 1536, 1550, 1575, 1585, and 1600. It was displayed for the last time in 1606. Some historians surmise that the Veronica may in fact have been stolen in 1527, during the sack of Rome, when the city was overthrown by Emperor Charles V and his Spanish and German forces. Pope Clement VII managed to escape to Orvieto. The basilica was defended to the death, with most of its guards dying at their post on May 6, 1527. To mark this date, every year on May 6 new papal guards are sworn in to the Vatican.

The invaders plundered the city for a total of five months, committing brutal murders, raping nuns, and pillaging churches. L'Urbano di Messer wrote to the duchess of Urbino, saying: "Holy relics have been thrown out onto the streets. The Veronica has been stolen. It was passed around in taverns from person to person without a word of protest. A German, who sat sharpening the spear that had pierced Christ's side, tripped over its staff and ran brandishing it throughout the whole Borgo."

233

CONSTRUCTION OF ST. PETER'S BASILICA lasted from
1506 to 1626. The dome itself weighs 14,000 tons, and its
height – from street level to the tip of the cross above – is
133.3 meters. For several centuries (up until the building of
the Yamoussoukro Basilica in Ivory Coast) it was the largest
church in the world, with a surface area of 23,000 square
meters.

Some of the scientists who have examined the relic believe that it vanished during the sack of Rome and that later a copy was displayed—ever more infrequently—to visiting pilgrims. Others claim that the Veronica disappeared at the start of the seventeenth century. In 1617, Pope Paul V issued an edict stating that anyone found making copies of the veil would be excommunicated. A few years later, Pope Urban VIII ordered that every reproduction of the holy image in the Papal States be destroyed. He also stopped displaying the relic to the public.

Given that Urban was pope between 1623 and 1644,

he would have known if the Veronica had disappeared, although he and the papacy never officially admitted to it. For the next hundred years, it was made out that the relic was still hidden in St. Peter's Basilica. No one was allowed to see it, however, and no photos of it existed. Not even a single travel guide to Rome mentioned its existence, and gradually the relic faded into obscurity. It was shown in public only once a year, during vespers on the Fifth Sunday in Lent and only very briefly and from a distance (specifically, a balcony atop St. Veronica's column). One pilgrim visiting the church wrote: "The veil itself, which was protected by a glass screen, was brownish in color. On this background, one could only just make out—with the use of some imagination—some rather blurred contours."

In 2005 a Vatican-based correspondent for the German newspaper *Die Welt*, Paul Badde, was allowed into the treasury within St. Veronica's column. The image, presented to him as once the most precious relic in Rome, didn't make a great impression on Badde. With some difficulty he was able to make out the face of a person, although the cloth was very darkened. Badde did note, however, that Christ's eyes were closed in the image.

Badde continued his research by scouring the archives for documentation on the relic. Every description of the image that he found dating from the eighth to the sixteenth century made the point that Christ was always shown with His eyes open. This stood in radical contrast with every one of the veil's reproductions from the seventeenth century, in which Christ's eyes were always closed. Badde discovered that some time between 1618 and 1633, a huge change occurred in the way Christ was portrayed: the face of a living man, as found on numerous copies, was replaced with the visage of a dead man with his eyes closed.

Similar observations were made by Sr. Blandina Paschalis Schlömer, who noticed that "until the start of the seventeenth century, every one of the most well-known artists in Europe portrayed Christ according to the same model." ▶

POPE BENEDICT XVI during his visit to Manoppello in 2006. Beside him stand Bishop Bruno Forte of Chieti, Fr. Andreas Resch, Fr. Heinrich Pfeiffer, and Paul Badde.

GERMAN APOLOGISTS

GERMANS HAVE BEEN NOT ONLY RESPONSIBLE FOR DISCOVERING THE VEIL OF MANOPPELLO but also very active in spreading its reputation and fame. Among those influential people are Sr. Blandina Paschalis Schlömer, a Trappist nun; Professor Heinrich Pfeiffer, a priest and lecturer in art history at the Pontifical Gregorian University in Rome; Werner Bulst, a priest and sindonologist; and Paul Badde, Vatican correspondent for *Die Welt*. They have all written books on the veil.

In 2005 another German, Cardinal Joachim Meisner, visited the small town of Manoppello. Meisner was so taken by the Veronica image that he persuaded his fellow cardinal and countryman Joseph Ratzinger to pay a visit to the town. Ratzinger did visit a year later—on August 1, 2006—as Pope Benedict XVI.

In Manoppello, Benedict met Sr. Blandina, who had moved to Italy for good in 2003. She had received permission from her superiors to leave her convent and settle in a small hermitage in Manoppello, about half a kilometer from the Capuchin church where the veil is kept. Blandina supports herself by fashioning icons, and almost every day she spends numerous hours at the church, helping pilgrims from all over the world.

PAUL BADDE, who for years was the Rome correspondent for the German newspaper *Die Welt*. During his time there he wrote his book entitled *The Face of Christ*.

FR. ANDREAS RESCH is the founder and director of the Institute for the Field Limits of Science in Innsbruck, Austria. One of the phenomena he has examined is the Veil of Manoppello, writing a book on the subject entitled *Das Antlitz Christi* (*The Face of Christ*).

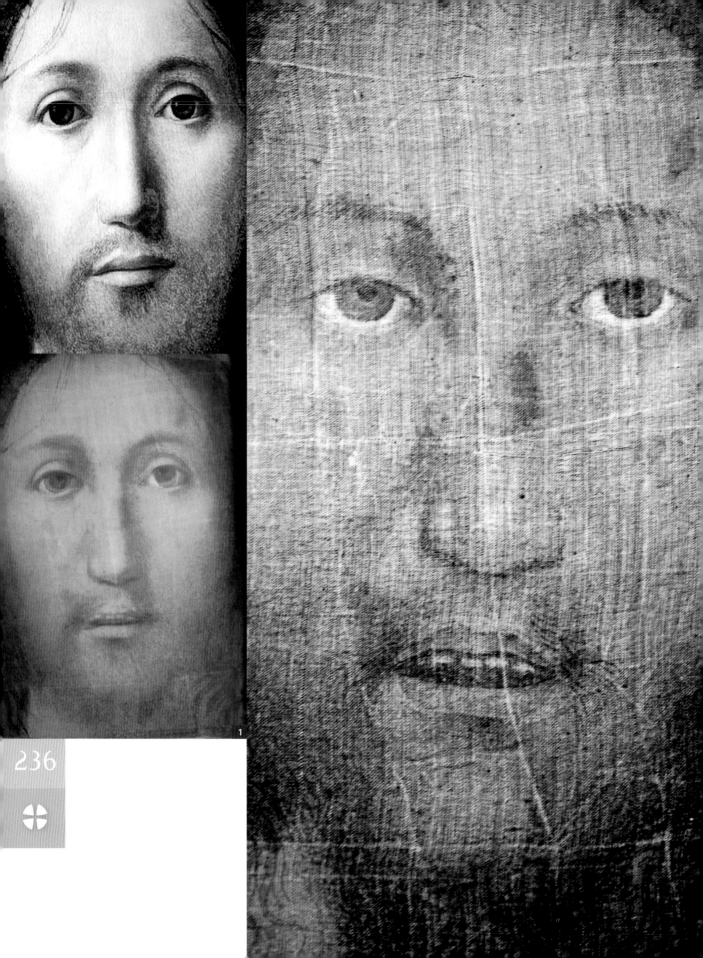

236

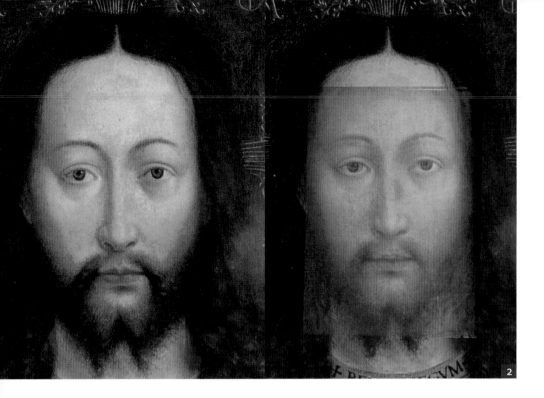

THE FACE OF MANOPPELLO bears a striking resemblance in terms of proportion and facial details to numerous portraits of Christ painted by medieval Christian artists. These include 1) *Salvator Mundi* by Antonello da Messina, 1450; 2) *Portrait of Christ* by Jan van Eyck, 1430; and 3) *St. Veronica with the Sudarium* by unknown artist, c. 1420.

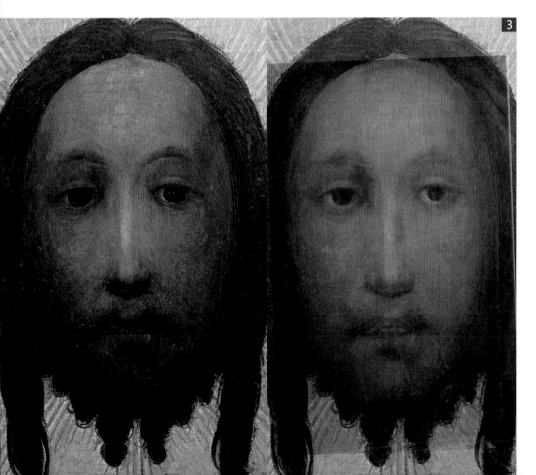

COMPARE
page ▶ 28

CHRIST
IN MANOPPELLO in
an image reflected
from the veil and in
the Eucharistic host.

▶ Cimabue, Masaccio, Bellini, Raphael, Titian, Bosch, El Greco, and Rublev all subscribed to this particular model, or impression. In 1510 Albrecht Dürer even painted his self-portrait based on this accepted image of Christ. The start of the seventeenth century, however, witnessed a sudden move away from this accepted model—almost as if it had disappeared altogether.

Badde concluded that the Veronica must have been stolen around the time the basilica was being rebuilt. His suspicions were given further credibility after he visited the Vatican treasury, where he found an empty frame that had once contained the Veil of Veronica, dating from 1350. It bore an inscription that read: "Until the seventeenth century, a famous relic was kept between these two panes of glass." This is interesting for two reasons: first, the relic could presumably be examined from two sides, and secondly, the crystal glass had been broken into five pieces, with one piece missing altogether. The damage suggested that someone had stolen the relic in a hurry.

Heinrich Pfeiffer also agreed that the relic preserved

in St. Peter's Basilica was not, in fact, the genuine Veil of Veronica. When Pfeiffer first traveled to Manoppello, the settlement was not even officially a town; it obtained that status only in 2004. When he entered the settlement's Capuchin monastery and saw the image of Christ, he immediately posited the theory that this was the relic that had disappeared from the Vatican.

Upon commencing tests on the relic, the most important thing was to figure out how it found its way to Manoppello. Local legend had it that the veil was brought to Abruzzo in 1506 by an angel. There is no evidence, however, to suggest that the relic could already be found in the small town in the sixteenth century. The first mention of it comes in 1608, when it apparently formed the subject of a dispute between two families: the Leonellis and the Petruccis. In 1638 another of the relic's owners, Don Antonio De Fabritiis, donated the veil to the Capuchin monastery, where it is found to this day.

According to Pfeiffer, the relic must have arrived in Manoppello between 1506 (when the first part of St. Peter's Basilica was demolished) and 1608 (when the second part was demolished). It was during this time that the veil must have been stolen.

In 1645 the Capuchin Donato da Bomba wrote his *Relatione historica*, in which he mentioned that he and his order had come across the cloth seven years earlier. Da Bomba related how his brother monk Clemente da Castalvecchio had received a veil, whose edges were in a lamentable condition. The veil, according to da Bomba, was four hands in length—which roughly matches the size of the shattered frame Badde found in the Vatican treasury (34 by 31 centimeters).

From 1638 to 1923, the image of Christ was kept in a semi-dark side chapel in the Capuchin church, receiving hardly any natural light. Devotees could make out only its grayish hue. In 1866 anticlerical authorities expelled the Capuchins from their monastery, and the relic spent the next three years hanging in a deserted,

SR. BLANDINA uses a flashlight to illuminate Christ's face on the veil. The image changes under beams of light.

locked church. The Capuchins continued their veneration of the relic, however, as they had done every year since 1686. The festival of the *Volto Santo* (Holy Face) coincided with the Feast of the Transfiguration (August 6).

Renovation works at the church in Manoppello began in 1960, and the veil was moved to a more prominent place—above the main altar, where it is still kept today. It is housed in a glass monstrance, so that it can be viewed from both sides. The cloth, much like images in medieval paintings, shows a man with curled sideburns, wisps of hair in the middle of a high forehead, and a thin beard forked in two. At first glance, it is recognizable as an image of Christ.

The experiences of pilgrims who come to see the Veil of Manoppello are reminiscent of those of medieval pilgrims who had come to worship the Veronica. Everyone sees it somewhat differently. It's enough to look at the cloth from another angle or in a different light to get a completely different view. Badde

notes that 10 people standing in front of the Volto Santo will see ten different images. In his opinion, however, although much is gained from looking at photos of the Turin Shroud, the same is lost by looking at prints of the veil. Even medieval paintings of the Veronica are more realistic and faithful to the original than photographs, which simply "flatten it out". In person, it changes like a rainbow and seems to combine traits of holograms, photographs, paintings, and drawings. Furthermore, when a beam of light falls on the veil, the image of Christ's face disappears, and the cloth becomes almost entirely transparent. This seems to accord with the account of Martin Luther, who instead of seeing a face, saw emptiness.

In 1993 Pfeiffer presented his findings, stating the following: "This unusually thin fabric is more than transparent. One can even read a newspaper placed within a certain distance behind the veil without any difficulty. The image does not in any way disrupt reading. It becomes invisible, however, under a black light and disappears completely under UV light. This proves that we are not dealing with a painting, in other words, a piece of work made by an artist using paints applied using some form of tool. I found no evidence of printing. One must therefore conclude that the image is the result of some internal change in the fiber. It causes light to reflect off the fabric in such a way that the human eye is able to discern colors. These colors change depending on the angle of light and the position of the viewer. They vary between brown, gray, and red. The eyes on the veil are brown,

THE PUPILS IN THE IMAGE are the only places on the veil that show signs of charring.

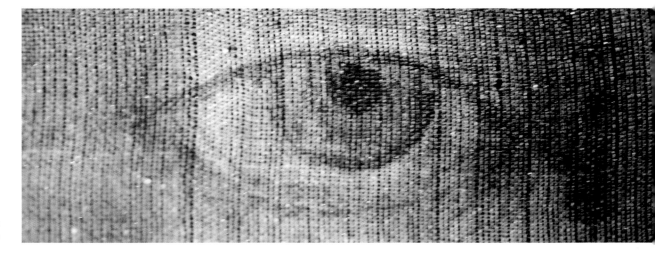

while the lips are light red. The pupils in both eyes seem slightly uneven. The hair looks like a lit-up shadow of natural hair. It seems like the whole image is a lit-up shadow of an entirely illuminated and transparent visage. No photograph can capture a true representation of the original."

To determine why the veil possesses such unique characteristics, it was decided to examine the material from which it was made and how the image became imprinted on the fabric. Upon examination, it turned out the cloth was made of byssus, a rare and expensive fiber used in ancient times, sometimes known as woven gold. This material, referred to as sea silk, is obtained from mother-of-pearl, of which one needs a thousand samples to make just one kilogram of byssus. The best sort of mother-of-pearl for producing the fabric is obtained from a Mediterranean species known as the noble pen shell (*Pinna nobilis*), which can reach up to a meter in length. This could explain why the oldest

Syrian source, dating from the sixth century, described the veil as having been "drawn from water".

Byssus is unique in its properties. It's as thin as a spiderweb. It has an iridescent coloring and transparency and a certain sheen that likens it to a hologram. It's the only material of its kind known to allow light to pass through it and to change color depending on the light surrounding it. It's as fireproof as asbestos. It doesn't dissolve in water. It's resistant to alcohol, ether, diluted acid, and lye.

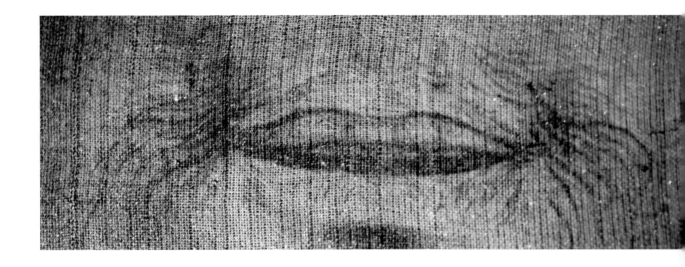

JESUS' LIPS show traces of blood.

Byssus is mentioned in the Bible: in the Old Testament, an archpriest's exterior robe, or ephod, is said to be made of byssus. Similarly, in the book of Revelation, the robe adorning the Bride of the Lamb (Christ's bride, the Church) is described as being made of byssus.

Today, as in ancient times, byssus is the most expensive material in the world. Only one place still produces it: a small island called Sant'Antioco, which lies off the coast of Sardinia. The island is home to a specialist in sea silk, Chiara Vigo, who describes yet another of byssus' qualities: "One cannot paint on byssus. It's simply impossible." This has to do with the residue of sea salt found on the material. It gives the fabric a specific sheen and also prevents the absorption of pigments. As a result, paint runs off byssus as it does off mother-of-pearl. One could dye the entire fabric purple but still couldn't draw anything on it. After her visit to Manoppello in 2004, Vigo claimed that she didn't know how the image on the veil was produced but that it definitely couldn't have been painted by man.

243

The Veil of Manoppello

COMPARE
page ▶ 156

PLACING THE TWO CLOTHS—the Turin Shroud and the Veil of Manoppello—one on top of the other reveals that the facial imprints are of the same person. The anatomical details and the patterning of the facial wounds correlate with each other to such an extent that scientists have claimed that the shroud is the negative imprint and the veil is the positive imprint of the same image.

Vigo's assumptions were confirmed by the Italian scientist Donato Vittore, from Bari University. Using a high-definition scanner, Vittore discovered that there were absolutely no traces of paint on the veil. The image, therefore, could not have been produced using any known painting technique. Likewise, it cannot be a print, since the image's resolution is identical on both sides. However, Vittore did discover some slightly charred fibers within the darkest parts of the pupils, as if exposure to a high temperature had burned the threads.

Another Italian scientist, by the name of Giulio Fanti, confirmed in turn that the image had a three-dimensional character, although less distinctive than that of the Turin Shroud. This is because byssus is much thinner and more delicate than linen. Nevertheless, using computerized imaging, one can discern a three-dimensional effect around the nose and eye sockets. The image is not a painting; rather, it is an imprint of a three-dimensional object.

This is not the only similarity between the Veil of Manoppello and the Turin Shroud. Andreas Resch, founder and director of the Institute for the Field Limits of Science in Innsbruck, which is affiliated with the Pontifical Lateran University, continued the comparative studies started by Sr. Blandina Paschalis Schlömer. Overlaying enlarged high-definition prints of both images, Resch concluded that "the images on the shroud and the Veronica are a 100-percent match and in no way a result of coincidence." Furthermore, "this similarity proves that we are dealing with imprints of the same person."

The only difference between both imprinted faces was that on the Turin Shroud the wounds were still fresh and bleeding, and the eyes covered with coins. On the Veil of Manoppello, on the other hand, the wounds were already healed over, and the eyes were open. Saverio Gaeta, author of the book *L'Altra Sindone* (*The Other Shroud*), attributes this to the fact that the former cloth was imprinted with the image of a dead man, while the veil was imprinted with a live (or even resurrected) man.

Resch and his team also noted that, much as with the Turin Shroud, attempts to reproduce the veil faithfully ended in failure. The main obstacle was the fact that the image wasn't created using any sort of pigment, but rather through the modification of the fabric's fibers. The scientists were not able to account for this "modification", however. They could only surmise that its source must have been some as yet unidentified eruption of energy.

While the image on the Turin Shroud appears as a photographic negative, the corresponding image on the veil is positive. The laws of physics dictate that such an image could have been formed only by placing one fabric on top of another.

VEIL OF
ST. VERONICA
in a painting in
the Church of the
Invention of the Holy
Cross in the Vilnius
Calvary.

The similarity between both relics drove the scientists to the conclusion that they must both have been among Christ's burial clothes. St. John, who arrived at Christ's tomb on Easter morning with St. Peter, mentions in his Gospel more than one burial cloth: "Peter therefore went out, and the other disciple, and were going to the tomb. So they both ran together, and the other disciple outran Peter and came to the tomb first. And he, stooping down and looking in, saw the linen cloths lying there; yet he did not go in. Then Simon Peter came, following him, and went into the tomb; and he saw the linen cloths lying there, and the handkerchief that had been around His head, not lying with the linen cloths, but folded together in a place by itself. Then the other disciple, who came to the tomb first, went in also; and he saw and believed" (Jn 20:3–8).

The most interesting part of this passage is the final phrase: "and he saw and believed". What did John see that made him believe? Seeing only the burial cloths, he must have been impressed by something about them. In his Gospel, St. John does not say that the cloths (*othonia*) in which Jesus was wrapped were scattered about, as if He had attempted to disentangle Himself from them. Rather, he implies that, apart from the cloth around his head, they lay seemingly untouched, as at the time of burial when they were wrapped around Christ's remains. The body the cloths had been wrapped around had disappeared, and perhaps it looked as if the corpse had simply passed through the surrounding fabric. Furthermore, perhaps the shroud and the veil had been visibly imprinted with Christ's image. All this would explain why even a mere glance at the cloths was enough to make St. John believe.

All the objects found in the empty tomb would most likely have been removed by the Apostles. The oldest known text that makes reference to Christ's burial clothes—the sixth-century apocryphal narrative *Transitus Mariae*—tells us that after Jesus' Ascension, Mary prayed continually before one of the burial cloths until the moment of her own Assumption. It's highly likely that the veil, much like the Turin Shroud, found its way to the Osroene Kingdom, where Christians were free to practice their faith under the rule of King Abgar V. This would account for why the relic found itself in Camulia, near Edessa.

One more bit of evidence regarding the similarity between the Turin Shroud and the veil ought to be mentioned. It comes from the writings of the Italian mystic Maria Valtorta, who lived from 1897 to 1961 and was purported to have had numerous conversations with Christ. Below is an extract of the proclamation she received on February 22, 1944:

"The veil of Veronica is also a goad to your skeptical souls. Since you, O rationalists, O tepid people vacillating in your faith, proceed through arid examinations, compare the face of the Veronica with that of the Holy Shroud. One is the Face of a living person, the other of a dead one. But length, width, somatic types, form, distinctive features, are identical. Superimpose the images. You will see that they correspond. It is I. I Who wanted to remind you how I was and how I had become out of love for you. If you had not gone astray, if you were not blind, those two Faces should be enough to bring you to love, to repentance, to God."

Commenting on this passage, Andreas Resch has written the following: "Even if we treat these opinions critically and concede that we cannot consider them from a scientific point of view, we must admit that we are dealing with a proclamation that exceeds the natural bounds of Maria Valtorta's knowledge. In those days, no one had yet considered the similarities between these two images. Ignorance on the topic extended to such an extent that in the German published edition of her writings, this fragment was simply missed out. However, contemporary analyses interpret this proclamation as the result of paranormal activity and the experience of a mystic."

One needn't rely solely on mysticism, however, when modern science is able to reach the same conclusions. The one moment in which both of these remarkable images could have been made was the point when they were subjected to an as yet unidentified surge of energy, while lying one on top of the other in the tomb.

247

The Veil of Manoppello

DISCOVERY

TRADITION

HISTORY

TRUTH

A B

THE PILLAR
OF SCOURGING

CHAPTER VIII

THE PILLAR OF SCOURGING

Rome

ITALY

Scientists examining the pillar at which Christ was supposed to have been beaten and scourged were faced with a much greater challenge than those scientists tasked with examining the holy cloths. The stone bears far fewer traces than the cloths. Nevertheless some interesting discoveries have been made.
The oldest document describing a trip to the Holy Land is a seventh-century copy of a journal written by the Christian pilgrim Egeria, who traveled to Palestine between 381 and 384. In 383, while celebrating Good Friday in Jerusalem, she noticed that many devotees "were making their way to Zion to pray before the pillar at which Christ was scourged".

SCOURGING POST in the Church of St. Praxedes, kept within a glass reliquary. The place where the iron ring, to which the convict would have been tied, is visible toward the top of the pillar.

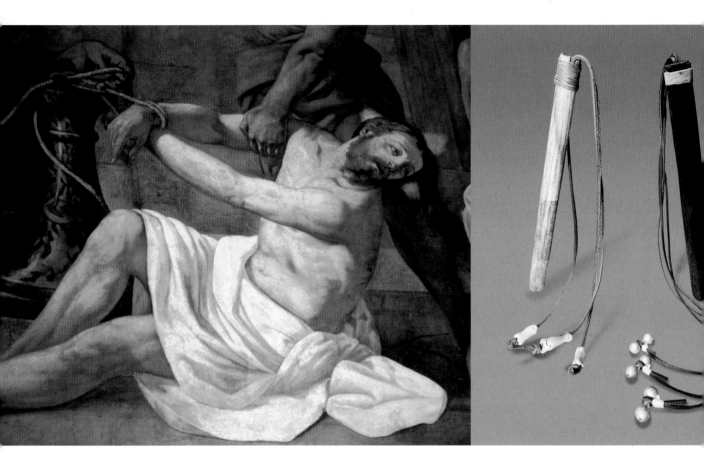

JESUS IS TIED TO
THE PILLAR.
Detail of a painting
by Francesco Gai
(1835–1917) in
the Chapel of St.
Zeno in the Roman
Basilica of St.
Praxedes.

✠

CONTEMPORARY
reconstruction of
a Roman whip used
in ancient times to
scourge prisoners.

Specifically, the Christian worshippers were heading for the Church of the
Apostles, atop Mount Zion. According to Eusebius of Caesarea and other historians of the early Church, this was a Judeo-Christian temple, whose community worshipped Christ as the Messiah and Son of God but also preserved
numerous Old Testament traditions that the modern Church had abandoned.
According to some of the oldest Christian sources, after the Romans destroyed
Jerusalem in A.D. 70, the salvaged scourging post was moved to the church on
top of Mount Zion.

Chroniclers state that the Judeo-Christians were becoming more and more
isolated within Jerusalem. In 375, Bishop Epiphanius wrote that "the pilgrimage up to Zion used to mean something, but now it has become cut off
from the public." The Jewish-Christian and the Gentile-Christian communities were reconciled only toward the end of the fourth century, largely thanks
to the mediation of St. Porphyry of Gaza. Evidence of the reconciliation can ▶

COMPARE
pages ▶ 48–49

JUDEO-CHRISTIANS

JESUS OF NAZARETH and His first followers were all Jews. From the Acts of the Apostles we know that after Christ's Ascension, the disciples practiced their faith in the risen Lord while still adhering to the laws of Judaism. Jerusalem's first Christian community, which was eventually led by James the Apostle, known as "the Just" and "the brother of the Lord", observed Jewish practices and customs. Although the early Christians encountered opposition from the Pharisees and the Sadducees, the conflict remained largely within the confines of the Jewish community.

An important event marking the breakdown of relations between the nascent Church and the synagogue took place at an ecumenical council in Jerusalem in about A.D. 50, when the Apostles declared that any Gentile who was baptized would no longer be obliged to follow all the Jewish laws. Both sides drifted further apart after the Jewish rebellion broke out against the Romans in A.D. 66. The Judeo-Christians, heeding a prophecy made by Christ Himself, escaped to the town of Pella, to the east of the Jordan, thereby surviving the Roman destruction of Jerusalem in A.D. 70.

The loss of the Temple in Jerusalem had fateful consequences for the future of Judaism. The Jews had to redefine the practice of their faith, which was now bereft of its sacrifices and its priests. The synagogue came to occupy the most important position, with readings from the Scriptures and prayers forming the main activities.

One of the sects that survived this period was Christianity, which acknowledged the New Testament as the fulfillment of the Old Testament and Jesus Christ as the Messiah foretold by the prophets. Rabbinic Judaism also survived and underwent development by Pharisees who needed to make adaptations to the Jewish faith in the absence of the Temple. Its identity was influenced to a large extent by its opposition to Christianity, as can be seen in the newly introduced Shmoneh Esreh, a prayer that spoke disparagingly of the Judeo-Christians.

Initially the Judeo-Christians formed the majority of Christ's followers, but as the faith grew it admitted Gentiles who converted from paganism. As the Church spread throughout the Roman Empire, the Judeo-Christian proportion of the faithful diminished.

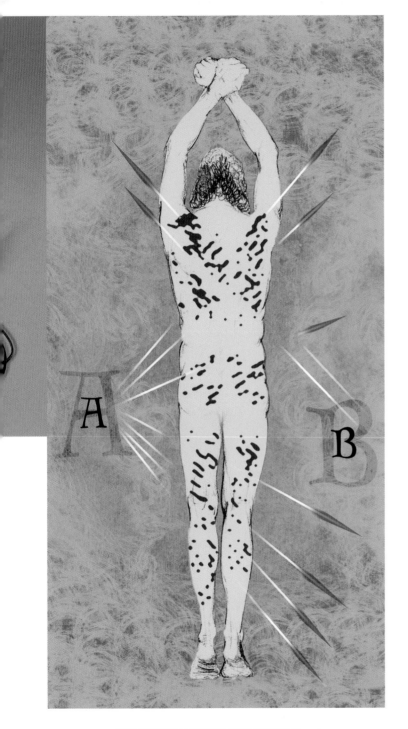

WOUNDS FOLLOWING SCOURGING. Based on the traces of blood found on the Turin Shroud, it is possible to determine how the scourging was carried out by two legionnaires, A and B.

Colonna della Flagellazione di Gesù Cristo
The Column of the Flagellation of Jesus Christ
Colonne de la Flagellation du Christ

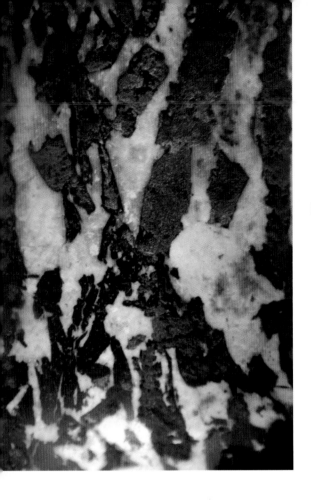

SCOURGING POST, made from Egyptian marble quarried in Faiz Abd El Shebid, near Umm Shegilat.

▶ be found in Rome's Basilica of St. Pudentiana, in which a mosaic dating from 395 shows both communities reunited on either side of Christ. Following this reconciliation, the pillar once again became a relic for all pilgrims to worship.

The marble pillar remained the Judeo-Christians' most precious relic for some time. Historians attribute this to the fact that, while Jewish custom dictated that any object coming into contact with bodily remains is made unclean and had to be removed beyond the city walls, the pillar itself did not break any Jewish law.

But where did the marble pillar come from?

The Evangelists tell us that Christ was scourged in the place where His hearing occurred—in the praetorium of Pontius Pilate, who was Judea's Roman prefect. For centuries, academics disagreed as to the exact whereabouts of the praetorium, positing such locations as Herod's Palace, the Antonia Fortress, and the Hasmonean Palace. Today most archeologists believe it was located on the site of the Hasmonean Palace: we know from historian Titus Flavius Josephus that Herod the Great had ordered that the palace be renovated and redecorated so that it would overflow with splendor and wealth. After the palace and the town were destroyed by the Romans, the Judeo-Christians were able to salvage the pillar.

We know from St. Jerome of Stridon and St. Paula of Rome that the pillar was initially incorporated within the portico of the Church of the Apostles. Soon afterward, however, when the church was being rebuilt, the pillar was moved to the church's interior. The relic has been documented by numerous pilgrims, among them

SCOURGING POST made from marble quarried near modern-day Egyptian-Israeli border.

MAIN ENTRANCE to the Basilica of St. Praxedes in Rome, where the relic of Christ's scourging post is kept. The church's facade is not visible from the main road as it's surrounded by numerous other buildings.

St. Antonino di Piacenza and the archdeacon Theodosius in the sixth century, and Arculf and St. Bede the Venerable in the seventh century.

When the Fatimid caliph Al-Hakim ordered that the Church of the Apostles be destroyed in 1009, the pillar managed to avoid destruction. Instead, it was transported to Constantinople and rehoused in another Church of the Apostles. Here, it was documented by the likes of Anthony, bishop of Veliky Novgorod, and Robert de Clari, a chronicler of the Fourth Crusade. They referred to it as had earlier pilgrims to the Holy Land, namely, by its Latin name, *columna mormorea* (marble column).

In 1223, the pillar was transported from Constantinople to Rome. This was precipitated by Cardinal Giovanni Colonna, who had acted as papal legate during the Fifth Crusade. The rulers of the Latin Empire of Constantinople needed to rely on the good favor of Pope Honorius III, and so they presented the pillar to his legate. Colonna saw this as quite an auspicious gift, as his own crest bore an image of a column, or colonna. Upon arrival in Rome the cardinal ordered that the relic be housed in his titular church, the Basilica of St. Praxedes.

The Basilica of St. Praxedes is one of the oldest Christian places of worship in Rome. It was built on the site of an ancient oratory toward the end of the fifth century, although its current structural shape dates back to 822, after it was rebuilt by Pope Paschal I, who also ordered that the church be decorated using Eastern-style mosaics.

In particular, the church's St. Zeno Chapel is regarded as a very fine example of early Byzantine art. The chapel would eventually house the remains of Pope Paschal's mother, as well as the holy pillar.

Thanks to the relic, the Basilica of St. Praxedes became one of the most popular pilgrimage sites of the Middle Ages. The Holy See even decided to institute a Feast of the Holy Pillar, celebrated the Fourth Sunday in Lent. At that time, the pillar also had an iron hoop, to which Christ was presumably tied.

In 1240 this hoop was donated to King Louis IX of France in return for three spikes from the Crown of Thorns. Similarly, in 1585 Pope Sixtus V donated a fragment of the pillar to the city of Padua. From 1898 onward, pilgrims could view the pillar in a gilded bronze reliquary.

In time, thanks to growing secularization, the relic was gradually forgotten. Today, most pilgrims and even the majority of people in Rome are unaware of its existence. For centuries, St. Praxedes served as the titular church of many renowned cardinals, including Charles Borromeo and Robert Bellarmine and more recently Rafael Merry del Val and Paul Poupard.

JESUS' SCOURGING. Painting by Italian artist Agostino Ciampelli (1565–1630) in the Basilica of St. Praxedes in Rome.

BENEATH the Basilica of St. Praxedes is a crypt containing the remains of two sisters, St. Praxedes and St. Pudentiana, daughters of the Roman senator St. Pudens. They were supposedly executed for unlawfully burying the remains of Christian martyrs.

The Pillar of Scourging

257

The Pillar of Scourging

THE BASILICA OF ST. PRAXEDES, while one of the oldest churches in Rome, owes its current architectonic layout to extensive renovations that took place in the eighteenth century.

CHRIST PANTOCRATOR. The mosaic on the vaulting of St. Zeno's Chapel in the Basilica of St. Praxedes, Rome, is one of the finest surviving examples of early Byzantine art.

Is the relic in the Basilica of St. Praxedes the actual pillar at which Christ was beaten? Analysts have claimed that its height (sixty-three centimeters) corresponds with that of ancient pillories. The pillar's shape—wider at the bottom (forty centimeters in diameter) and thinner at the top (thirteen centimeters in diameter)—is typical of the architectonic style that dominated in the Hellenist era. A similar pillar dating from the beginning of the Christian era can be found in a mausoleum in Jerusalem's Kidron Valley. Scientists also found where the iron hoop would have been attached near the top of the pillar. It was to this hoop that the convicted person would have been tied. The pillar's elegant style suggests that it was made during a very rich and elaborate architectonic period. This could have coincided with the redecoration of the ornate Hasmonean Palace.

Samples of the pillar have allowed scientists to deduce what material it was made of—a rare kind of diorite marble. Mineralogical experts have also discovered that the marble was quarried in Egypt. Sources tell us that King Herod had materials shipped from abroad while rebuilding the Hasmonean Palace. It's not

unlikely, therefore, that this marble was brought over from Egypt.

Tests carried out on the pillar have not been conclusive enough to allow us to state categorically that the relic is authentic, although there is a high likelihood that it is. None of the tests have contradicted what we know about the pillar from Christian tradition. Neither have they yielded results that disprove the relic's authenticity outright.

It's also worth adding that during the early Christian era, two pillars were venerated in Jerusalem. The second is mentioned by an anonymous pilgrim from Bordeaux in a source dating from 333, as well in one of the catechisms written by St. Cyril of Jerusalem dating from 348. The practice of venerating two pillars has to do with the belief, held by many Christians, that Jesus was tied up and flogged twice—once in Pilate's praetorium and then again at the palace of Caiaphas (where the Gospels mention only that He was interrogated and beaten). The second pillar would most likely have been found among the palace ruins, after the Romans destroyed Jerusalem in A.D. 70.

German historian Michael Hesemann believes that fourth-century pilgrims venerated the pillar from the palace of Caiaphas—even though the Gospels make no explicit mention of it—simply because they weren't aware that the other pillar (hidden away on Mount Zion) existed. The Caiaphas pillar was effectively a substitute relic in the eyes of pilgrims. As mentioned, it was only at the end of the fourth century that the Zion pillar was first displayed to the public.

Since that time, the pillar from Caiaphas' palace has diminished in importance. Midway through the fifth century, the pillar was moved to the newly built Basilica of St. Peter in Jerusalem, whose construction—on the site of the old palace of Caiaphas—had been ordered by the empress consort Eudokia (today the same site is occupied by the nineteenth-century Church of St. Peter in Gallicantu, run by an order of French nuns). The Basilica of St. Peter was demolished by the Persians in 614. The pillar was saved and then moved to the Church of the Holy Sepulchre.

COLUMN FRAGMENT in the Church of the Holy Sepulchre, Jerusalem, venerated as the pillar at which Christ was flogged. It most probably comes from the palace of the high priest Caiaphas. However, experts do not believe this is the authentic scourging post of Christ.

The Pillar of Scourging

261

HISTORY

TRADITION

TRUTH

DISCOVERY

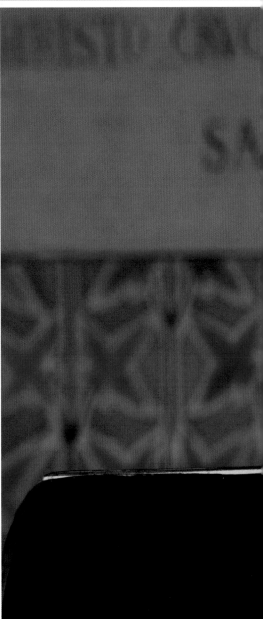

SIXTY WOUNDS TO THE HEAD

THE CROWN
OF THORNS

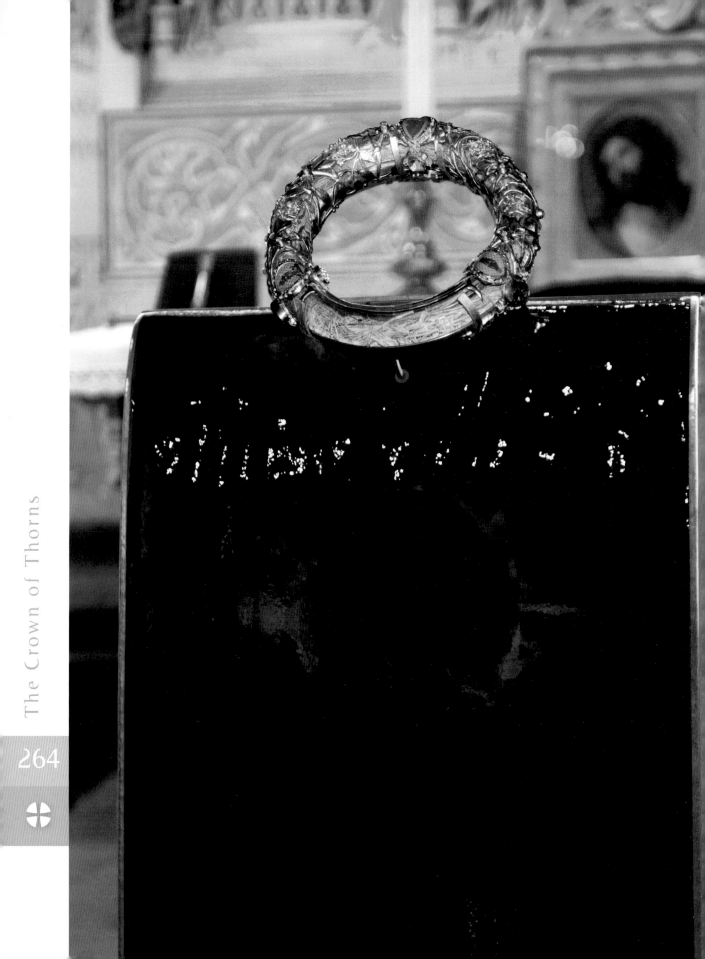

CHAPTER IX

THE CROWN OF THORNS

On certain Fridays at 3:00 P.M. (the hour of Christ's death), a relic venerated as the Crown of Thorns is put on public display at Notre Dame Cathedral in Paris. The relic was sold to King Louis IX in 1239 by the young ruler of the Latin Empire of Constantinople, Baldwin II. Despite his position of power, Baldwin endured tough times. He ascended the throne at the age of 12 and out of necessity had to mature very quickly. His early rule was beset by the need to preserve not just his dynastic line but also his life.

265

CROWN OF THORNS, or more specifically the surviving band, in a circular reliquary at Notre Dame Cathedral, Paris.

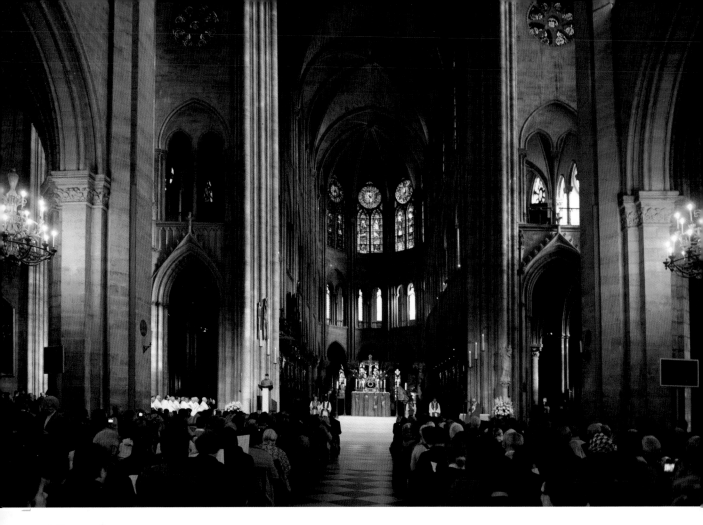

PUBLIC SHOWING of the Crown of Thorns, which takes place in the cathedral on the first Friday of every month at 3 p.m.—the hour of Christ's death—and on every Friday during Lent.

NOTRE DAME CATHEDRAL in Paris is a gem of Gothic architecture. Its construction lasted over 180 years, from 1163 to 1345.

The Byzantine capital was invaded several times by Greek and Bulgarian forces, and in 1237 the 20-year-old emperor traveled to the West to seek help from other European powers.

Pope Gregory IX, remembering the slaughter committed by the Crusaders in Constantinople in 1204, refused Baldwin any help. He feared that the intervention of Western soldiers might again result in the pillaging of the Byzantine capital.

Having been unsuccessful in Rome, Baldwin traveled to Paris. France's ruler at the time, King Louis IX, was a deeply religious man who possessed a number of Christian relics. He was reluctant to provide military help to Baldwin, but he made the Byzantine ruler an attractive proposition. Louis offered the huge sum of

135,000 pounds in gold in exchange for the Crown of Thorns kept at the imperial palace in Constantinople.

The Crown of Thorns was one of only a few relics that survived the pillaging of the Crusaders in 1204. It was also the most precious symbol of the imperial rule. Baldwin had little choice in the matter, however.

Indeed, he had already put up the relic as collateral with a Venetian banker, Nicolo Querino, in exchange for a large sum in credit. He decided therefore to accept the French king's proposal.

Louis was wary that the Venetians might try to replace the relic with a forgery and sent two Dominican monks, Andrew and John, as special emissaries ▶

GUARDING THE RELIC during its public showing are knights of the Equestrian Order of the Holy Sepulchre of Jerusalem.

267

COMPARE
page ▶ 61

KING LOUIS IX represented the ideal monarch for many generations of European rulers. He was canonized in 1297, just 27 years after his death, by Boniface VIII. He is buried in the Church of St. Denis near Paris, while his heart is kept in Monreale Cathedral in Sicily. St. Louis is the patron saint of pilgrims, France, and many cities including Paris, Munich, and Berlin. He is also the patron of many professions such as teachers, merchants, soldiers, and doctors.

THE HOLY **COLLECTOR**

ST LOUIS IX (1214–1270) OF THE HOUSE OF CAPET became king of France at the tender age of 12, following the death of his father, Louis VIII. He did not receive full powers until the age of 22, however, and his mother, Blanche of Castile, acted as regent during the interim period. Louis set himself the tasks of building an empire on Christian foundations and of completely reforming the government so that it was fair to all. He made administration more efficient, oversaw a financial recovery, created a standardized currency, and introduced a royal bureaucratic system controlled by monks. In the case of unfair decisions, victims were granted compensation and dishonest clerical workers were dismissed. Louis also introduced royal courts (called parlements) to which one could appeal the decisions of feudal courts presided over by the barons. He banned duels, the carrying of arms, and the conducting of private wars within France. He also planned to rebuild those towns that he entrusted with certain privileges.

Louis IX became known as a peaceful ruler, mediating in disputes not only between the French nobility but also between countries, such as Aragon and England. He also mediated in a disagreement between Pope Innocent III and Emperor Frederick II. His peaceful disposition did not stop him from resorting to war altogether, however. Upon hearing of the Mamluk invasion of Jerusalem, Louis personally led the Seventh Crusade to the Holy Land in 1248. The crusade ended in defeat, and Louis himself was captured. He returned to France in 1254 after paying a huge ransom. In spite of this, in 1270 he organized the Eighth Crusade, which ended in disaster when the Crusaders and the king himself succumbed to an epidemic of dysentery.

Louis IX earned a reputation as the most ardent defender of Christianity among all of Europe's rulers. Fascinated by the life and deeds of St. Francis of Assisi, he gave much support to the Franciscan Order and was himself a member of the Third Order of St. Francis. He was a collector of relics, the most precious of which was the Crown of Thorns. He was utterly devoted to his wife, Margaret of Provence, with whom he had 11 children.

▶ to examine the crown and to verify its authenticity. After the transaction was concluded the relic was placed in the care of Archbishop Gauthier Cornut of Sens. He also organized a tour from Venice to Paris. Louis, his brother Robert of Artois, and their mother, Blanche of Castile, joined the party in the Burgundian town of Villeneuve-l'Achevêque, and the entire cortege continued on toward the French capital.

The day on which the Crown of Thorns arrived in Paris—August 18, 1239—was declared a feast day. From a large tribune that had been constructed outside the city walls, clergymen greeted the relic, which was then placed in a gold reliquary. Louis and his brother Robert, both barefoot and wearing only linen robes, carried the reliquary through the streets of Paris, while whole crowds fell to their knees and blessed themselves. As one eyewitness account put it: "The kingdom had never experienced a day so full of festivity and joy."

CROWN OF THORNS arriving in procession to Paris in 1239. Almost the entire population of the French capital came out to experience the event.

The Crown of Thorns

269

THE SAINTE-CHAPELLE in Paris, founded as a treasury for Christ's relics, in particular the Crown of Thorns. During the French Revolution, the church was desecrated and then turned into a flour mill.

A Mass was said after the brothers had reached Notre Dame, and the crown was housed in the royal Chapel of St. Nicholas. Soon pilgrims from all over Europe began traveling to Paris to see the relic, and before long it became evident that the chapel was too small to accommodate their numbers. Louis therefore decided to build a new church to house the relic.

He started by making several other purchases from Baldwin, who was close to bankruptcy. Two large fragments of the True Cross, the shaft of the Holy Spear, a fragment of the purple robe in which Jesus had been cloaked, a piece of the sponge that had quenched His thirst on the Cross, and a 30-centimeter-wide piece of Christ's burial cloth were all acquired by the French king.

Despite his efforts, Baldwin II was not able to maintain his rule in Constantinople. The money for funding his army of mercenaries was quickly depleted, and the loss of the Passion relics proved a blow to morale. Baldwin fled the capital, and on August 15, 1261, Michael VIII Palaiologos led his Greek forces

FRESCO in the Sainte-Chapelle showing Christ adored by the angels. Painted by the Alsatian artist Louis Steinheil (1814–1885) during the church's renovation after the damage from the French Revolution.

into Constantinople. Fifty-seven years after the Fourth Crusade and the founding of the Latin Empire of Constantinople, the empire came to an end.

Louis IX issued an immediate decree for a new chapel to be built in the Capetian royal palace on the Île de la Cité. The Sainte-Chapelle, as the chapel became known, is a sublime example of Gothic architecture, inspired by descriptions of the royal chapel in Constantinople. To this day, the Sainte-Chapelle makes a great impression on its visitors. In his 1323 work *De Laudibus Parisiis*, French philosopher John of Jandun describes the chapel thus: "When a person crosses its threshold, he has the impression that he has been lifted into heaven and has entered one of the most beautiful rooms in paradise."

The lavish chapel cost 40,000 French livre in gold to build—three times less than the amount Louis paid Baldwin for the Crown of Thorns—which reveals just how much the relic meant to the French king. He paid another 100,000 French livre for the huge revolving gold reliquary, which was placed in the center of the Sainte-Chapelle. He carried the only key to the reliquary around his ▷

271

STATUE OF JOHN THE APOSTLE. One of 12 statues fitted in the columns that separate the church's stained glass windows.

COMBINED SURFACE
AREA of the stained
glass windows in the
Sainte-Chapelle is 618
square meters.

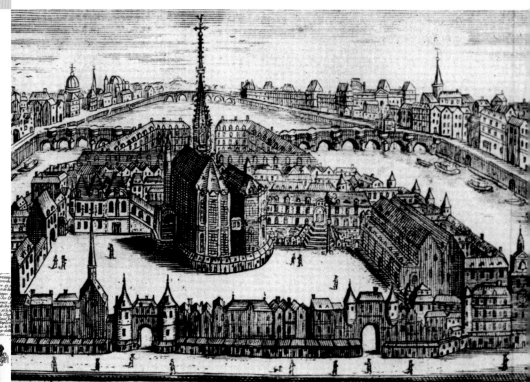

LE PALAIS en la Cité Ancienne demeure des Roys jusqua Philippe le Bel qui y etablit le Parlement en 1286 La Sᵗᵉ Chapelle a été batie par Sᵗ Louis l'an 1230 le batim. est estimé le plus hardy de france ayant 2 Eglise l'une sur l'autre

GOLDEN
RELIQUARY
in the Saint-
Chapelle. Pierre
Ransonnette's
(1745–1810)
illustration, dating
from 1790, gives
an idea of what
the reliquary
looked like before
it was melted
down by French
revolutionaries.

THE STAINED
GLASS WINDOWS
in the Sainte-
Chapelle depict
1,134 scenes from
the Old and New
Testaments, as well
as scenes of the
history of some of
Christ's relics.

272

THE SAINTE CHAPELLE

THE FRENCH KING ST. LOUIS IX
funded the building of the Sainte-Chapelle.
From its inception, the chapel was designed as
a shrine in which to store relics, above all the
Crown of Thorns, which the king bought from
Latin Emperor of Constantinople Baldwin II in
1239 for 135,000 pounds in gold. Two years later,
the architect Pierre de Montreuil began work
on the two-storey chapel in the courtyard of
the Capetian royal palace on the Île de la Cité
in Paris. It was finished in 1248 and became one
of the medieval gems of Gothic architecture,
acting as a design model for numerous chapels
throughout Europe.

For centuries the chapel served as a
repository for Christian relics. Apart from the
Crown of Thorns, other relics preserved in the
Sainte-Chapelle included two fragments of the
True Cross, the shaft of the Longinus Spear, a
piece of the purple cloak wrapped around Christ
when He was mocked before the crucifixion, a
fragment of the sponge used to moisten Christ's
lips on the Cross, and a piece of burial cloth. The
chapel also housed the remains of several saints,
including Martin of Tours, Louis of Toulouse,
and Séverin.

The Sainte-Chapelle suffered extensive
damage during the French Revolution and was
turned into a flour mill. Golden reliquaries were
melted down, and several precious relics were
lost for good. Restoration work on the chapel
was not begun until 1853. Today the chapel
forms part of the Palais de Justice and is open
to the public. The chapel no longer contains
any relics, but visitors can marvel at its huge,
15-meter stained-glass windows, which present
scenes from the Old and New Testaments, as
well as the history of some of Christ's relics.

neck, occasionally showing the relic to his guests. The crown was put on public display once a year, on Good Friday, so that people could venerate it and the sick could touch it.

What did the Crown of Thorns, used as a symbol of mockery and an instrument of torture, look like? It was a cap made of a thorny shrub that covered the whole head. Its skeleton structure included a hoop made of entwined twigs, to which other thorny branches were attached, probably tied together with string.

The Crown of Thorns was most likely taken away by a witness of the crucifixion after Christ was taken down from the Cross. Since Christianity was persecuted in its early history (by both Romans and Jews), relics were often hidden. It was only after Constantine the Great issued the Edict of Milan in 313, granting religious freedom to all Christians, that the relics resurfaced.

MODERN RECONSTRUCTION of the Crown of Thorns based on analysis of bloodstains on the Turin Shroud.

The Crown of Thorns

✛

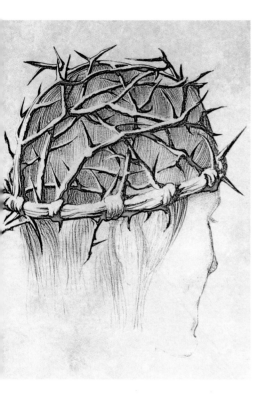

The oldest historical document referring to the Crown of Thorns, a pilgrimage account written by St. Paulinus of Nola, dates from 409. Other surviving fifth-century accounts include one written by St. Vincent of Lérins, who states that the crown was shaped "like a pileus [helmet], so that it covered the whole of [Christ's] head". Over the next few centuries, while it was kept in the Church of the Apostles on Mount Zion, numerous pilgrims, including Cassiodorus and St. Antonino di Piacenza, wrote about the relic.

In 650 St. Gregory of Tours wrote that only a hoop made of bulrushes remained of the original crown, since many of the branches forming the cap had broken off and the thorns had fallen away. It also began to appear in this form in Christian paintings, no longer in the shape of a cap, but a narrow entwined band of thorny branches.

In 1063 the Byzantine emperor Constantine X ordered that the relic be moved from Jerusalem to Constantinople, where along with a number of other relics it was housed in the Boukoleon Palace chapel. It was not stolen or destroyed during the Fourth Crusade, but it didn't remain in Constantinople for much longer, as it was sold to the king of France. The relic arrived in Paris in the form of a band, together with numerous thorns that had previously fallen off. Louis IX sent these thorns to various churches in France and ordered that the crown be rehoused in the Sainte-Chapelle, where it remained for over 450 years.

The French Revolution was a dangerous time for the relic. In 1793 an incensed crowd of Parisians destroyed the Sainte-Chapelle's interior. The relics were mockingly paraded through the streets before being destroyed. Among those objects lost was a fragment of the True Cross (which was considered the largest fragment in the world), the staff of the Longinus Spear, a shroud fragment, and the sponge used to quench Christ's thirst on the Cross. Another fragment of the True Cross, one of the Holy Nails, and, most importantly, the

THE CROWN OF THORNS was not shaped like a ring, as is often depicted in paintings, but like a thorny helmet.

The Crown of Thorns

275

Crown of Thorns were all saved. In 1804, the crown was housed in the Notre Dame repository. Two years later, it was given a reliquary in the shape of a golden sphere, funded by Napoleon Bonaparte.

Botanists who have examined the crown have determined that the hoop, which has a diameter of 21 centimeters, is made of a bulrush species called *Juncus balticus*, which grows in the Eastern regions of the Mediterranean Basin. They have not discounted its authenticity.

Much more difficult is the task of identifying the individual thorns. According to the botanists' estimations, there must have been about 50 to 60 thorns.

In 1870 French architect Charles Rohault de Fleury located as many as 139 thorns venerated in churches throughout Europe. This suggests that a number of the thorns are fakes, or else they could be third-class relics that have come into contact with the genuine articles. Only in a few cases can we find documents that allow us to reconstruct a thorn's history and determine whether it came from Constantinople or from Paris.

The thorns preserved in churches throughout Europe belong to three species of plant. The first is a shrub called *Zizyphus vulgaris* Lam. (or *Zizyphus spina Christi*). This thorny shrub, which can reach a height of seven meters, grows in regions around Jerusalem, and its spikes have a length of up to five centimeters.

The second species is the *Rhamnus lycioides* (black hawthorn): a tangled, thorny, many-branched shrub that can grow to a height of three meters. It grows mainly within the Mediterranean Basin. The third species is the thistle-like plant *Gundelia tournefortii*, which grows in the semi-desert areas of the Near and Middle East, from Palestine to Azerbaijan. American scientist Alan Wangher found a very high concentration of pollen grains from the *Gundelia tournefortii* embedded in the fabric of the Turin Shroud, specifically around the imprinted figure's head. In his opinion, the Crown of Thorns was made of this particular plant species. Other scientists, however, haven't discounted the possibility that the crown was made of two or even three species of thorny plant.

The comparatively easier task is determining the authenticity of those thorns that were donated by Louis IX and can be found today in churches in France (including Reims, Saint-Denis, Toulouse, and Bordeaux) and Italy ▶

TUMBLE THISTLE *Gundelia tournefortii*, from which—according to Prof. Alan Wangher—the Crown of Thorns was formed.

THE THORNY SHRUB known as *Zizyphus vulgaris* Lam. (shown in photographs below) is considered to be one of the materials from which the Crown of Thorns was made.

PUBLIC SHOWING of the Crown of Thorns, which attracts crowds of pilgrims every month to Notre Dame in Paris. Devotees must wait in line for hours to be able to kiss the relic.

279

✛

RELIQUARY OF THE TWO THORNS in the Basilica of the Holy Cross in Jerusalem, Rome.

CHAPEL OF THE THORN on the bank of the Arno River in Pisa—home of the precious relic.

▶ (including Rome, Pisa, and Vicenza). The thorn bequeathed to Pisa received an especially sumptuous home. In the thirteenth century it was moved to a specially built miniature Gothic chapel on the banks of the River Arno—the Capella della Spina. Botanists have confirmed that this thorn belongs to the *Zizyphus vulgaris* Lam. species. Tests carried out on the thorn preserved in the Basilica of the Holy Cross in Rome yielded the same results.

In 1356 Emperor Charles IV acquired two thorns from Paris and housed them in Karlštejn Castle, built especially to house the emperor's collection of relics. Later his cousin King Charles V transported one of the thorns from the Sainte-Chapelle to a newly built chapel in his castle in Vincennes.

Other thorns that are venerated as fragments of the crown arrived in the West from Constantinople somewhat earlier. Usually they were gifts from

Byzantine emperors that later ended up in various churches or monasteries, such as in Compiègne and Saint-Germain-des-Prés in France and Malmesbury in the United Kingdom. In 1206 two thorns were embedded in the crown of Henry of Flanders, second emperor of the Latin Empire of Constantinople, who then sent it to his brother Philip I of Namur. This imperial insignia is kept in the Diocesan Museum of Namur to this day.

In Poland, thorns venerated as relics can be found in the Cathedral of the Resurrection and St. Thomas the Apostle in Zamość, in the Church of the Holy Sepulchre in Miechowie, and in the Church of St. Joseph and St. Anthony of Padua in the village of Boćki.

SCIENCE

HISTORY

TRADITION

DISCOVERY

THE INVESTIGATIONS
CONTINUE

CHAPTER X

THE INVESTIGATIONS CONTINUE

✤

THE LONGINUS SPEAR

Over the centuries and in churches throughout Europe, relics other than those discussed in earlier chapters have been venerated as holy objects linked with the suffering, death, and burial of Christ. Among them is the spear with which a Roman soldier is said to have pierced Jesus' side. It's known as the Longinus Spear, since—according to the oldest Christian sources available—Longinus was the soldier's name.

Rome

ITALY

285

✤

LONGINUS SPEAR. Detail of a sculpture in St. Peter's Basilica, Rome. According to old Christian sources, Longinus was the centurion in the Gospels who said of Jesus, "Truly, He was the Son of God."

ST. PETER'S BASILICA, Vatican. The church's treasury holds the spearhead of the Longinus Spear. Pope Innocent VIII obtained the relic in 1492 from Turkish Sultan Bayezid II.

According to sources, he suffered from cataracts, which were supposedly cured by the blood and water that flowed from Christ's side. Later he was baptized and even died as a martyr for his faith.

The spear, which according to Christian tradition remained in Jerusalem, was mentioned by a number of pilgrims visiting the Holy Land in the sixth and seventh centuries, including Breviarius, Antonino di Piacenza, Cassiodorus, Arculf, and St. Gregory of Tours. According to their testimonies, the spear was divided in two parts, one kept in the Church of the Apostles on Mount Zion, the other in the Martyrium Basilica. The spear fell into the hands of Khosrau II when the Persians invaded the city in 614. Fourteen years later, however, it was retrieved by the Byzantine emperor Heraclius after he routed the Persian forces.

Pilgrimage accounts from the Holy Land ceased to mention the Longinus Spear in the eighth century, while it received mention from pil-

THE LONGINUS SPEAR

is also known as the Spear of Destiny. Its stem disappeared in Paris during the French Revolution, while the spearhead can be found in the Vatican. It's kept in a priceless reliquary made of gold and crystal, encrusted with precious stones. For centuries the Spear was considered to be one of the four most precious relics owned by the Catholic Church.

COMPARE
page ▶ 20

The Investigations Continue

287

grims traveling to Constantinople. Here, the spear's staff was kept in a decorated golden icon called the Yeona, found in the Hagia Sophia Cathedral, while the spearhead was kept in the treasury of the Boukoleon Palace.

In 1204 the Franks and Venetians invaded the city during the Fourth Crusade. The Crusaders didn't steal the spear, however, which remained in Constantinople. In 1241 Baldwin II sold the spear's staff and its container (the Yeona) to Louis IX of France. The relic was kept in the Sainte-Chapelle in Paris until 1793, when it was lost during the French Revolution.

The spearhead remained in Constantinople, however, until the Ottoman Turks invaded the city on May 29, 1453, under Mehmed II. Many of the city's inhabitants were murdered, and the Turks decided to make Constantinople their new capital. Hagia Sophia was turned into a mosque, and the spearhead became the Turks' possession.

In 1492 Mehmed's successor, Sultan Bayezid II, came to an agreement with Pope Innocent VIII. In return for the Longinus Spearhead, Bayezid requested that his brother Cem, who was a pretender to the Ottoman throne, never leave the Holy See. Innocent welcomed the sultan's brother with great honor, allowed him freedom of movement within Rome, but forbade his crossing the papal borders. The relic, as promised, was delivered to Rome.

In 1492 the Turks transported the relic by boat to Ancona. From there it was delivered to Rome by two cardinals: Rodrigo Borgia and Giuliano della Rovere. Interestingly, both men would later become popes— Alexander VI and Julius II, respectively. The eighteenth-century pope Benedict XIV decided to determine whether the relic was authentic and asked the French king to send the spear's staff from the Sainte-Chapelle so that he could compare it with his spearhead. The comparison proved successful when both pieces fitted together perfectly. Today, the relic is kept in St. Veronica's column in St. Peter's Basilica in the Vatican. Every Easter Saturday it is displayed from the column's balcony and used to bless the congregation.

Is this the real spear used to pierce Christ's side? We don't know for sure, since the relic was never subjected to rigorous tests. We do know that it is a hasta spear, the sort used by Roman legionnaires in the first century. Historians have, on the other hand, dismissed the supposed authenticity of the spear kept at the Hofburg Palace in Vienna, which for years was part of the imperial insignia of the Holy Roman Empire.

STATUE BY BERNINI of the Roman centurion Longinus, in St. Peter's Basilica in Rome. The sculpture is found in the column of St. Longinus, which is one of the four pillars supporting the church's dome.

The Investigations Continue

289

Prüm
Berlin

GERMANY

THE SANDALS OF PRÜM

Another relic believed to have belonged
to Christ is a pair of sandals, found today
in Prüm Abbey, in the German Rhineland.
In the eighth and ninth centuries, this was
one of the most important places in the
Frankish Kingdom. In 722, Princess Bertrada
(wife of Pepin the Younger and great-grandmother
of Charlemagne) funded the construction of the
Benedictine abbey.

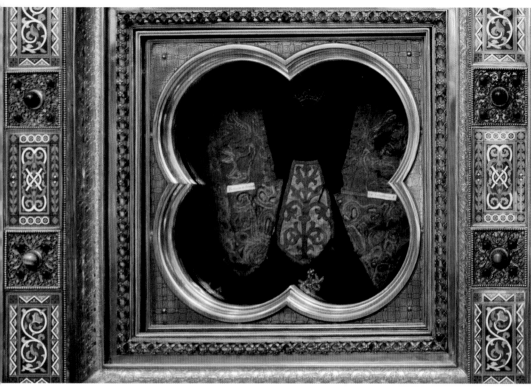

RELIQUARY WITH CHRIST'S SANDALS in the Holy Savior
Basilica in Prüm. French scientist Gérard Lucotte has traced the
sandals back to the Roman-occupied Holy Land.

POPE ZACHARY
was head of
the Catholic
Church between
741 and 752. He
bequeathed
Christ's sandals
to Pepin the
Younger. A bas-
relief depicting the
pope is found in
Prüm's Holy Savior
Basilica.

The abbey was closely linked with the royal family that would become the
Carolingian dynasty, whose landed possessions reached west from the Rhine to
as far as Brittany. The Benedictine monks ran a school within the abbey at which
the royal family's children were educated. Charles II, "the Bald", the grandson of
Charlemagne, was also educated there.

**Pippin the Younger became the first King of the
Franks** of the Carolingian dynasty and was crowned in 751 by St. Boniface.
Pepin made a strategic alliance with the pope, protected Rome against the
Lombard invasion, and oversaw the foundation of the Papal States, which exer-
cised political power until 1870. In 752 Pope Zachary (the last pope of the

291

BASILICA OF THE
HOLY SAVIOR in
Prüm. The first
Benedictine abbey on
this site was founded in
720, while the current
church was built a
thousand years later,
in 1721.

Byzantine Papacy) donated to Pepin the Younger the sandals thought to have belonged to Christ. The gift was a symbol of the amicable union between the pope and the Carolingians and legitimized the dynasty's rule.

The Frankish king ordered the relic to be housed in Prüm Abbey, which in turn became one of Europe's most important pilgrimage sites. In time, however, the abbey's popularity among pilgrims was eclipsed by that of two nearby towns: Trier and Aachen. The sandals, or more specifically, large remaining pieces of the sandals, are found in Prüm to this day and are contained in a gold reliquary.

Historians are unable to say how the sandals came into the hands of Pope Zachary in the eighth century (perhaps they were brought to Rome by St. Peter himself). At the start of this century, Gérard Lucotte (who also conducted a thorough examination of the Tunic of Argenteuil) examined the sandals. He noted that this particular sort of footwear was worn during the period of the Roman Empire, while the sandals' shape and method used to tie them were typical of the sort of shoe worn throughout the Holy Land. Based on this evidence, we cannot dismiss the possibility that the sandals constitute an authentic relic once belonging to Christ.

THE HOLY BLOOD

RELICS ASSOCIATED WITH THE BLOOD OF CHRIST were venerated in a number of towns in medieval Europe. The place preserving the most well known among them is the Basilica di Sant'Andrea in Mantua, whose relic's history is based on the story of St. Longinus—the Roman soldier who pierced Christ's side with his spear. According to legend, the mixture of blood and water that flowed from Christ's side cured Longinus of his cataracts. This resulted in the conversion of the Roman soldier, who proceeded to scoop clumps of the bloodied earth into his helmet. Although Jews considered blood to be unclean, the Roman soldier had no qualms about handling Christ's blood, but, wary of being accused of profanity, Longinus supposedly buried the relic of Christ's blood in a box under the city walls.

Chroniclers inform us that in 804 St. Andrew appeared in a dream to a man of faith and revealed the location of the hidden relic. Pope Leo III traveled to Mantua to give thanks for the newly discovered blood of Christ. Then, in 924, around the time of the Hungarian invasion, the relic was hidden again, only to be discovered in 1048. Swedish chronicler Hermann of Reichenau writes that once again St. Andrew revealed the relic's location, this time in a dream to a blind man. Pope Leo IX, like his predecessor, visited Mantua to worship the relic. His initial plan to take the blood of Christ back with him to Rome was abandoned following a great protest by Mantua's citizens.

In 1472 the building of the Basilica di Sant'Andrea was begun on the exact spot where the relic had been discovered. For centuries the church attracted pilgrims from all over Europe. In 1848, however, the basilica was desecrated by the Austrians, and several of the containers holding the blood of Christ were destroyed. Today, the remaining small lump of blood is preserved in an eighteenth-century reliquary and displayed every Good Friday. For the remainder of the year it is kept in a green marble urn. Scientists have never tested the relic, although the Church—beginning with Pope Leo IX in 1053—regards it as authentic.

In 1998 the Missionaries of the Sacred Blood in Częstochowa, Poland, acquired a fragment of the relic and with it founded the Precious Blood Shrine a year later.

RELIQUARY OF THE BLOOD OF CHRIST in the sanctuary of the Missionaries of the Precious Blood in Częstochowa, Poland.

ST. GASPAR del Bufalo (1786–1837), founder of the Missionaries of the Precious Blood.

THE AACHEN RELICS

Aachen
Kornelimünster
Berlin

GERMANY

THREE AACHEN RELICS on a nineteenth-century print: Jesus' swaddling cloth, His loin cloth, and the veil in which John the Baptist's head was wrapped following his execution.

For centuries, certain woven relics other than those discussed in previous chapters have been venerated throughout Europe as Christ's burial cloths. Jewish burial customs necessitated the use of numerous cloths, all the more in the case of Jesus since His body was very bloody and contact with blood or a dead body made a person unclean. Among the relics are another shroud, bands, and a burial cap.

Based on their studies, sindonologists claim that there must have been a second shroud, which was used to cover Christ's body as it was taken down from the Cross and moved to the tomb. It could not have been the Turin Shroud, which doesn't bear traces of such use and which covered Christ's body only when it was already in the tomb. Bishop Arculf was said to have seen this second shroud toward the end of the seventh century in Jerusalem during his pilgrimage to the Holy Land and noted that the shroud measured eight feet in length, slightly shorter than the Shroud of Turin.

Sources tell us that the emperor Charlemagne collected a number of the Passion relics, including numerous burial cloths donated to him in 799 by the patriarch of Jerusalem. The emperor stored these relics in Aachen. After his death, Charlemagne's son Louis the Pious decided to donate four cloths to the Benedictine monastery in Kornelimünster, near Aachen. In 876 Charles the Bald proposed a swap of relics between Kornelimünster Abbey and the Church of St. Cornelius in Compiègne. The German monks received the skull and arm of St. Cornelius, while the French brethren received the second shroud from Christ's tomb. Charles the Bald wanted to raise the profile of Compiègne, which was also his official residence, and after completing the

RELIC FROM KORNELIMÜNSTER VENERATED as the *Linteum Domini*, or the towel that Jesus used at the Last Supper to dry the feet of the Apostles.

AACHEN – THE CITY OF RELICS

AT THE TURN OF THE NINTH CENTURY, AACHEN, GERMANY, became Western Europe's most important city. It was built during the Roman Empire, in the first century A.D., under the name of *Aquisgranum* or *Aquae Grani* (meaning "waters of Grannus", after the Celtic deity of healing and thermal springs). Pepin the Younger, who valued the waters' medical properties, built a chapel and his residence in the town. His son and successor, Charlemagne, decided to make the town his capital.

In 790, Charlemagne built the Carolingian Palace of Aachen, which included the famous octagonal chapel that today is found in the Cathedral of St. Mary. The palace served as the imperial residence but also as a treasury, filled with numerous Christian relics imported from all over Europe. Four so-called Great Relics of Aachen are preserved to this day in the Gothic presbytery, which for centuries attracted great numbers of pilgrims, while the cathedral museum exhibits three other lesser relics.

VOLUME ABOUT THE RELICS of Aachen, published in 1867.

AACHEN CATHEDRAL has many objects pertaining to Emperor Charlemagne, including the sarcophagus containing his remains and his imperial throne.

PUBLIC SHOWING OF THE AACHEN RELICS in an illustration
from 1664 and a photograph from 1993.

LOINCLOTH, ▶ thought to have belonged to Christ, is one of the four Great Relics of Aachen.

exchange of relics, the French town became a popular pilgrimage site. In 1840 one of the shrine's workers tried to estore the shroud's original whiteness by immersing it in a tub of boiling water. The shroud was completely destroyed.

Apart from the newly acquired skull and arm of St. Cornelius, three textile relics remained in Kornelimünster Abbey. The first is venerated as the *Linteum Domini*, or the towel with which Jesus girded Himself when washing the disciples' feet at the Last Supper. The second is the *Sindon Munda*, which is a piece of linen shroud measuring 180 by 185 centimeters, thought to have covered Christ's body as it was being transferred from the Cross to the tomb. The third relic is the *Sudarium Domini*, a veil made of byssus measuring 39 by 22 centimeters, believed to have covered Christ's face in the tomb. These cloths have never been subjected to any scientific testing. An Italian sindonologist and doctor, Professor Pierluigi Baima Bollone, believes they are not, in fact, Christ's burial cloths, since they are bereft of any images or even traces of blood. German scientist Ernst Hönings is inclined to agree, stating that "in all likelihood [the relics] are not authentic, but they do certainly date back to ancient times."

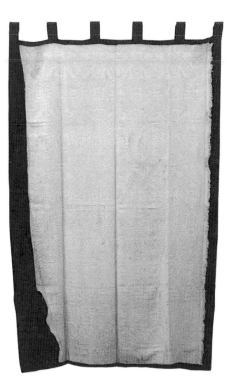

The main part of Charlemagne's collection remained in Aachen, thanks to which the town became one of the most popular pilgrimage sites in medieval Europe. It prided itself on the seven relics kept in its famous octagonal cathedral. Most prized were Aachen's four Great Relics, which include the Virgin Mary's cloak, Christ's swaddling clothes, St. John the Baptist's beheading cloth, and Christ's loincloth (*perisonium*). Since 1239 these relics have been kept in their own reliquary—the Shrine of the Virgin Mary—located in the cathedral's presbytery. The town was also in possession of three lesser relics, which included Christ's band, Mary's band, and a fragment of the scourging whip used to flog Jesus.

In 1349 Charles IV instituted the tradition of displaying the relics in Aachen and in Kornelimünster every seven years. For centuries the cloths were shown from the cathedral balcony and later inside the building itself. The seven-year cycle has lasted to this day, and the relics were most recently displayed in 1993, 2000, and 2007. Interestingly the number of pilgrims visiting Aachen was at its largest in the twentieth century, not in the Middle Ages. This took place in 1939, when Hitler was in power. The public showing of relics, or *ostensiones reliquiarum*, became a silent protest against Nazi rule.

Can the Aachen relics be considered authentic? The cloths have never been examined using scientific methods, such as bloodstain or pollen-grain analysis. In the last decade of the twentieth century, however, they underwent rigorous ▶

SUDARIUM DOMINI, a byssus veil, kept in Kornelimünster and venerated as a relic of Christ

SINDON MUNDA, a fragment of linen shroud, venerated in Kornelimünster as one of Christ's burial cloths.

CEREMONIAL PROCESSION with the great reliquary, making its way through the streets of Aachen in 1951.

AACHEN CATHEDRAL. Birthplace of the Holy Roman Empire and a gem of Carolingian architecture. Its most important part is the old palace Chapel of Charlemagne, which contains the four Great Relics and the emperor's remains.

GREAT **RELIQUARY** of Aachen, also known as the Marian Reliquary: of all the objects stored within it, a robe thought to belong to the Holy Mother has for centuries been regarded as the most sacred.

PUBLIC SHOWING of relics in Kornelimünster in 1657. Illustration by Gerard Altzenbach.

restoration, from which we know that all the relics originated in the Near East and can be dated back to the Roman Empire. The most damaged burial cloth is Christ's loincloth, a triangular piece of material with rounded points that measures 151 by 123 by 127½ centimeters. Scientists believe the cloth was cut from a larger garment, most likely a tunic. These days the perisonium looks more like a bloodied rag, which is why the decision was made to display it folded up in a rectangle and tied with a silk ribbon. The cathedral's governing clerics don't judge the relics to be authentic, but they stress the relics' importance as symbols of the Christian faith.

Spanish scientist Domenico Leone and Salesian priest Fr. Luigi Fossati have counted as many as 52 shrouds, each found to be copies of the Turin relic. Some of them, such as the samples found in Cadouin, France, and in Lier, Belgium, were for many years considered authentic burial cloths from Christ's tomb.

Other burial cloths that have for centuries attracted the attention of pilgrims include the two shrouds of Besançon. Scientists believe that these could be the cloths that were wrapped around the top of the Turin Shroud. Sources

FIGURE OF CHRIST on the Marian Reliquary, showing Jesus as a
king bearing royal insignia: a crown and an orb.

tell us they were looted when Constantinople fell during the Fourth Crusade.
Three years earlier, in 1201, the Byzantine *skeuophylakion* (guard to the treasury) Nicholas Mesarites wrote that two kinds of burial relics were contained
within the treasury: *entaphioi sindones* (burial shrouds) and *kai othonia kai
ta soudaria* (sheets and scarves).

As mentioned in the chapter on the Turin Shroud, its owner at about this time
was Burgundian knight Otto de la Roche. In 1208 Otto's son Ponce de la Roche
offered the archbishop of Besançon, Amadeus de Tramelay, two linen cloths that
he had received as a gift from his father. Each of them measured 260 by 130 centimeters and bore the image of a dead man known to us from the Turin Shroud.
We will never know whether these relics were authentic or forgeries, as the first
was lost in a fire at Besançon Cathedral on March 6, 1349, and the second was
burned in public under the orders of the National Convention in 1794, during the
French Revolution.

PUBLIC
SHOWING of
relics in Aachen,
1958. The cloths
were shown from
the gallery of the
cathedral's tower.

303

THE CAP
OF CAHORS

CHRIST'S BURIAL
CAP, venerated
in Cahors since
medieval times.

The history of the burial cap of Cahors is altogether another matter. In accordance with Jewish funereal customs, a special sort of hood (called a *pathil* in Hebrew) was placed on the head of the deceased and tied under the chin to stop the jaw from opening and the tongue from protruding. The cap wrapped the head but left the face exposed. If, in Christ's case, all the traditional funereal customs were followed, He must have also had a burial cap placed on His head.

How did the cap end up in a small French village on the southern border of the Massif Central? One hypothesis is that it was part of Charlemagne's collection of Passion relics. We do not know, however, who donated the relic to the emperor. Some believe it may have been the patriarch of Jerusalem, others that it was the Byzantine empress consort Irene. Still others believe Charlemagne received the cap from the caliph Harun al-Rashid. In any case, according to this theory, in 803 Charlemagne gave the relic to Bishop Aymatus of Cahors.

EMPEROR CHARLEMAGNE bequeaths the Holy Cap to Bishop Amatus. Painting from the cathedral in Cahors.

Another hypothesis is that the cap was brought back from the Holy Land by another bishop of Cahors, Gérard de Cardaillac, who also built the Cathedral of St. Étienne. In 1119 the cathedral was consecrated by Pope Calixtus III. The cap, stored in the cathedral, attracted pilgrims from all over the continent. For centuries it was displayed to the public on prominent feast days, such as Pentecost, although this tradition ended in 1960. Today the relic is kept in a nineteenth-century reliquary in the cathedral's Chapel of St. Gaubert.

The Holy Cap has never been subjected to such rigorous tests as the Sudarium of Oviedo or the Tunic of Argenteuil. In the nineteenth century, the father of modern

ST. STEPHEN'S CATHEDRAL in Cahors, where the relic of Christ's burial cap is kept.

305

THE CATHEDRAL in Cahors, consecrated in 1119 by Pope Calixtus III, combines both Romanesque and Gothic architectural styles.

Egyptology, Jean-François Champollion, claimed the cap was ancient in form and typical of examples originating in the eastern regions of the Roman Empire. It's composed of eight layers of delicate cloth, which are sewn together to create a thicker piece of material. Tests carried out in the nineteenth century also revealed traces of blood within the cap. In 2001 Robert Babinet published the results of his analyses, which reveal that the patterning of wounds on the cap's interior matches the layout of the wounds visible on the Turin Shroud. In particular, the extensive abrasion on the right cheek and the spike wounds to the back of the head and the lower part of the neck match up on both relics. According to Babinet, this is proof that the Cap of Cahors was among Christ's burial cloths. The cathedral's rector is more reticent, however, claiming that one ought to await the results of more detailed and varied tests before making any final judgment.

RELIQUARY, dating from the nineteenth century, in which the Cap of Cahors is kept.

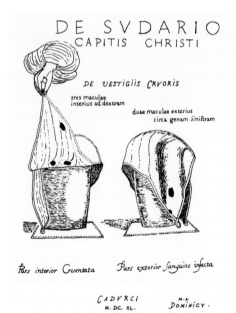

TRACES OF BLOOD ON THE CAP OF CAHORS, as seen in a book illustration by Justin Gary, dated 1899. The inside of the cap shows three bloodstains, while the outside shows two, on the left cheek.

HISTORY

TRADITION

TRUTH

DISCOVERY

GOLGOTHA
AND THE EMPTY TOMB

CHAPTER XI

GOLGOTHA AND THE EMPTY TOMB

Few churches in the world have received the same level of scientific scrutiny as Jerusalem's Church of the Holy Sepulchre. For a while it might have seemed that nothing new could ever be discovered there, but in 1986 two Greek conservators—art historian Georg Lavas and architect Theo Mitropoulos—did just that.

During their restoration work in the shrine built on top of Golgotha (where Christ was crucified), which is visited daily by thousands of pilgrims, they happened upon a carved limestone ring, measuring 11.5 centimeters in diameter. According to the scientists, the ring was large enough to support a 3-meter cross and keep it vertical.

Jerusalem

ISRAEL

310

THE CHURCH OF THE HOLY SEPULCHRE contains the Anastasis Rotunda, at the center of which stands a chapel measuring 8 meters long and 5.9 meters wide. It's made up of two parts: a vestibule known as the Chapel of the Angel, and the Holy Tomb itself. The entrance to the chapel is low, and one needs to crouch to enter it.

A GREEK ORTHODOX MONK opens the door leading to the area beneath the Golgotha Chapel.

THE ROCK OF CALVARY, which is found beneath the Church of the Holy Sepulchre in Jerusalem. Scientists have calculated that the base of the rock is 6.75 meters beneath the current floor level of the basilica, while its crest is 4.2 meters above floor level.

STONE RING ON THE ROCK OF CALVARY, discovered in 1986 by Greek conservationists. Archaeologists claim it may have been used to keep the cross in its vertical position.

It would have been possible to drive the cross into the earth, but not through stone. The discovery of the limestone ring, therefore, was confirmation for many that the rock on which the basilica was built was indeed the site of Christ's execution.

The Gospels tell us that Christ was crucified outside Jerusalem atop a small hill by the name of Golgotha (from the Aramaic *gulgolta* and the Hebrew *gulgolet*, meaning "skull"). It lay on a disused quarry site, about 45 meters west of the town wall, and had been used to extract limestone between the seventh and first centuries B.C. The stone was then used to build Jerusalem's walls. In Christ's time, the limestone extraction stopped and the quarry site was transformed into a garden, although a jagged rock 7 meters long, 3 meters wide, and 4.8 meters high jutted out from its center, reaching an altitude of 755 meters above sea level. From afar it looked like a skull, which is why the spot was also given the name the Place of the Skull. The biblical details of the location have been confirmed through archaeological excavations.

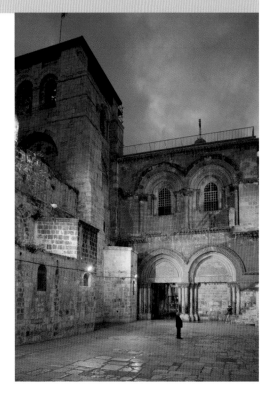

THE CHURCH OF THE HOLY SEPULCHRE

is divided among five Christian communities: Orthodox (Greek), Catholic (administered by the Franciscans), Armenian, Ethiopian, and Coptic. The church contains communal areas as well as sections dedicated solely to particular denominational groups.

THE THREE MOST IMPORTANT PLACES

in the Church of the Holy Sepulchre in Jerusalem:

1) The Rock of Calvary, where Jesus of Nazareth was crucified

2) Chapel of the Holy Sepulchre, which contains Joseph of Arimathea's tomb, where Christ was buried

3) Chapel of the Invention of the Cross, which contains the cistern where St. Helena found the three crosses.

CROSS-SECTION of the Church of the Holy Sepulchre. The original structure dates back to 1149 and was built by the Crusaders. The church was restored on two occasions: following a fire in 1808 and after an earthquake in 1927.

JERUSALEM BEFORE CHRIST

CHRISTIANS REGARD JERUSALEM, which was the site of Jesus' suffering, death, and Resurrection, as a holy city. It was from here that all the relics associated with Christ began their journeys into the wider world.

Above all, however, Jerusalem is most important for the Jews. During the tenth century B.C. King David conquered Jerusalem and made the city his capital. His son Solomon built the First Temple, which also became the repository for the Ark of the Covenant. The town became an influential center for religion, culture, politics, and economy, initially as part of the Kingdom of Jerusalem and then of the Kingdom of Judah.

Around 586 B.C., the Babylonians captured Jerusalem, destroyed the Temple of Solomon, and took the Jews into captivity. It was almost half a century later that the Persian king Cyrus the Great allowed the Israelites to return home and rebuild the Temple, which was completed (and commonly known as the Second Temple) in 516 B.C.

As a result of Alexander the Great's invasion of Jerusalem in 332 B.C., Judea found itself under Greek control, but not until the city fell in 198 B.C. to the Seleucids, was a Hellenized culture imposed upon the Jews by force. The resulting tension came to a head in 167 B.C. with the successful Maccabean revolt and the declaration of a new kingdom.

In the first century B.C., Judea found itself under Roman rule. Many Jews could not accept being governed by a pagan empire, and many aspired strongly to independence. Revolts broke out every so often in protest against the Romans. Such was the atmosphere in Jerusalem upon Christ's arrival to the Holy City.

THE TOMB DISCOVERED by British General Charles Gordon in 1884, which lies north of Jerusalem's Damascus Gate, gives an idea of what Christ's tomb might have looked like.

THE PLACE OF THE SKULL, where Christ was crucified, was located 45 meters to the west of Jerusalem's city walls. Golgotha is shown circled.

COMPARE
page ▶ 24

▶ The Gate of Ephraim, which was one of Jerusalem's main gates, stood close to the execution site, and Christ must have passed through it during the Way of the Cross. This was also one of the town's busiest thoroughfares, leading as it did from Jerusalem to the Roman provincial capital of Caesarea. The choice of Golgotha as the crucifixion site was not a coincidence. Indeed, Roman rhetorician Quintilian wrote the following in the first century: "Whenever we crucify criminals, we choose the busiest roads, so that as many people as possible can see the crucifixion and fear it."

Christ's burial place was also located outside the city walls, only 38 meters from Golgotha. A Jewish necropolis had been built on the site of the quarry, with graves hewn from the rock. One of these prepared tombs belonged to Joseph of Arimathea—a Pharisee and a member of the Sanhedrin who followed Christ, but hid that fact from the other religious leaders.

THE STONE OF ANOINTING
in the Church of the Holy Sepulchre is not the actual stone upon which Christ's body was anointed after death. It was added to the church in 1810, following a devastating fire two years earlier. It's located exactly halfway between Golgotha and the Empty Tomb, exactly 19 meters from either of the two sites.

A CATHOLIC PRIEST says Mass in the Chapel of the Holy Sepulchre.

OSSUARY of the high priest Caiaphas in the Israel Museum, Jerusalem.

A CATHOLIC PRIEST says Mass in the Chapel of the Holy Sepulchre.

We can guess what the grave looked like based on British General Charles Gordon's discovery of a first-century tomb to the north of the Damascus Gate in 1884. While Gordon asserted that this was Christ's tomb, most historians and archaeologists don't believe this to be the case. They do agree, however, that this was exactly the same kind of tomb as the one that belonged to Joseph of Arimathea. It comprised two rooms: a vestibule and a burial chamber. There were no coffins inside. Instead, bodies were lain in carved niches or alcoves about two meters long. Burial practice dictated that after the entire body had been decomposed, the remaining bones were transferred to a stone ossuarium. In 1990, archaeologists discovered one such ossuary, bearing an inscription claiming that the bones of the high priest Caiaphas were preserved inside.

Italian sindonologist Pierluigi Baima Bollone writes the following: "One can presume that after the Ascension, the places of Christ's death and burial remained in the hands of the Judeo-Christians and quickly became pilgrimage sites. It seems clear that the Christians had no authority over these places. Eutyches, a patriarch of Alexandria, tells how devotees came to give thanks at what was effectively a rubbish dump. This would account for the play on words, whereby the Arabic *al-kayama* ('church of the tomb')

OLIVE TREES
in the Garden
of Gethsemane,
dating back
to the time of
Christ.

became *al-kamana* ('church of the dump')—a distortion that would later be taken up among opposers of the Christian faith."

The urban and topographical layout of Jerusalem today, however, is nothing like what it was during Christ's time or even several decades after His death. The current Via Dolorosa dates back to the era of the Crusades and does not match the exact route walked by Jesus as He carried the Cross. Similarly, the current city walls were built under Muslim rule.

A critical point in Jerusalem's history was the Jewish rebellion against the Romans in A.D. 66. The Judeo-Christians took no part in the rebellion, having left Judea and made their way several dozen kilometers east, to the town of Pella, in modern-day Jordan. Historians presume that they had fled because of predictions made by Christ Himself, as St. Luke relates in his Gospel: "But when you see Jerusalem surrounded by armies, then know that its desolation is near. Then let those who are in Judea flee to the mountains, let those who are in the midst of her depart, and let not those who are in the country enter her. For these are the days of vengeance, that all things which are written may

Golgotha and the Empty Tomb

319

✛

ROMAN LEGIONNAIRES carrying their loot following the destruction of Jerusalem. Fragment of a bas-relief sculpture from the triumphal arch of the Emperor Titus, in Rome.

be fulfilled. But woe to those who are pregnant and to those who are nursing babies in those days! For there will be great distress in the land and wrath upon this people. And they will fall by the edge of the sword and be led away captive into all nations. And Jerusalem will be trampled by Gentiles until the times of the Gentiles are fulfilled" (Lk 21:20–24).

The Romans quashed the rebellion and besieged Jerusalem, which fell in the spring of A.D. 70. Titus' legions destroyed the city, and the Temple of Jerusalem was reduced to rubble. Only three towers of Herod's palace remained intact, along with part of the western wall. According to Tacitus, 600,000 Jews lost their lives. Titus Flavius Josephus wrote that during the period of rebellion from 66 to 73, over a million Jews were killed, and almost 100,000 ended up in captivity.

In 130 the emperor Hadrian ordered the rebuilding of Jerusalem, but in a completely different style, based on the Hellenistic model and under the new name of Aelia Capitolina. A temple dedicated to the Roman god Jupiter Capitolinus was built on the site of the old Temple of Jerusalem. The Jewish population considered this a huge affront, and in 132 another rebellion broke out. It was led by Simon bar Kokhba, whom the Jewish elders under Rabbi Akiva came to regard as a prophet and Messiah. Judeo-Christians once again refused to participate in the revolt, not wanting to declare bar Kokhba their Messiah.

CAIAPHAS' PALACE

JOSEPH, SON OF CAIAPHAS, was a Jewish high priest from A.D. 18 to 36 and led the Sanhedrin during their interrogation of Christ. One of the hearings took place in his palace, which, according to scientists, was found on the side of Mount Zion, on a site that is occupied today by the Church of St. Peter in Gallicantu (named after the Apostle's three-time denial of Christ). This church was built by French Catholics in 1931. Two other churches had also been built on this site in the past—one erected by the Byzantine empress Eudokia and another by the Crusaders. Both churches, however, were destroyed by invading forces.

A number of small, dark cellars can be found under the modern Church of St. Peter, once used as storerooms and places to keep prisoners. Some scientists believe that Christ may well have spent His last night alive in one of these underground cells. There is no concrete evidence for this assertion, but it remains a likelihood.

UNDERGROUND CISTERNS AND CELLARS in the old palace belonging to Caiaphas.

STONE STEPS that Jesus trod on His way to appear before Caiaphas.

THE CHURCH OF ST PETER IN GALLICANTU, erected on the site of Caiaphas' palace.

321

THE HOLY STAIRS

A SMALL CHAPEL STANDS NEAR THE PAPAL ARCHBASILICA OF ST. JOHN LATERAN IN ROME and is approached by 28 steps known as the Holy Stairs (*Santa Scala*). According to medieval sources these are the stairs that led to Pontius Pilate's palace, upon which Christ is believed to have been led on the way to His sentencing. They were supposedly brought from the Holy Land to Rome by St. Helena in 325, although the steps are not mentioned in any commentaries on the empress' trip. Indeed, they receive their first mention only around the ninth century: the oldest document referring to Pilate's stairs dates from the papacy of Sergius II, who was pope from 844 to 847.

For centuries, the Lateran Palace was the official residence of the bishops of Rome, before they moved to the Vatican. The Holy Stairs led to the Church of San Lorenzo, which contained the papal treasury, known as the *Sancta Sanctorum*, or "holy of holies". To this day, a sign appears above the altar stating, "There is no holier place on earth" (*Non est in toto sanctior orbe locus*). Medieval sources inform us that the *eikon acheiropoietos* (image not made by human hand), which may well be a reference to the Veronica Veil (known today as the Veil of Manoppello), was preserved here.

The building's current structure dates back to the sixteenth century. In 1589 Pope Sixtus V ordered the building of another set of stairs alongside and parallel to the Holy Stairs. The latter could be ascended only on one's knees, while the newer stairs could be climbed normally. Since they have been worn down considerably over the centuries by pilgrims' knees, the Holy Stairs were lined with wooden decking. Recent tests carried out on the steps have revealed that they are made of a marble quarried in Tyre, a town in modern-day Lebanon.

SANCTA SANCTORUM, or the Holy of Holies, is the name given to the old papal treasury in the Lateran Palace in Rome.

SANTA SCALA in Rome, or the Holy Stairs, are venerated as the steps over which Jesus walked on his way to appear before Pilate.

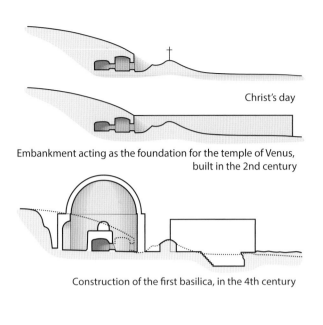

Christ's day

Embankment acting as the foundation for the temple of Venus,
built in the 2nd century

Construction of the first basilica, in the 4th century

HORIZONTAL PROJECTION of Golgotha and
the Holy Sepulchre showing the changes in
topography over the centuries.

The second rebellion was crushed in 135, with 580,000 dead. Jews were refused entry into Jerusalem under punishment of death, and a new Roman colony was built in the city's place. The Temple Mount was destroyed and a new temple dedicated to Jupiter was built instead, with a giant statue of the emperor Hadrian built at its entrance. The colony's second-largest temple, dedicated to Aphrodite (Venus), was built on Golgotha, which itself had been covered over with soil. The new colony was in no way reminiscent of the architectonic layout of the old Jerusalem.

Entry into Aelia Capitolina was restricted to the territory

within the city walls. Jews could continue living outside the city limits, which is perhaps why so many settled on Mount Zion. Christ's devotees remained divided: the Judeo-Christians, like the Jews, resided on Zion, while Christians converted from paganism were allowed to live within the limits of the new city.

Aspects of Christ's life, as well as places associated with Him continued to live on in the memory of Christians. One person who most certainly worked at preserving this memory was Jesus' cousin Simon, who was head of the Christian community in Jerusalem until A.D. 107. On visiting Jerusalem in 160 Bishop Melito of Sardis noted that the local Christians showed him around all the places associated with Christ's ministry and teaching. Origen had a similar impression of the city when he visited in 215 and 230. No wonder, then, that when Bishop Macarius of Jerusalem met Constantine at the First Council of Nicaea in 325, he was able to

THE CHAPEL OF ADAM in the Church of the Holy Sepulchre in Jerusalem. The Rock of Calvary, with crack in the stone, is visible through a window on the chapel's altar wall. Christian legend states that the blood of Christ crucified flowed through this crack and down onto Adam's remains, buried below.

323

tell the emperor that his citizens knew exactly where to find the holy places associated with their Lord.

Influenced by these stories, Constantine sent his mother, Helena, to Jerusalem, where she found the True Cross. She was also able to locate the place of Christ's death and burial. The Temple of Aphrodite (Venus) was destroyed, and a field of graves dating from the first century was discovered beneath it. Only one of these graves was empty, bereft of any remains or ossuaries. All the evidence suggested that it had been used only once. Helena concluded that the tomb must have carried great significance since others had not been buried there afterward.

Under orders from Constantine, a great new basilica

was built near Golgotha and the place of Christ's burial. It was three times larger than the current church, which was built by the the Crusaders. In the middle of the large compound was a churchyard, above which loomed the skull-shaped rock with a golden cross at its summit. Five large buildings surrounded the courtyard. ▷

VIEW OF JERUSALEM from Hartmann Schedel's *World Chronicle* published in Nuremberg in 1493.

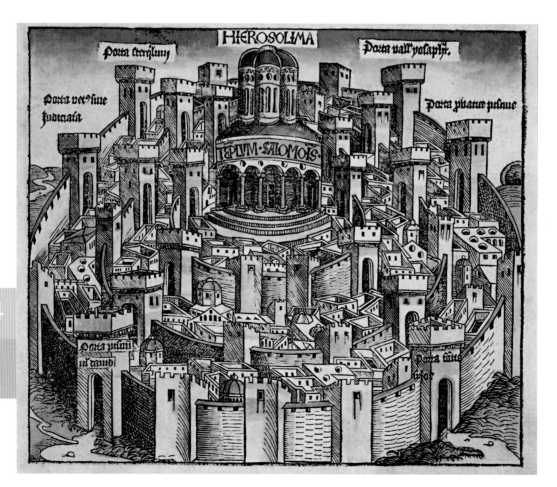

ECCE **HOMO**

ON THE LAND BELONGING TO THE CONVENT of the Congregation of Our Lady of Zion in Jerusalem is a large courtyard that is paved with massive stones dating back to the Roman Empire. The courtyard was discovered in 1857 during excavation work led by Alphonse Ratisbonne, a French Jew who became a Catholic priest. According to Fr. Ratisbonne, the discovery was none other than the *Lithostrotos*, or tribunal, which St. John describes in his Gospel and where Christ was crowned with thorns and mocked prior to His crucifixion.

The remains of a stone arch can also be seen above the small road leading to the convent of the Congregation of Our Lady. Pilgrims refer to this arch as the Ecce Homo Arch, under which Pilate, after sentencing Jesus, said, "Behold the man."

Archaeological tests do not support this assertion, however. The supposed *Lithostrotos* is in fact a part of the eastern Roman forum, constructed under the emperor Hadrian during his rebuilding of Jerusalem (or Aelia Capitolina, as it came to be known) in A.D. 135. The Ecce Homo Arch is in fact the remains of a triple triumphal arch that served as the entrance to the ancient forum.

PAVED COURTYARD from Roman times, considered by Fr. Alphonse Ratisbonne to be the *Lithostrotos* where Jesus was tried, but which actually dates to a later period, specifically A.D. 135.

ECCE HOMO ARCH, a remaining structure from the developments carried out under Emperor Hadrian (A.D. 135).

COMPARE
page ▶ 329

325

GOLGOTHA CHAPEL. The site of Christ's crucifixion is marked by a crucifix surrounded by oil lamps. Pilgrims kneel before the altar and kiss the Rock of Calvary.

Among them was a huge shrine built on the site of Christ's tomb and whose cupola was modeled on the Pantheon in Rome. Another church with five naves, called the Martyrium Basilica, was erected on the site where the True Cross was discovered.

Pilgrims who traveled to Jerusalem between the fourth and sixth centuries left accounts of their visit to the Holy Sepulchre. From them we have been able to learn that the rock face in which the tomb was found was cut in the shape of an octagonal prism whose entrance was so small that one had to bend over to pass through it. Barely two people could fit inside. The tomb's hollowed niche was fashioned as an arcosolium, meaning it was crowned with an arch. It was two meters long and one meter wide.

In 614 Jerusalem was invaded by the Persians under Khosrau II, who ordered the destruction of every Christian monument in the city, including Constantine's shrine complex. After Heraclius had expelled the Persians, he ordered the rebuilding of the complex but on a much smaller scale. The Byzantine ruler did not control the city for long, however, as it was once again invaded in 638, this time by the Arabs. Caliph Omar ordered that two mosques be built near Golgotha, but he didn't touch the church built upon the Holy Sepulchre. This was carried out by the

STATUE OF MARY in the Golgotha Chapel. The Holy Mother's heart is pierced by a sword, in accordance with the prophecy made by Simeon.

fanatical caliph al-Hakim, who in 1009 ordered the destruction of every Christian place of worship in Jerusalem, including Christ's tomb.

In 1072, the Seljuk Turks controlled Jerusalem and forbade Christians from entering the city. At this time, the Turks ruled over a vast empire, stretching from Turkey to Afghanistan. Meanwhile, Christian Byzantium was in decline. In 1095, Pope Urban II enjoined the Crusaders to liberate the Holy Land from Muslim rule. On July 15, 1099, an army of European knights occupied Jerusalem. Their leader, Godfrey of Bouillon, became the first ruler of the Latin Kingdom of Jerusalem. Another church was built on the site of Christ's burial place, which has lasted to this day (notwithstanding numerous renovations). The shrine remained intact even when Saladin invaded Jerusalem in 1187.

The status of the Church of the Holy Sepulchre has been preserved over the centuries, despite the city's having changed hands on several occasions. In 1517 and in 1917 the city came under Ottoman and British rule, respectively, and in 1948, as a result of the Arab-Israeli conflict, the city was split between Israel

327

and Jordan (with the Old Town and the Holy Sepulchre Church on the Arab side). Following the Six-Day War in 1967, Israeli forces occupied the whole of Jerusalem, with the Knesset (Israeli parliament) declaring it their capital 13 years later.

Today the Church of the Holy Sepulchre attracts pilgrims from all over the world. Due to its numerous renovations, the basilica exhibits an eclectic architectural style that draws on several influences. The most important parts of the church include the rotunda built above the Holy Tomb and crowned with a cupola called the Anastasis; the Golgotha Chapel; the Greek Choir; the St. Helena Chapel; the Franciscan church with its Chapel of the Blessed Sacrament; an Orthodox monastery and several chapels, including those of the Franks and the Syrians, the Longinus Chapel, and the Place of the Three Marys. The Church is under the pastoral care of Orthodox (mainly Greek), Armenian, and Catholic (Franciscan) clerics. The Coptic and Ethiopian Christians likewise have their own areas within the church.

Golgotha is found to the south of the main altar and is approached by two stone stairways leading to Calvary. The altar there is built above the Rock of ▶

CHAPEL OF THE ANGEL, or the vestibule next to the Holy Sepulchre, with a rectangular altar at its center. Made of solid rock, it's supposedly the remaining fragment of the stone that was rolled in front of Jesus' tomb. Historical sources tell us the Persians destroyed this boulder when they invaded in A.D. 614.

Golgotha and the Empty Tomb

STONE TABLET with an inscription dedicated to Emperor Tiberius from Pontius Pilate.

WHERE DID THE ROAD TO CALVARY START?

TODAY'S WAY OF THE CROSS, or Via Dolorosa, which runs along the streets of Jerusalem's Old Town, doesn't correspond exactly with the route taken by Christ on His journey to Calvary. Its route and stations were planned by the Dominican friar Rinaldo de Monte Crucis in 1294. At the time, however, Jerusalem's urban and architectonic layout was not at all reminiscent of the city that Christ knew. As a result, the locations of many of the stations were highly dubious. While the road's ending point—Golgotha—was fairly certain, its starting point was far less obvious. We know that Christ was sentenced in Pilate's praetorium, but where was it located?

In his version of the Via Dolorosa, Rinaldo de Monte Crucis located the route on the grounds of the Antonia Fortress, a Roman military barracks. Archaeologists, however, claim that Pilate's residence while he was in Jerusalem must have been either Herod's Palace or the old Hasmonean Palace. Christ's sentencing would have taken place in one of these two locations.

In 1961 Italian archaeologists carrying out excavation in Caesarea Maritima (the seat of the Roman prefect of Judea) discovered a limestone block bearing an inscription with a dedication from Pontius Pilate to Emperor Tiberius. The stone, currently located in the Israel Museum in Jerusalem, is the only piece of archaeological evidence we have that mentions by name the man who sentenced Jesus to death.

THE WAY OF THE CROSS traces a different path to the one that Jesus actually trod on his way to Golgotha. Similarly, Christ would not have walked over the paving stones in the Old Town, as they were laid many years after His death.

329

THE HOLY
SEPULCHRE
is never empty
during the
day. Someone
can always be
found praying
inside.

THE GOLGOTHA GATE

IN JERUSALEM'S OLD TOWN, not far from the Church of the Holy Sepulchre, stands a Russian Orthodox mission called the Imperial Orthodox Palestine Society. The Church of St. Alexander Nevsky constitutes its religious center, and within the church one can view a unique artifact. During excavations carried out in 1883, Archbishop Antonio Capustin discovered remains of the city's original walls and a hidden gate. Many Orthodox pilgrims believe that this was the gate through which Christ walked on the road to Calvary. It was often also called the Golgotha Gate, the Judgment Gate, or Jesus' Gate.

Archaeological tests, however, have revealed it to be a triumphal arch representing the entrance to the western forum. It was constructed in A.D. 135, when the emperor Hadrian rebuilt Jerusalem as a Roman colony. It was made of the same stone used for the city walls that had been demolished in 70 by Titus' legions. Although the gate does not date back to the time of Christ, it still has great historical significance, being one of very few surviving monuments from when the city was known as Aelia Capitolina

THE GATE OF JUDGMENT in the Church of St. Alexander Nevsky is in fact a triumphal arch from A.D. 135, constructed by Emperor Hadrian as part of his rebuilding of Jerusalem as a Roman colony.

▶ Calvary, where Jesus is believed to have been crucified. The level below contains the Chapel of Adam, from where one can see the cracked part of the Rock of Calvary through a glass screen. Legend has it that the skull of Adam was buried beneath Golgotha and that Christ's blood flowed from His crucified body through the cracked rock into the resting place of the first man. This was supposed to symbolize Christ's blood washing away original sin.

The chapel containing the Holy Sepulchre itself is made up of two parts. The first room, acting as a vestibule, is called the Chapel of the Angel and contains a small stone altar called the Angel's Stone—a reminder of the stone that was placed in front of the entrance to Christ's tomb. A stone like this had been venerated by pilgrims until 614, when it was destroyed by the invading Persians. The second room is on the site of the tomb itself, which had been destroyed by the Muslims in 1009. Inside is found the Aedicula, a marble reliquary of the Holy Sepulchre, which serves as an altar. At the end of the twentieth century, British archaeologist Martin Biddle, of Oxford University, conducted photogrammetric tests on the Holy Sepulchre, concluding that there was indeed evidence of an ancient rock tomb beneath the Aedicula.

TOMBSTONE
in the chapel of the Holy Sepulchre. An icon of the Resurrected Christ is found above it.

331

TIMELINE

ANTIQUITY

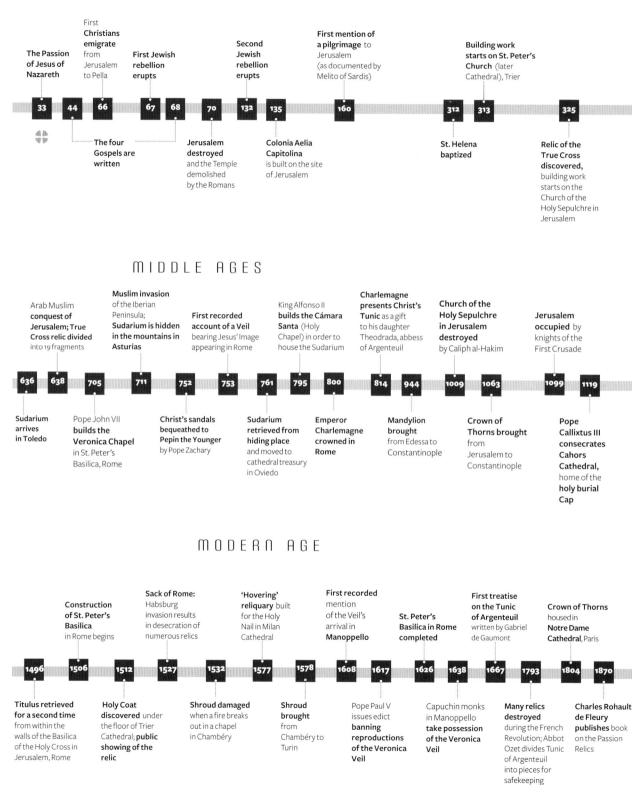

The Passion of Jesus of Nazareth
33

44
The four Gospels are written

First Christians emigrate from Jerusalem to Pella
66

First Jewish rebellion erupts
67

68

70
Jerusalem destroyed and the Temple demolished by the Romans

Second Jewish rebellion erupts
132

135
Colonia Aelia Capitolina is built on the site of Jerusalem

First mention of a pilgrimage to Jerusalem (as documented by Melito of Sardis)
160

312
St. Helena baptized

Building work starts on St. Peter's Church (later Cathedral), Trier
313

325
Relic of the True Cross discovered, building work starts on the Church of the Holy Sepulchre in Jerusalem

MIDDLE AGES

Arab Muslim conquest of Jerusalem; True Cross relic divided into 19 fragments
636

638

705
Pope John VII builds the Veronica Chapel in St. Peter's Basilica, Rome

Muslim invasion of the Iberian Peninsula; Sudarium is hidden in the mountains in Asturias
711

752
Christ's sandals bequeathed to Pepin the Younger by Pope Zachary

First recorded account of a Veil bearing Jesus' Image appearing in Rome
753

761
Sudarium retrieved from hiding place and moved to cathedral treasury in Oviedo

King Alfonso II builds the Cámara Santa (Holy Chapel) in order to house the Sudarium
795

800
Emperor Charlemagne crowned in Rome

Charlemagne presents Christ's Tunic as a gift to his daughter Theodrada, abbess of Argenteuil
814

944
Mandylion brought from Edessa to Constantinople

Church of the Holy Sepulchre in Jerusalem destroyed by Caliph al-Hakim
1009

1063
Crown of Thorns brought from Jerusalem to Constantinople

Jerusalem occupied by knights of the First Crusade
1099

1119
Pope Callixtus III consecrates Cahors Cathedral, home of the holy burial Cap

Sudarium arrives in Toledo

MODERN AGE

Construction of St. Peter's Basilica in Rome begins
1496

1506

1512
Holy Coat discovered under the floor of Trier Cathedral; public showing of the relic

Sack of Rome: Habsburg invasion results in desecration of numerous relics
1527

1532
Shroud damaged when a fire breaks out in a chapel in Chambéry

'Hovering' reliquary built for the Holy Nail in Milan Cathedral
1577

1578
Shroud brought from Chambéry to Turin

First recorded mention of the Veil's arrival in Manoppello
1608

1617
Pope Paul V issues edict banning reproductions of the Veronica Veil

St. Peter's Basilica in Rome completed
1626

1638
Capuchin monks in Manoppello take possession of the Veronica Veil

First treatise on the Tunic of Argenteuil written by Gabriel de Gaumont
1667

1793
Many relics destroyed during the French Revolution; Abbot Ozet divides Tunic of Argenteuil into pieces for safekeeping

Crown of Thorns housed in Notre Dame Cathedral, Paris
1804

1870
Charles Rohault de Fleury publishes book on the Passion Relics

Titulus retrieved for a second time from within the walls of the Basilica of the Holy Cross in Jerusalem, Rome

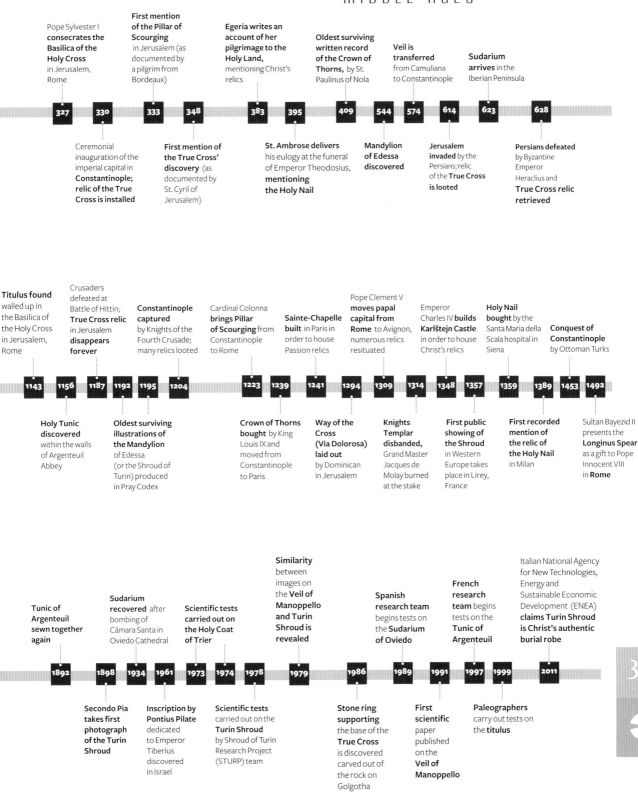

Pope Sylvester I consecrates the Basilica of the Holy Cross in Jerusalem, Rome

First mention of the Pillar of Scourging in Jerusalem (as documented by a pilgrim from Bordeaux)

Egeria writes an account of her pilgrimage to the Holy Land, mentioning Christ's relics

Oldest surviving written record of the Crown of Thorns, by St. Paulinus of Nola

Veil is transferred from Camuliana to Constantinople

Sudarium arrives in the Iberian Peninsula

327 **330** **333** **348** **383** **395** **409** **544** **574** **614** **623** **628**

Ceremonial inauguration of the imperial capital in **Constantinople; relic of the True Cross is installed**

First mention of the True Cross' discovery (as documented by St. Cyril of Jerusalem)

St. Ambrose delivers his eulogy at the funeral of Emperor Theodosius, **mentioning the Holy Nail**

Mandylion of Edessa discovered

Jerusalem invaded by the Persians; relic of the **True Cross is looted**

Persians defeated by Byzantine Emperor Heraclius and **True Cross relic retrieved**

Titulus found walled up in the Basilica of the Holy Cross in Jerusalem, Rome

Crusaders defeated at Battle of Hittin; **True Cross relic** in Jerusalem **disappears forever**

Constantinople captured by Knights of the Fourth Crusade; many relics looted

Cardinal Colonna brings **Pillar of Scourging** from Constantinople to Rome

Sainte-Chapelle built in Paris in order to house Passion relics

Pope Clement V **moves papal capital from Rome** to Avignon, numerous relics resituated

Emperor Charles IV **builds Karlštejn Castle** in order to house Christ's relics

Holy Nail bought by the Santa Maria della Scala hospital in Siena

Conquest of Constantinople by Ottoman Turks

1143 **1156** **1187** **1192** **1195** **1204** **1223** **1239** **1241** **1294** **1309** **1314** **1348** **1357** **1359** **1389** **1453** **1492**

Holy Tunic discovered within the walls of Argenteuil Abbey

Oldest surviving illustrations of the Mandylion of Edessa (or the Shroud of Turin) produced in Pray Codex

Crown of Thorns bought by King Louis IX and moved from Constantinople to Paris

Way of the Cross (Via Dolorosa) laid out by Dominican in Jerusalem

Knights Templar disbanded, Grand Master Jacques de Molay burned at the stake

First public showing of the Shroud in Western Europe takes place in Lirey, France

First recorded mention of the relic of the Holy Nail in Milan

Sultan Bayezid II presents the **Longinus Spear** as a gift to Pope Innocent VIII in **Rome**

Tunic of Argenteuil sewn together again

Sudarium recovered after bombing of Cámara Santa in Oviedo Cathedral

Scientific tests carried out on the Holy Coat of Trier

Similarity between images on the **Veil of Manoppello and Turin Shroud is revealed**

Spanish research team begins tests on the **Sudarium of Oviedo**

French research team begins tests on the **Tunic of Argenteuil**

Italian National Agency for New Technologies, Energy and Sustainable Economic Development (ENEA) **claims Turin Shroud is Christ's authentic burial robe**

1892 **1898** **1934** **1961** **1973** **1974** **1978** **1979** **1986** **1989** **1991** **1997** **1999** **2011**

Secondo Pia takes first photograph of the Turin Shroud

Inscription by Pontius Pilate dedicated to Emperor Tiberius discovered in Israel

Scientific tests carried out on the **Turin Shroud** by Shroud of Turin Research Project (STURP) team

Stone ring supporting the base of the **True Cross** is discovered carved out of the rock on Golgotha

First scientific paper published on the **Veil of Manoppello**

Paleographers carry out tests on the **titulus**

GLOSSARY

ACHEIROPOIETOS (Gr.) made without human hand

ANASTASIS (Gr.) resurrection

ARCOSOLIUM (Lat.) early-Christian form of a tomb with an arched recess

ARMA CHRISTI (Lat.) instruments of Christ's Passion

BASILEUS (Gr.) king

CAMARA SANTA (Lat.) Holy Chapel

CHETONEH (hebr.) type of robe worn over clothes; a chiton

COLUMNA MORMOREA (Lat.) marble column

CRUX BONI LATRONIS (Lat.) cross of the good thief

CYBORIUM (Lat.) azure altar with a baldachin

DULIA (Lat.) veneration

EFOD (hebr.) Jewish high priest's liturgical robe

EXACTOR MORTIS (Lat.) death sentence

GOLGOTA (aram.) skull

HAGIA SOPHIA (Gr.) *Holy Wisdom*

HASTA (Lat.) type of Roman spear

HEMATIDROSIS (Lat.) disease causing a person to sweat blood

HORRIBILE FLAGELLUM (Lat.) horrible whip

LABARUM (Lat.) standard of Roman legions led by the emperor

LATRIA (Lat.) adoration and worship

LEPTON (Gr.) Roman coin worth 1/100 of a drachma (see: Pathil)

LINTEUM (Lat.) apron, towel

LITHOSTROTOS (Lat.) cobblestone, pavement

MANDYLION (Gr.) veil, towel

NISSAN (hebr.) month at the start of spring in the Jewish calendar

NIVOLA (wł.) cloud

NUMINOSUM (Lat.) something unknowable, triggering fear, but also compelling

OSTENSIONES RELIQUIARUM (Lat.) public exhibition of relics

OTHONIA (Gr.) cloths

OSSUARIUM (Lat.) container used to store the bones of dead people; ossuary

PARS PRO TOTO (Lat.) *a part for the whole*

PATHIL (hebr.) burial cap

PATIBULUM (Lat.) horizontal beam on a cross

PERISONIUM (Lat.) loincloth

PILEUS (Lat.) helmet

POST MORTEM (Lat.) after death

PRUTAH (hebr.) Roman coin worth 1/100 of a drachma (see: Lepton)

REX (Lat.) king

RIGOR MORTIS (Lat.) stiffening of the body after death

SADIN (hebr.) tunic

SANTA SCALA (ital.) Holy Stairs

SANTO CHIODO (ital.) Holy Nail

SIMBA (hebr.) cloak, coat

SINDON (Gr.) shroud, sheet

SOLIDUS (Lat.) Roman gold coin

STAUROPHYLAX (Gr.) custodian of the cross

STAUROS (Gr.) cross

STAUROTHEKA (Gr.) reliquary of the cross

STIPES (Lat.) vertical beam on a cross

SUDARION (syr.) veil

SUPPEDANEUM (Lat.) support beam nailed to the cross under the feet

TETRADIPLON (Gr.) four doubles, an earlier name for the Turin Shroud

THEKA (Gr.) packaging, casing

THEOTOKOS EIKON (Gr.) image of God

TITULUS DAMNATIONIS (Lat.) sign of the condemned

VERA EIKON (lat.-gr.) *real image*

VIA DOLOROSA (Lat.) Way of the Cross

VOLTO SANTO (ital.) Holy Face

ACKNOWLEDGMENTS

The authors and editors wish to thank the following people and institutions for their help in the realization of this book:

Marek Adamski, Janina Andrearczyk, Fr. Marek Arciszewski CSMA, Gherardo Avogadro, Paul Badde, Fr. Jan Henryk Bałdyga, Wiesław Banach, Marcello Bandettini, Debora Barbagli, Lucia Barocchi, Beata&Dariusz Bartczakowie, Jean-Paul Barth, Grzegorz Bierecki, Joanna Bogdanowicz, Daniela Bonucci, Fr. Bernard Briks OMI, Fr. Piotr Burek CSMA, Łukasz Bytniewski, Fr. Paweł Cebula OFMConv., Fr. Waldemar Chrostowski, Fr. Dariusz Cichor OSPPE, Card. Angelo Comastri, Fr. Bohdan Dutko MS, Bruno Fabbiani, Birgitta Falk, Fr. Benito Gallego, Mirella Garda, Markus Gross-Morgen, Fr. Piotr Guzik, Fr. Michał Janocha, Monika&Michał Kamińscy, Angelika Korszyńska-Górny, Fr. Jerzy Kraj OFM, Tomasz Kuczborski, Fr. Witold Kuman MS, Fr. Kazimierz Kurek SDB, Fr. Gonzalo Lobo, Gérard Lucotte, Fr. Roman Majewski OSPPE, Colette Marion, Rodolphe Marion, Jolanta&Jacek Mycielscy, Fr. Ryszard Niziołek CSMA, Jaime Garcia Noriega, Fr. Jan O'Dogherty, Sr. Maria Róża Pacocha CSSE, Elisa Pezzana, Fr. Sebastian Pięta CPPS, Giorgio Pogliano, Fr. Karol Porczak MS, Sr. Michaela Rak ZSJM, Włodzimierz Rędzioch, Fr. Paolo Ristori, Franz Ronig, Filippo Rossi, Damian Rybak, Roberto Cesaro Sanfilippo, Fr. Giovanni Scarabelli, Sr. Blandina Paschalis Schlömer, Peter Schwarz, Barrie Schwortz, Franca Silletta, Fr. Łukasz Skawiński, Fr. Wojciech Skóra MIC, Fr. Zdzisław Sochacki, Petrus Soons, Małgorzata&Zbigniew Spytkowie, Barbara Sudnik-Wójcikowska, Andrzej Swat, Catherine de Thieulloy, Enrico Toti, Lidia&Kazimierz M. Ujazdowscy, Fr. Timothy Verdon, Sławomir Wawer, Fr. Roman Wcisło MS, Roland Wentzler, Hanna Werblan-Jakubiec, Paweł Wilk, Piotr Wojcieszek, Fr. Tadeusz Zawadzki, Iza Zygmuntowicz.

Brotherhood of the Passion in Góra Kalwaria, Poland; Milan Cathedral Council, Rome Basilica Council in the Vatican.

Polish edition *Świadkowie Tajemnicy*
Published 2012 by **Rosikon Press, Warsaw, Poland**

Text © 2012 by **Grzegorz Górny**
Photographs © 2012 by **Janusz Rosikoń**

With the permission of the Warsaw Metropolitan Curia no.749/D/2012, 09.03.2012

Graphic design by **Maciej Marchewicz**

Maps and illustrations by **Piotr Karczewski**

Collaboration **Jan Kasprzycki-Rosikoń**

Production by **Kasper Kasprzycki-Rosikoń**

English translation by **James Savage-Hanford**

Editing and corrections by **Mary Murphy**

Photographs taken from the following collections: Budapest National Library p. 22, 23, 122; © St Peter's Basilica, Rome p. 91 right, 287; Brotherhood of the Passion in Góra Kalwaria p. 106 right; Museum of Santa Maria della Scala p. 127; Spanish Center of Sindonology CES p. 154; Polskie Wydawnictwo Encyklopedyczne p. 235; Kornelimünster Abbey p. 295, 299; Aachen Cathedral p. 297, 298, 301 top, 303 bottom
Photographs: © 1978 Barrie M. Schwortz Collection, STERA, Inc. cover, p. 4, 19, 43, 44, 45, 46–47, 51, 52, 55 upper, 59 top right, 61 bottom left, 62–63, 68, 69; © 1997 Barrie Schwortz Collection STERA, Inc. p. 60; © 2005 Barrie M. Schwortz Collection, STERA, Inc. p. 53, 54; © 2005 John Brown Collection, STERA, Inc. p. 54; © 1978 Mark Evans Collection, STERA, Inc. p. 22 upper; © 2001 Barrie M. Schwortz Collection, STERA, Inc. p. 55 bottom; Dariusz Bartczak p. 29, 32, 33; André Marion p. 57, 167, 168, 188, 191; Barbara Sudnik p. 58, 59 top left, 157 bottom, 189, 277 bottom; Gherardo Avogadro p. 90, Fr. Piotr Guzik p. 141; Gérard Lucotte p. 193; Zbigniew Spytek p. 290–292; Jean-Paul Barth p. 304 left, 306 left

English edition © 2013 by **Ignatius Press, San Francisco**

ISBN 978-1-58617-844-4

Library of Congress Control Number 2013943143

Printed in Poland